A Sense of Place II

A Sense of Place II:
The Benedictines of Collegeville

Edited by
Colman J. Barry, O.S.B.

The Liturgical Press
Collegeville, Minnesota
1990

Cover design by Don Bruno.

2	3	4	5	6	7	8	9

ISBN 13: 978-0-8146-1910-0
ISBN 10: 0-8146-1910-X

Library of Congress Cataloging-in-Publication Data

A Sense of place / edited by Colman Barry.
      p.   cm.
    Contents: —2. The Benedictines of Collegeville.
    ISBN 0-8146-1910-X (v. 2)
    1. St. John's Abbey (Collegeville, Minn.) 2. St. John's
University (Collegeville, Minn.)—History. 3. Collegeville (Minn.)—
Church history. 4. Benedictines—Minnesota—Collegeville—History.
I. Barry, Colman James, 1921–
BX2525.S226S46   1990
255' .1'00977647—dc20   87-62925
                                                CIP

CONTENTS

CONSIDERABLE COMMENTARY HAS BEEN written about Saint John's Abbey and University during its formative, developing, and maturing periods over more than one hundred and thirty years. Fr. Hilary Thimmesh, president of Saint John's University, suggested that some contemporary essays and comments be assembled in a volume that could be available as a record for interested readers. He asked Robert L. Spaeth, then dean of the College of Arts and Sciences of Saint John's University, and me to invite contributors and edit such a volume which was published as *A Sense of Place: Saint John's of Collegeville* (Collegeville: Saint John's University Press, 1987).

The thirty-one invited contributors to this first volume all had associations with the life and ministries of both our Collegeville monastery and its schools. Oblates, alumni, faculty, and friends were included. Guests of Saint John's, professional observers of American religious life, educational colleagues, and ecumenical friends are all found in this volume. Their reactions and judgments are invaluable for objective evaluation as well as for future historians. These essays were in no way intended to be a complete overview of the Collegeville scene. They are one composite collection from friends, associates, and observers who generously expressed their judgments about this American monastery and university in its vocation of worship and work, listening, studying, teaching, and producing.

The book was widely read and its title "A Sense of Place" was subsequently used by some institutions and states for similar productions. Several readers wrote or said that they would be most interested in Saint John's publishing a second, corresponding volume made up of comments "from the inside," that is: What do the Benedictines of Saint John's Abbey think of this place? After discussion and consultation a decision was made to prepare a second volume of *A Sense of Place* consisting of essays from monks of Saint John's and published by The Liturgical Press.

Rabbi Mark W. Verman, current occupant of the Jay Phillips Chair of Jewish Studies in Saint John's University, made a valuable observation in commenting on the first volume of *A Sense of Place*. He pointed out that "place" [*makom*] is one of the epithets used for God in the Hebrew tradition. This basic insight into our original and authentic Jewish roots as a Christian community was a spiritual inspiration in the development of this collection.

Those invited to submit an original essay to this volume were asked to write on the meaning to them of Saint John's monastery, its place in worship and work in our apostolates, our varied heritage of service, as well as what Saint John's has meant in their lives: "What might be included in such an essay? Reflections on your own experience that the monastic life at Saint John's has offered; the faith, vision, and experience that inspire or inform. Whether your essay stresses the monastic presence in the world or its place in your life, or both, we will be happy to include it."

Several contributors characterized their essays in creative fashion: Can Anything Good Come from Collegeville; A Monastic Space; The Place Around Us; A Place of Sense; High Above the Sagatagan; A Landscape Paradise; What You Thought You Came For; Nice To Know; This I Remember. These themes are often repeated in the collection with interesting variations.

Several of the essays are expressions about a process that was begun in the '20s at Saint John's and continues as the century winds down. It had several characteristics while developing. The first, the American liturgical movement brought from European monastic centers, was applied in the monastery, seminary, prep school, college, and parishes. It was carried forward by The Liturgical Press as an educational and pastoral development. Vatican Council II in its first decree on the liturgy made the goals and values of a liturgical spirituality official and universal.

The social action essentially resulting from and necessary to liturgical living was applied at Collegeville in on-going sequences of organized regional and national meetings and workshops conducted by experts at liturgical conferences; workshops in rural life values; mental health institutes for clergy of all faiths by representatives of psychiatry and religion; Scripture and spirituality institutes for Christians and Jews; summer sessions for sister formation and theological studies. Journals such as *Orate Fratres (Worship)*, *Sponsa Regis (Sisters Today)*, and *The Bible Today* became popular influences in the English-speaking world for a deepening of spiritual values. The Institute for Ecumenical and Cultural Research formalized several pioneering ecumenical dialogues in Collegeville between separated Christians. The Marcel Breuer architectural planning brought the arts and religion into modern focus. The Jay Phillips Chair of Jewish Studies helped direct theological teaching to the Hebrew roots of Christianity. Radio Station KSJR-FM, which developed into Minnesota Public Radio, is a unique educational, ecumenical, and cooperative expression of quality broadcasting. The Hill Monastic Manuscript Library became the largest deposit of classical and medieval manuscripts transcribed before printing and available to students on microfilm. Co-institutional, coordinate cooperation with our neighboring College of Saint Benedict has enriched and expanded the curricular, cultural, and social programs of both Saint John's and Saint Benedict's.

As this volume is being prepared for publication, another giant leap of faith is under construction. For the first time in 400 years the Episcopal Diocese of Minnesota is building an Episcopal Center, a House of Prayer for contemplation and reflection, at a Benedictine abbey, on the banks of the Watab and adjoining the Ecumenical Institute. Five acres of land have been leased by Saint John's to our Minnesota Episcopal Diocese for this purpose. The leadership of Episcopal Bishop Paul Anderson, as well as the central work of Dr. R. William Franklin, director of the Christian Humanism Project in Saint John's University and chairperson of the Board of Directors of the Episcopal Center/Collegeville, is an example to all separated Christians who look for ways to respond, to be involved, to experience and be connected to the Eucharistic prayer of Jesus: "That they may be one . . . ." Saint John's is honored to participate in this creative and grace-filled *glasnost.*

All of these endeavors have meaning as work in relation to worship in the monastic tradition. They offer an environment for contemplation in a society opening steadily to the spiritual dimension of life and reality in an age of mobility, individualism, technology, and over-stressed human sexuality. A hospitable place is being provided for students of all ages who want to seek, listen, and converse about God. Those who participate are offered an opportunity freely to search for a meaningful relationship with God and persons; or look for a sense of stewardship, covenant, stability, and sources for service. There exists a contemporary search for an experience of faith in models both authentic and original. America is more than an expression of the values of market economy capitalism, the competitive process of political democracy, or an organized therapeutic thrust for self-actualization or human potential. There is also a deep awareness in our society from its pluralistic beginnings of the core spiritual values imbedded in the sanctuary of the individual person.

Engraved over the entrance to the famed library of the former Monastery of Saint Gall is the unique invitation: "Enter Here the Pharmacy of the Soul." Today a state museum, this great, ancient Swiss abbey is a rich depository of classical and medieval manuscripts of both Irish and Benedictine monastic origins. These priceless manuscript books handwritten by dedicated monastic scribes preserved the heritage of classical, early Christian, and medieval culture—both religious and civil. Included in all monastic libraries such as Saint Gall is a wide range of literary and legal records, charters, wills, and biographies. Scripture, sermons, theological and philosophical commentaries, medical, scientific, mathematical, musical, and artistic sources—all can be found in these collections.

Also included among the more important documents helpful in reconstructing the ancient and medieval story are chronicles by monk authors of events with interpretations of the passing scene. These monastic authors were unique early reporters about the infra and extra structure of their institutions and society at large.

A collection such as follows of essays by participants in contemporary monastic life in one place stands in that long line of chronicles of the monastic tradition. Its historical value will be determined in the future. The assembling, editing and preparation for publication of this volume of essays by thirty monks of Saint John's Abbey has been an enriching experience for this editor. It is a pleasant obligation to express appreciation to those confreres who so graciously and generously responded to this invitation to write an essay on their sense at this time "from the inside" of this beloved place in the Indianbush, Saint John's of Collegeville.

Colman J. Barry

And what you thought you came for
Is only a shell, a husk of meaning
From which the purpose breaks only when it is fulfilled
If at all. Either you had no purpose
Or the purpose is beyond the end you figured
And is altered in fulfillment. There are other places
Which are also the world's end, some at the sea jaws,
Or over a dark lake, in a desert or a city—
But this is the nearest, in place and time . . .
  T. S. Eliot, "Little Gidding" from *Four quartets*

IN SOME WAYS MY EXPERIENCE AT SAINT JOHN'S Abbey confutes Eliot's notion. I chose to enter the monastery because I loved God, wanted to give my life to this love, wanted to seek realization of this love in my work, prayer, leisure, and companions. I remain for the same reason. Moreover, I remain because, whatever unsuspected realizations I've had about what such a life entails, it seems to be working. Saint John's Abbey is a place to learn how to love God.

However, if I look back now at how and when and why I first came to the college as a freshman in 1974, I find Eliot's reflection more compelling. Then, seeking independence and excitement rather than stability, and considering Saint John's as a toe-hold in what I vaguely conceived to be the "Great Northwest," I had no idea what Saint John's was to come to mean in my life. What drew me to Saint John's must have had something to do with the truth about this place, its being simultaneously for people and for God, but this was a truth that dawned only slowly.

Almost whenever I meet people who find out that I attended Saint John's University, they presume that I came to Saint John's with a purpose: "Somehow you must have known, or at least suspected, that one day you would be a monk." Wrong, I say. "Oh? When did you first think about entering the monastery? On your first contact with the sanctity of the monks? As a result of some inspired course on Scripture or the burning issues of theology?'' No. The truth be told, I never once during my undergraduate years at Saint John's considered myself to have a vocation, let alone one to be a monk. Within a year after graduation I did, but until then it never crossed my mind. This reply never fails to astonish, and it seems worth wondering why.

In fact, I first heard of Saint John's as a school with a great wrestling team. That was in the early 1970s, at the end of the Terry Haws era, and Haws's successor managed to recruit the senior co-captain from my high school wrestling team in the suburbs of Chicago to come to Collegeville. As a sophomore I had wrestled behind this all-stater, challenging him every Thursday for the starting slot on the varsity and getting my tail whipped just as often, but he taught me to work hard and I finished the junior varsity season with only one loss. The next year I made it far enough—sectional finals—to think that someone might be interested in having me wrestle at their college, and I arranged to visit another teammate who had moved to the Minneapolis area. I arrived during spring break, and the two of us made the drive up old Highway 152 to see Saint John's.

We reached the campus on one of those spring days that never cease to work their magic in Minnesota. The ice had only days before released the waters of the Sagatagan to sparkle hypnotically in the mid-April sunlight, and about 3:00 on the afternoon we arrived scores of Johnnies were heading to the playing fields for the annual ritual of intramural softball, either jogging or riding on the seats, hoods, or trunks of the dilapidated cars then preferred by the few students who could afford them. It was a scene calculated to bewitch a seventeen-year-old dreamer intent on heading West, not East, for college; to a smaller world, not a bigger; away from civilization, not towards it. The very air seemed to breathe promise of life and discovery, and I succumbed to its spell completely.

My former teammate left Saint John's after one year, and I spent half of my senior wrestling season on the sidelines with a dislocated elbow. I was turning more and more towards academic interests and pushing sports to the purely recreational side of my life. Saint

John's, as I explored the sheaves of college brochures that arrived in my mailbox, fostered both these interests, and it compared favorably with both the University of Illinois and the University of Notre Dame, my other choices.

Money permitting, I wanted a private college, and Saint John's offered generous financial aid on top of a scholarship I had already received. Of course, Notre Dame was Notre Dame, and I had entertained visions of going to college in the shadow of the golden dome ever since watching Terry Hanratty throw touchdown passes to Jim Seymour when I was in grade school. But as I visited and corresponded with South Bend, something was missing that I had experienced at Saint John's. Notre Dame expected me to be impressed that they were entertaining me, but they never communicated any real feeling of wanting me to come there. In South Bend I felt that Notre Dame was the important thing; I could ally myself to that importance or not, but I couldn't really expect it to pay much attention to me.

Saint John's, on the other hand, did little things, like exchange through the mail a jersey I had bought in the bookstore that turned out to be too big. Like send me chaplain's letters because I had expressed an interest in youth ministry. Now I realize that these attentions reflected not merely the gimmicky marketing tactics of a crack admissions crew, but the first signs of a truth about this place that has endured for me for over fifteen years: I counted. And this premium on the person ran deeper than the kind of superficial personalism that almost any small place can offer compared to a bigger, more prestigious one. It is a value that begins with the monks: Saint John's exists that they might better seek to love God; it is a value that flows from a belief that the truth of human lives resides deeper than the moment and therefore should be served, honored, manifested in the moment, no matter how ordinary.

Of course, Saint John's suffers too from human foibles; it can succumb to the tendency of any institution to nurture its myths at the expense of its realities. And no one knows these foibles and myths better than the monks. Yet, the spirit that I experienced in those early contacts survives and thrives because the central myth at Saint John's is not really a myth at all, but the message of the Gospel. Moreover, Saint John's "myth" is incarnate in the monastery itself, in the attempt to live that gospel message in all the unspectacular everyday ways that life affords: Love one another as I have loved you.

I didn't think in these terms then; I merely understood that I meant more to Saint John's than I did to Notre Dame. Arriving in Collegeville by Greyhound bus on September 1, 1978, I remember that Saint Cloud that day recorded the coldest temperature in the nation, 32 degrees! What would January bring? I found out. Snow. Twenty-seven inches of it. Enough to stop the Benny-buses in their tracks and force the monks to man the kitchens in place of the dining service workers. The students didn't starve; the monks probably depleted three days worth of food in the day and a half that they ran things, so worried were they that we'd go hungry.

All of this adds up, slowly, and rather uncomprehendingly, to a force that eventually compelled me to return and make Saint John's my home. My mother, I remember, telephoned Fr. Rene McGraw, the prefect on "Third Tommy" in advance of my birthday to ask him to order a cake and tell her what it cost. He did the first but not the second. We ate the cake in Rene's room, went on to popcorn, and munched that on into the night through rounds of a name-guessing game he called "Botticelli." In only two of my classes that year did I have monks for teachers—Br. Louis Blenkner in English and Fr. Alberic Culhane in Old Testament. But I got to know others as characters around the place, in the dorms especially.

Some monks I knew only by hearsay—horror stories of the pace of "Speedy Bede's" chemistry lectures or Father Bertram's zoology tests. But even the horror stories were good material; they were told of Brother Louis, he of the black habit and rubber beach sandals even in the dead of winter, he who was reputed to tell classes that he would probably give God an A in the class, himself a B, and we should all prepare ourselves for Cs. The story may have been apocryphal; the grading scale was pretty accurate.

As the years went on and I switched from the sciences to English, I got to know Louis better, and also Frs. Alfred Deutsch, Hilary Thimmesh, Pat McDarby, and J. P. Earls, not to mention Mr. Stephen Humphrey, who wasn't a monk but about as close as you could come, and who was as good a guide to the characters in Collegeville as Virgil was for Dante in the *Inferno* Steve so loved to teach. When the new course bulletins came out, about a half-dozen of us at a time would sit in his room listening to advice: "Take Godfrey," "take Rene," "take Alex," "take Chrysostom." Indeed it was uncannily similar to the Latin poet pointing out the denizens of hell to his amazed disciple, while the relish in his voice, the twinkle in his eye hinted that these characters and this place too comprised a kind of divine comedy, a realm where all things signified the wonderful and therefore comic grace of God.

However strong these impressions were and remain, it still seems odd that they didn't cause me to think of becoming a monk myself. True, I had switched majors to English, where even the non-monks seemed vaguely Benedictine. For example, Dr. Eila Perlmutter, who fashioned as formidable a *persona* for herself as any monk and who, with Louis, sits on my shoulder to this day, a literary conscience as I write this essay. For three years I had intended to train as a parish youth minister, but during my senior year I forsook this idea and began thinking of graduate studies and an eventual academic career. First, however, a year or two off from studies to see something of the world and decide between classics and English, or so I thought.

Perhaps because I was so immersed in what was good about Saint John's, I didn't match what it truly was with what I wanted for my own life. As a matter of fact, I didn't actually have much of an idea of what I wanted in my life. My turning away from youth ministry had meant, thus far, an invitation to confusion and rootlessness in matters of belief and experimentation and indulgence in matters of behavior. At first, this freedom seemed exciting, an autonomy unbounded by conventional values.

But as time went on, the sweetness of this dispensation began to cloy. It's hard to say when my disillusion began, but not until it did, did I begin to discover what I have been discovering ever since: how Saint John's nurtures faith, helps me to grow, helps me to love and be loved by God. One night, sitting in front of a fireplace in a rented house in Saint Paul when I had stayed behind from a New Year's Eve outing, I began to take inventory of my life and especially my beliefs. Perhaps I only then discovered that I truly had beliefs. Two years earlier in a youth ministry leadership meeting we spent an evening in teams constructing personal creeds. I remember thinking then that too many people seemed almost glibly sure of what they believed. I was more afraid of faith than any of them—or they hid their fear as well as I. Two years later, staring into the flames, I began to realize that I believed. In what I didn't exactly know, although I felt sure it had something to do with God and the Gospel, with Jesus Christ and sin and grace and redemption.

But what really seems to have come to me that New Year's Eve is the fundamental intuition that the question "How do I believe in God?" would occupy me for the rest of my life. Furthermore, I knew that the world in which I now lived either frowned contemptuously on such weak-willed soul searching or smiled indulgently as one would at an idiot child, "There but for the grace of—something, not God—go I." Today this judgment of my world seems unfairly harsh. I met two of my best friends during this time, but the world did appear in rather dire terms then. I also knew I couldn't pursue this question on any born-again, personal-Lord-and-savior route. I had a penchant for intellectual and unsentimental inquiry, at times a cynical streak, and I knew that my pursuit of God would have to make room for such baggage, checked as it was for the duration.

As I mentally catalogued what I would require to be able to live this question, Saint John's appeared to me almost corporeally. Here were people committed to the same search, people who lived the question of God neither simplistically nor contemptuously, but honestly, daily. In a strangely trinitarian way, Saint John's not only embodied a fundamental respect for the life of the mind; it kept in mind an equal respect for the life of the body, all the while remaining dedicated to the truest life, the life of the spirit. I sensed Saint John's then not as a kind of greenhouse nursery for life, but a place where one might—where people did—live life itself.

One of the things I remembered that night was a senior seminar class in which we discussed the medieval tale of *Gawain and the Green Knight*. I had presented a paper for the class, but what I remembered was a comment by Fr. Hilary Thimmesh (all available English faculty attended the seminar classes) about how, in the old days, seasons of the year and the liturgical cycle had been marked so concretely in the monastery's way of life.

A little review. The tale of Sir Gawain recounts the Christmastide feast at which the Green Knight appears to challenge the chivalry of Arthur's round table. Gawain takes up the challenge and deals the knight what should be a death-blow; however, the Green Knight miraculously survives, reminds Gawain to seek him at the Green Chapel a year and a day hence to receive an answering stroke, and gallops from Camelot, literally holding his severed head in his hands. As Gawain passes the coming year, the poet recounts the passing seasons: Yuletide that gives way to "the crabbed Lenten" fast, in turn replaced by the "sweetness of the soft summer," Harvest with its warning to "wax to ripeness," until finally Michaelmas brings the year full circle to winter.[1]

Hilary spoke of the symbolic way in which the monastery table, for example, was stripped during Lent of all but the basic condiments—salt, pepper, sugar. Jellies and syrup succumbed to the general fast but came back in glorious style on Easter morning, which still features pancakes and waffles with fresh berries and whipped cream. Brother Louis recalled the pared down music of the Lenten liturgies, with a capella singing the rule until the organ erupted in the thunderous *Alleluia* of the Easter Vigil. Though Hilary and Louis spoke even then of a bygone era, one that even the most romantic would admit had as many abuses as glories, something in the practices spoke to me of a conscientious effort to symbolize basic truths of the human experience, especially the spiritual dimension of that experience.

It is this conscientiousness about how we live our lives that I recalled as I stared into the fire on New Year's Eve, appropriately the day when Gawain prepares to receive the return axe-blow of the Green Knight. Moreover, I recalled people whom I respected, people who had given their varied lives to a common endeavor, the search for God. I didn't think about the *Rule of Benedict;* I was hardly familiar with it, but I did think of monks whose lives embodied that rule without reducing it to a repressive uniformity.

When I first talked to Fr. Julian Schmiesing, then vocations director, and listed for him the monks who had influenced my interest in monastic life, he was amused that I could mention Father Alfred (then rector of the seminary) and Brother Louis (an independent and sometimes irreverent cuss) in the same breath. He knew what

1. The quotations are from a modern English translation by the late J.R.R. Tolkien (Boston: Houghton Mifflin, 1978).

I could only guess: such variety is the rule rather than the exception in monasteries. His smile signified approval that I had somehow accepted a heterogeneity I couldn't yet understand, rather than, as I first suspected, laughter at my naïveté.

I entered the monastery as a candidate in 1981. One night during the first week, I was scanning the paper between supper and evening prayer when Fr. Dunstan Tucker introduced himself to me. Eighty years old then, Father Dunstan was spoken of with reverence and awe even by those I had held in reverence and awe— as a teacher, a scholar, dean of the college, coach of the baseball team. After introducing himself, Father Dunstan said he hoped I would be patient "with us." He went on, "We can be a little daunting at first, but once you get to know us, we're really very human." He spoke the words with reverence. That spring and summer I watched him tend a small but spectacular flower garden just off the back porch of the monastery, a task he approached with the care and patience he must have given to his Dante scholarship. Concerned with the repositioning of flagstones near his garden, he wouldn't bring himself to criticize another monk's deplorable taste, but said instead that he "disagreed with his aesthetics."

Eight years later, more realistic about the life of the community and more aware of the blemishes and bonuses of personalities, I find these impressions only growing stronger. I watched Father Dunstan stand, on All Souls Day, at the grave of Fr. Conrad Diekmann, offering a silent prayer. Then I stood by his own grave as his body was brought to rest with the colleague and brother he loved. And two falls ago I myself stood on the grave of Fr. Otto Weber, not so much praying as cursing: "Otto, what the hell are you doing in there? We've got work to do!"

Both my own parents' fathers died before I was born, but at the age of twenty-five, in the monastery, I could still learn for the first time how a grandfather indulged a grandson. At age thirty-four I'm still one of the "youngsters" and will continue to be until I'm well into my fifties, I suppose. Most wonderful of all is finding monks who were once my teachers or distant figures in the procession become confreres, colleagues, friends, heart and soul companions.

Teaching at the prep school helps keep me young too, and I love being able to quote Hamlet from memory to one student, help another discover her ability to write vivid stories, yet find time to tip another's frisbee toss three times before catching it behind my back—in habit! If someday a prep graduate thinks of me and decides that one can love God and love life, I hope I'll have helped keep alive what Saint John's was for me.

But I remember that Eliot says even what I thought I came for "is altered in fulfillment." Monks whom I didn't know or had never seen are now brothers. Those I entered novitiate with are close companions. I sing full-voiced as I hadn't done since fourth grade when Sr. Rose Nicholas told me to "mouth the words." The daily current of psalms, a far-off mystery in college, washes over me again and again, my own voice part of the rhythm that sustains us all.

While I can't say that I've learned to prefer nothing whatever to Christ, I think that I have to at least begun to run on the path of his commandments, have felt in small measure my heart overflow with the inexpressible delight of love. That, after all, is what Saint Benedict asks of and promises his monks:

> "May God, who has begun this good work in you,
> bring it to perfection" (Monastic profession liturgy).

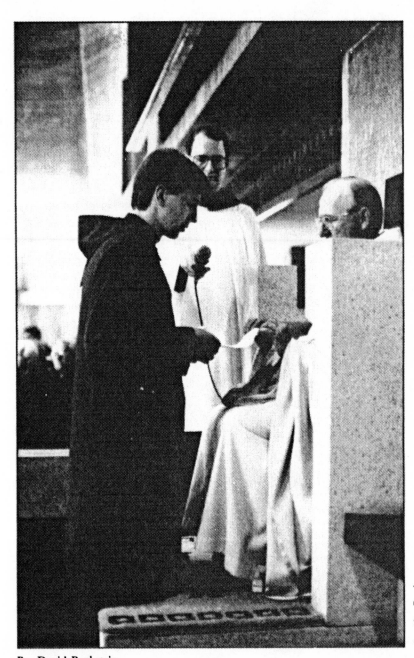

Br. David Rothstein

Br. Alan Reed

SILVAN BROMENSHENKEL

S IR ETIENNE DUPUCH STATED IN THE NASSAU
Tribune on March 11, 1987:

> Because of the educational facilities provided by the Catholic mis-
> sion in the Bahamas, and especially the work of the Sisters of Charity
> among the poor, the Catholic Church under the direction of Bishop
> Bernard Kevenhoerster, O.S.B., and Bishop Leonard Hagarty,
> O.S.B., became the fastest growing religious organization in the
> Bahamas.

The Catholic Church had a distinct advantage in the Bahamas,
continues Sir Etienne, because it could collect funds from friendly
parishes in the United States and was generously supplied with both
funds and personnel from Saint John's Abbey in Minnesota.

The first two Catholic bishops of the Bahamas were monks of
Saint John's Abbey. They were examples of the abbey's considerable influence abroad, especially in countries where Saint John's
has made monastic foundations, namely, the Bahamas, Mexico,
Puerto Rico, and Japan.

The administration of Bishop Kevenhoerster and Bishop Hagarty
covered the half century from the '30s to the '80s. These two monks
were the leading diplomats among the clergy of the day. They were
the stuff from which bishops are chosen.

But they were also aggressive personalities, and they chose as their
closest associates men who were of the "pushy" type, in the bet-

ter sense of that word. Names that come to mind are Benedictine priests like Bonaventure Hansen, Frederic Frey, Cornelius Osendorf, and Brendan Forsyth, to name only a few, and later on, diocesan priests like the present vicar general, Msgr. Preston Moss. These men had much to do with shaping the views and policies of Bishop Hagarty's long and colorful thirty-one-year reign.

But the foundation and framework on which Bishop Hagarty could build was laid in the '30s and '40s during the administration of his predecessor, Bishop Kevenhoerster. This essay is concerned mainly with some recollections, and rather random ones, of the period just preceding the Hagarty years.

Bishop Bernard was deeply involved in the care and education of youth, both in the classroom and elsewhere. As a bishop, he considered himself to have a ministerial responsibility not only to Catholics but to all the people of the Bahamas.

Besides the fourteen grammar schools that were opened in Nassau and the Family Islands during his administration, there were twenty-seven Sunday schools opened during those twenty years. The Madonna Day Nursery operated by the Sisters of Charity had a daily average attendance of about forty children of pre-school age, and the tall stately bishop moved among these little ones as the symbol of goodness. He gave constant encouragement to the sisters and their dedicated lay helpers.

The care of youth outside the classroom mushroomed into many youth organizations. Athletic fields and clubrooms were provided in most of the Nassau parishes. The Catholic Band under the direction of Frs. Arnold Dittberner and Alban Fruth, and the Saint Benedict's Choral Club guided by the late Fr. Ambrose Wittman were among the leading musical groups in Nassau.

Another educational area that had the special interest of Bishop Bernard was the summer schools for Family Island catechists. These were carefully planned and attended by all catechists of the islands. Parish study clubs and even sewing clubs for women and girls flourished and had a lasting impact on the spread and deepening of the faith, especially because of the genuine personal affection between the people and the priests and sisters.

Bishop Bernard constantly encouraged the priests, sisters, and brothers to move about and meet the people where they were, which was often not in church but in their homes or out on the playing fields. The sisters who taught in the schools were also regular visitors in the homes of their pupils and were usually the ones who brought word to the pastor of illness or distress in a home. As many of the pupils were not Catholic, this was how many Protestant families made their acquaintance with a Catholic priest, and it was not unusual that entire families became Catholic because of the friendships that grew up in this way.

When I came to the Bahamas as a newly-ordained priest in the summer of 1947, Bishop Bernard was already in failing health, but the educational and social activities of the Catholic mission were everywhere in evidence and were an important part of life in the Bahamas. The antagonism toward Catholics that first greeted priests who came in the late 1800s and early 1900s had for the most part been laid to rest. As people began to have the advantages of education, fear and prejudice gradually disappeared. But more important was the fact that the gentle and diplomatic manner of Bishop Bernard proved a most contagious spirit which seemed to pervade both clergy and laity who made up the Catholic community in the Bahamas. Gentleness, kindness and hospitality are so much a part of the nature of the people of the Bahamas that they instinctively recognized the same qualities in Bishop Bernard. A deep affection was bound to develop between the chief shepherd and his flock.

Bishop Bernard died on December 9, 1949, and Prior Frederic Frey wrote in the *Bahama Benedictine:* "Without doubt His Lordship's greatest contribution to education in the Colony was the founding of the Convent of Blessed Martin de Porres and of Saint Augustine's Monastery."

Saint Augustine's Monastery and College was founded by Abbot Alcuin Deutsch of Saint John's Abbey and Prior Frederic himself in 1945 and was still in its infancy. At Saint Martin's Convent a Bahamian teaching sisterhood had been established and already five of its sisters were taking a full-time active part in the education of youth.

Just as now the basketball courts and the playing fields at Saint Augustine's College are daily after-school and weekend meeting places for hundreds of Bahamians, so in the days of Bishop Bernard the priory basketball court and the Saint Bernard cricket field were teaming with youth every day after school, and often the priests were there. Certainly not all of these young people would show up in church on Sunday, but some of them did, and gradually many became converts to the faith.

However, Bishop Bernard was acutely aware that forming a faith community required patient teaching in doctrine and morals and well prepared and disciplined worship on the Lord's Day. He would personally check to see that every catechetical class and holy hour was taken seriously, just as seriously for an attendance of three people as for twenty or thirty.

When he died, after heading the Catholic community in the Bahamas for twenty years, thousands of people of all denominations came to pay their respects as his body lay in state in Bungalow Dunmore on the priory grounds. The Bishop Bernard Memorial Building constructed in his memory now houses the offices of the Haitian community apostolate.

Bishop Bernard's right-hand man was Fr. Bonaventure Hansen, a monk of Saint John's Abbey who had come to the Bahamas in 1921. Before that he had been a Dakota missionary for sixteen years between 1905 and 1921. He was a man in delicate health when he began pioneering for the faith in the semi-tropics, but he stayed with it for the next thirty-three years until his death on December 9, 1954.

Father Bonaventure was one of those men who believed deeply in his vocation as a missionary. He also believed deeply that one has to take many risks and perhaps make more than a few mistakes to give the Lord a chance to do his part, even with one's mistakes.

There was a more than natural explanation for Father Bonaventure's incurable optimism. It was the fact that he believed the Blessed Virgin Mary was assisting him in every decision to found "yet another" mission, and that from then on she was entrusted with the "impossibilities" of the future. This happened not only once and again, but every time he acquired another piece of property with the intention of turning it into a chapel, school, nursery, or convent.

Father Bonaventure never forgot that when he was an infant Our Lady had miraculously intervened to save his life, that she had preserved him on two other occasions when poor health found him near death, and that she had more than once rescued him from near shipwreck in the early and perilous days of out-island travel.

He did much to promote a fitting observance of the Marian Year in 1953–54 and was called to his reward the first day after its close.

Although a kindly person and a good listener to people of opposing views, Father Bonaventure was something of a controversial character. As vicar delegate to Bishop Bernard Kevenhoerster, he was more forceful in expressing his views and more daring in opening new missions. He was not only motivated but driven on in high gear by an overpowering desire to bring the Gospel to everybody, especially those outside the faith. He had quit smoking years before his death, not so much for health reasons but out of respect for the feelings of Protestants who were opposed to it. His fertile mind was always restless and full of ideas for new and untried approaches to make friends among Protestants. The fact that he was held in the highest regard by the descendants of previously anti-Catholic parents was proof to him that there is much evangelization to do among people who may never see the inside of a Catholic Church. Father Bonaventure took his cues from such gallant North American pioneers as Saints Isaac Jogues and Jean de Brébeuf. Failure or defeat never seemed to dishearten him but only made him more tenacious and resourceful.

For a vicar delegate he had the happy trait of refusing to fuss too much about the details of administration. He felt that if you regulate and program things too carefully, the Holy Spirit will leave you on your own. "Many times I missed the boat completely," he used to say, but he didn't seem to have time to brood over failures.

Father Bonaventure also remained interested in scholarly reading throughout his busy life. Scripture, theology, canon law were favorite subjects of his reading; books on Church history and the lives of the saints could be seen open on his desk. He studied carefully the encyclicals and decrees from the Holy See. It was a source of genuine pleasure to him when in 1942 the Holy See honored him with the medal *Pro Ecclesia et Pontifice*.

Not everyone saw eye to eye with his passion for opening new missions. Some of the missionaries felt it was more important to cultivate carefully that part of the vineyard where the Church was already established than to go too far afield. But one man who shared Father Bonaventure's view was Fr. (and later Bishop) Paul Leonard Hagarty. Bishop Leonard used to quote Father Bonaventure to explain his own passion for opening new churches, schools, and clinics right and left: "Father Bonaventure often said, 'Even if you have to go into debt, have this generation receive some Catholic education.'"

Because his views reflect so closely his respect for the wisdom of Father Bonaventure, it is worth quoting Bishop Leonard on this subject:

> If you just turn off education because you haven't got the money in hand, or refuse to open a new mission because you're short of funds, you will deprive the Family Island people of a church or a school just because they can't pay.
>
> There are two different policies in regard to expanding missions. One policy says, "Go slowly, prepare the people and they will become missionaries themselves." The other policy says, "Spread it thin, and go from one island to the next, one mission to another, even if you can't give them full instruction."
>
> There is a great deal to be said for each view, but I have always felt that the sacraments are for people.
>
> My policy has been that, even if your personnel is limited, try to extend as far as you can the basic teachings of the Catholic Church. Then people will at least have the chance to say yes or no to the teachings of the Church.
>
> I consider this a more valid missionary policy than just staking out certain places in order to stick right there and develop them as centers. Life is going by too fast for that. There are people getting sick and dying and having had no chance to get close to the Church. I figure that I am the bishop of all the people of the Bahamas, not just the Catholics.[1]

In spite of Father Bonaventure's rather brusque manner, which mellowed much in later years, there was in him an unmistakable trait of bigheartedness which prompted his most characteristic greeting, "What can I do for you?" Over the years he became known to old-timers of every denomination as the "grand old man." He had begun his work in the Bahamas at a time when there were still very few Catholics, thus finding himself in the delicate position of a priest surrounded almost entirely by unbelievers. Other missionaries of his temperament had felt themselves ostracized in

1. Colman J. Barry, *Upon These Rocks: Catholics in the Bahamas* (Collegeville: St. John's Abbey Press, 1973) 452.

such surroundings, but Father Bonaventure, even in his brusqueness, genuinely loved people. He sensed what was good and true in the tradition of the mainline Protestant denominations, and he set out to sow the seeds of Catholicism in a soil that was already prepared by the people's love of the Bible and their fidelity to the commandments. Father Bonaventure had a mind that was open enough to recognize good faith and zeal for Christ in the hearts of non-Catholic clergymen, even those strongly opposed to Catholicism.

In fact, the more a Protestant opposed Father Bonaventure, the more likely that person was to become his personal friend. He had an affinity for people of strong convictions. Many of his most trusted friends were Protestants of various denominations who were prominent in the business and political life of the country. He was regarded by them as a spiritual leader who was genuinely interested in common problems. They knew him as a trusted collaborator, a man who proved to them that Catholics shared the anxieties and hopes of all Christians and were anxious to work together with them in building a better Bahamian community. Here was a man who could walk into the midst of opposition day after day and batter it down, or rather, melt it away, by his massive and persistent presence coupled with a burning zeal to bring God's love into the picture. Clergymen of other denominations who at one time had been suspicious of the Catholic Church came to respect and love Father Bonaventure as a person. They respected him all the more because they saw in him a man of uncompromising loyalty to his Church and a living example of militant Christianity.

Writing in the centennial booklet commemorating one hundred years of Catholic education in the Bahamas (1989), the present minister of education, the Honorable Paul L. Adderley, observes:

> This centennial celebration is a superb opportunity for Catholic education to claim full recognition for its solid contribution to the birth of the Commonwealth of the Bahamas, made through its institutions and through the many thousands of men and women, boys and girls, who owe much to it.
>
> I believe that this deserves a higher profile in our national consciousness.
>
> Catholic education has survived many viscissitudes. Through the years it has been a valued partner of the government school system

in providing educational opportunities for pupils as well as teachers and administrators, and in the planning and production of curricular and other measures and matters aimed to improve the quality of education offered and of skills mastered in our country.

I hope that this will long continue to be the case and would again wish to congratulate the Roman Catholic Church on the occasion of its centennial celebration.

Writing in the same publication, the prime minister of the Bahamas, the Honorable Sir Lynden Oscar Pindling, remarks:

I do hope that as the second century of Catholic participation in the delivery of education begins, it would continue to be successful in giving Bahamian young people quality-exposure to primary and secondary education at home, and advise referrals of more able, experienced and matured candidates to Saint John's and Saint Benedict's in Minnesota.

I am ever so pleased that through your enthusiastic, stimulating and motivational exercises, education is now perceived as an instrument of power in the sense that it gives individuals human dignity as well as true freedom and responsibility to chart their own destiny.

THE CARPENTER SHOP
AND HUBERT SCHNEIDER

B Y THE VERY FACT THAT MONASTERIES TEND
to lengthen their lives into centuries and grow casual with their
histories, they don't expend a vast amount of energy in asking how
and why they grew old.[1] They let their history accumulate itself
without fanfare or fret, and if it gathers dust, monks just shrug
their shoulders and let the dust get thicker. They know that someday there will emerge a person who will worry about the history
and want to put it on paper lest it be forgotten. The wiser know
that it will be forgotten even though the dust gets thicker; yet even
the wiser make precautionary provision by creating the office of
archivist, whose role it is to amass the things which become history, provide some order among them, and keep the dust from
growing too thick.

Most archivists are hidden away in obscure parts of the monastery where their treasures which other than historians and anti-
quarians tend to call junk are guarded so carefully against those
who have no right to peer into the past that not even the abbot
has a key to the store house. The archivists themselves tend to become as quiet as the treasures they brood over. They do their work
wordlessly, need no supervision, rarely receive any notice of their

1. Reprinted from Alfred H. Deutsch, "Introductory Essay," *Saint John's
Furniture 1874-1974* (Collegeville: Saint John's Abbey, 1974) 2-7.

existence, and grow grey in their profession. Such are the official archivists in the monastery.

The unofficial archivists are not vastly different from the official ones, and are not usually looked upon as archivists, though they should be. They too are custodians of the past who with skill and peculiar memory can lead one to the exact holding of some artifact among a jungle of unsortable confusion. For example, much of the history of the monastery is buried at varying levels underground where tunnels and vaults hold pipes and conduits that have meaning only to the custodian. Given a need for the location of a definite article, the custodian will lead you off to a piece of field, put a shovel in your hands, and say "dig down eight feet at this spot."

One is led to wonder whether Benedict was thinking about these men in the chapter on the artisans of the monastery who "practice their crafts with all humility." They have to be "brethren on whose manner of life and character the abbot can rely." They are people who early in monastic formation accepted Benedict's admonition to handle the goods entrusted to them "as if they were the sacred vessels of the altar."

When that worried historian finds it necessary to reduce some facts to paper, one of the unofficial archivists that he will have to visit will be found in the carpenter shop. Saturday morning will be the time for the interview because the saws will not be whining nor the jointer screaming that work is in progress. If Br. Hubert Schneider is a bit annoyed that you are interfering with the sharpening of the saws and the oiling of machines, you will not be made aware of it. This is the morning when he finds no need to put cotton in his ears. The only noise may come from the vacuum sweeper which picks up the sawdust left over from the week's produce. The tour may be cause that the saws are somewhat less sharp in the next week, but there may be other moments when he can tend to them. One Saturday missed in forty years will not ruin the machine.

The carpenter shop has two archives which speak with some authority to those who know enough to interpret the data. Behind the shop is the long, undistinguished shed that gets painted occasionally with leftover colors; known simply as the lumber shed, it might more profitably be called a museum of spare parts and leftovers. The first look is the not unexpected view of shapeless confusion common to museums where the curator has not yet had the time to mark the dates and essential features of the pieces. The mind encompasses one vast image of boards without number—long boards, short boards, round boards, square boards, stained boards, painted boards, smooth boards, and rough boards. Galleys along the two sides of the shed appear to have some order, but the middle road between them is a chaos of ends and bits and leavings piled against each other or around anything that has a bit of stability. Given time, the curator will handle each of these, identify it, tag it in his own recollection, then tuck it away in spaces where someday it will be available. He does not know the day, nor does he fret about that day.

Long knowledge of the monastery and its inhabitants has taught him the changeableness of things and man's tendency to repeat himself. Tucked away out of sight, by way of example, are a set of beautiful oak panels, all of a size. "These," he tells the historian, "are from the college dining room. I have put them up twice, I have taken them down twice, I will put them up again." Such wisdom garnished with the innate sense of thrift forms the philosophy which accounts for the collection. Not all of these things bear his personal memories. Much of the collection grows from his willingness to loan space to those changeable persons who find themselves with objects no longer useful. "Take it to the carpenter shop." When a new school of piety no longer found statues appropriate in their usual repositories, the solution was easy: "Take them to the carpenter shop." When antique furniture seemed out of place in modern decor, it went to the carpenter shop. If buildings came down or alterations were made, the salvage flowed to the carpenter shop.

Once the eye has grown accustomed to the apparent confusion, individual objects begin to peer at him. This is when the curator easily brings out of his memory information the historian is worried about. "That piece of bannister hanging up in the cradle? It is the bannister that was in the stairwell just outside the student dining room. We keep it in case we need to repair other parts of the bannister." "Those large grills? They come from the auditorium. Once they were to the left and the right of the front curtain and were the screens for the organ."

The historian would suspect that Brother Hubert might have grown sentimental over some of the pieces, especially things which he had made and now saw discarded. The historian is reminded of a bit of by-play in Chekhov's *Cherry Orchard* when Gayev gazes at a bookcase: "That bookcase was made exactly one hundred years ago. What do you think of that? Perhaps we should celebrate its anniversary. True, it's just an inanimate object, but all, everything considered, a bookcase . . . ." Then Gayev fondles the bookcase and launches into an apostrophe: "Dear, esteemed bookcase, I salute your existence which, for more than a hundred years, has contributed to the ideals of goodness and justice. Your silent call to productive efforts has never weakened in the course of these one hundred years."

Though he will not get sentimental, Brother Hubert has shown fondness for the materials which he worked with. Tucked away in a top galley above a little board on which is printed "walnut" are bits and ends of walnut. He recalls the pleasure of receiving a couple walnut logs from Bishop Peter Bartholome with a request to decorate the interior of the bishop's chapel. Some of the end pieces he had set aside for high school boys who at one time had a hobby shop where Tommy Hall now stands. One could almost accuse him of fondling the wood as he studies the grain to determine where this board will best fit in a table top, or desk top, or panel.

All these things he passes through with a degree of detachment remarkable in a monastery where builders of kingdoms and monastic pack rats hate to see more than one key to any operation. To him these are all the property of the monastery and he is the custodian. They were always available to anyone who had need. Rarely does one walk into the carpenter shop without seeing an amateur carpenter fixing a hockey stick or building bird cages or making some shelves.

For a good many years the carpenter shop was the locale of the junior formation program. Almost without fail a new brother candidate was sent to the carpenter shop for his first days and months of work in the monastery. Although Brother Hubert did not draw the salary of a junior master, it was in the shop where the young monk learned to exercise the principles the junior master and novice master were preaching. Here he began to learn the meaning of the sacredness of work and the meaning of the *labora* part of the Benedictine motto. He began to learn the discipline of regularity and responsibility to the work which obedience had assigned. He learned to respect the tools he worked with and to use them with reverence. The first inklings of monastic obedience—how it is transferred from abbot to individuals in the monastery—quickened in him; he began to learn a craft under the guidance of a master craftsman.

Tucked up in one of the lofts of the carpenter shed are rows of chair backs which the historian can peg with the aid of Brother Hubert. Most nearly accessible are the fancy chairs which somehow could not withstand the weight and strength of the students in Tommy Hall. Over a rafter are the curved back ends of chairs that students for many decades squirmed on in the dining hall. Even further out of reach are the seats and backs of chairs which swiveled in posts screwed to the floors of the study halls. Here they gather dust until the antiquarian discovers nostalgic alumni who will buy the chair they sat in back in Saint Bede's Hall.

The antiquarian has made his inroads during the past five years, and many of the castoffs that hid in the lofts and in the other storage space in the attic of the carpenter shop have become treasures. Where tabernacles and statues and carved chairs once stood is now occupied with a variety of plywood, pegboard, plasterboard, compoboard, nuwood, and dozens of other substitutes for the oak and maple that the perfect craftsman once used.

Some of the oak and maple still lies in unfinished and unglamorous form in the alcoves of the shed, identified only with strange words that Brother Hubert needs to translate for the historian touring with him. "Double u, ee, i, d..o,k.? That's easy. That's white oak. That's the marking of Max Schmoeller who worked in this shed for a long time." Then Brother Hubert talked about the decades when the abbey crafted its own wood from the forest to the dining tables. Workmen combed the woods during the winter season and culled out mature trees and hauled them to a spot about where Bernard Hall stands. Here for a few weeks in spring, before the farm was quite ready for the ploughs, Br. Julius Terfehr and the workmen cut the logs for the presumed needs of the carpenter shop. The steam engine burned up the sidings from the logs and made more steam to rip more logs into usable sizes. For students and monks the scene became the place of daily pilgrimage in a period when the puffing of the steamer was the most excitement on the campus.

Another little wooden sign at one of the alcoves catches the eye of the historian, but this one he can interpret for himself: "Ok, no dri." That means "oak, not dry, right?" And Brother Hubert nods his approval of the accuracy of translation. After forty years that sign is hardly accurate. But it did recall the process of preparing wood which the master craftsman needed for his work: the long process of stacking the new boards in shapely stacks with breathing space for each; the next move to the carpenter shop for further drying, then the move to the kiln where the final application of heat assured there would be no warping; finally the move into the carpenter shop where each board was shoved through a screaming planer until it had the thickness the craftsman needed.

Some few stacks of those years rest easily in the alcoves waiting for their turn to become finished boards. Hidden away behind stacks of boards is one neat pile of finished maple, one foot to two feet in length, carefully tied into small bundles. They are reminders to the historian that most of the floors in the college section of the quadrangle had been replaced.

When the twin towers came down for the removal of the bells to their new position, the towers did not completely disappear. The curious eye will find a stack of dry, brown beams sitting solidly in one of the alcoves, waiting for the day when the right job will be found for them. Still another part of the tower, the topmost cupola out of which the cross rose, waits in the farthest corner of the south balcony, accessible to the man willing to tangle his legs in chair parts and clamber through an assortment of furniture frames.

Windows, doors, screens lean against walls, each having lived out its time of service and waiting for some one to finish their history. The custodian can tell which came from what building, but none is important enough to warrant a permanent memory.

Rarely does one come across an intact article, for there is always someone browsing through the shed searching out its treasures. Only when a new department head decides that the office needs a fresh look will whole articles flow back to the carpenter shed. These are moments which can evoke a tinge of chagrin in the curator because frequently the pieces had been tooled specially for a role in a designated office, built to minute specifications for a designated space, and there is no other place for them. Standing on this Saturday in the central corridor as a resting place for odds and ends not yet sorted is a cabinet some ten feet long of solid oak and three feet deep, divided into spaces of unusual size, unfinished at one end because it had been made to rest against a particular wall. Someday it will be discovered by a monk with a big enough room who has the right assortment of curios to bury in the various drawers.

A small stack of finished panels reminds Brother Hubert that Abbot Alcuin Deutsch had discovered in his early years as abbot that he liked wainscoting, a liking he may have uncovered on a trip to a foreign monastery. Brother refers the historian to the monastery dining room which is entirely walled with wainscot to a height of seven feet with magnificently matched wood. Next he is referred to the conference room which had been the office of Abbot Alcuin: matched bookcase and beautiful wainscot surround the room. However, Abbot Alcuin's liking for wainscot did not extend as long as his liking for stone walls so that few exhibits of this art remain.

Another relict of the regime of Abbot Alcuin is the awareness that one can go to the carpenter shop without an ID card or a billfold. If Brother Hubert keeps books or writes down charges—which surely in this university now has to be done—one does not catch him at it. At the carpenter shop it seems rather gross to ask what something costs; one does not get the feeling of customer dealing with proprietor when he wanders into the shop. Vaguely one senses that surely this product or these boards cost something but it seems unbecoming to ask. In this shop one feels the almost forgotten sense that this belongs to "us." One wanders into this shop, asks for the attic key which is handed over without any inquiry, shops around as long as he chooses, and on leaving is greeted with "Did you find what you want?"

On this particular Saturday morning the shop is almost free of assembled parts, but memory recollects the months when one threaded his way between machines and heaps of sections that were fitted into the clothes cabinets and book shelves for Mary Hall, and again for Tommy Hall. When the new monastery was built, Brother Hubert contracted for the floors and wardrobes and book shelves. The flooring machine was uncovered and greased, wood that had been drying for twenty some years was carted out, and everybody from the Huschle's to Flynntown heard that flooring was being made. Thirty thousand feet of flooring screamed through the machine, and the sound delighted the ears of monks who lived in memory of selfsubsistence and remembered what Benedict wrote "for then they are truly monks when they live by the labor of their hands, as did our Fathers and the Apostles."

History also notes that this was the last major production of flooring, for shortly after that job the machine was sold. Another casualty of that huge job was the loss of hearing in one ear for Brother Hubert.

Further reminiscence recalls the willingness of the curator to put aside whatever job may be in progress to cut a board for a monk or student who is afraid of the buttons on the machines and the edges on the saw. Neighbors can ask Brother Hubert to file a saw without being embarrassed. During the years when the prep school kept the hobby shop open in the old chicken barn, students wandered into the carpenter shop any day to pick through the bits of board in the wheelbarrow which always stood near the jointer, to get some advice on handling a particular piece of wood, or to borrow a bit of glue or a handful of nails. Occasionally a nickel or dime sheepishly changed hands.

One of these years the carpenter shop may be rebuilt and may succumb to the title now appearing over the door of "woodworking department" like the mathematics department and English department—evoking the awareness of associated terms like budgets, directors, personnel managers, and inventories. It will lose the spirit the porter's office lost when it grew into a reception center, when the procurator became the business manager, and the assistant procurator became the director of corporate enterprises.

The historian is tempted to pick up a dowel standing in the corner of the shop and break into the words of Chekhov's Uncle Gayev: "Dear, esteemed dowel, I salute your existence." But the historian has read through the rest of Chekhov's *Cherry Orchard* and knows some subsequent lines of Uncle Gayev: "Today I delivered a speech to the bookcase . . . so idiotic! Not until I got through did I see how idiotic it was." His niece responds: "That's right, uncle dear, you should keep quiet. Just keep quiet, that's all."

I N THE ENCHANTING DUET "DO YOU LOVE ME?"
in Act II of *Fiddler on the Roof,* Tevye and Golde rehearse decades
of personal meaning in their prescribed, arranged marriage. Not
strangely, aspects of their dialogue come to mind at the request
to write a personal essay about the meaning, the sense of Saint
John's in my life. For as high school graduation drew near, some
South Dakota friends and I had decided for the University of Michigan and pre-law studies. There had been no family debate about
whether I would continue on to college; somewhat unusual for those
times, both my mother and father were college graduates. That
matter was settled. But midsummer 1948 saw my parents newly
convinced and refusing tuition for me to any but a Catholic college; thus the persuasive power of my lately injured, for a time
home-bound World War II veteran and oldest brother, Fran, a
Saint John's alumnus. To keep me occupied, he arranged a double,
pre-med and philosophy set of majors for me. I was bewildered,
too incensed to shout, and cultivated that dismal change in my plans
as a grim reversal of values like the Witches' cry in Macbeth: "Fair
is foul and foul is fair. " Only later did I come to see it as a possible point of insertion of grace and, perhaps akin to Augustine's
oxymoron, a *felix culpa.* But that is another story.

At first blush, for me a long year after being enrolled in the college, I remained unsettled, rather sulkily unhappy to be here while,

simultaneously, I was becoming intrigued by the palpable intellectual ambiance and spiritual bent of many at this place. Still, late in my freshman year, the initial, grudging estimate of Saint John's held: the founding monks and their successors had molded an *ad hoc* community out of strangers, shaped a creditable set of schools, and made the whole of it work. It did not seem more to me then.

Now as then, Saint John's in all its complexity celebrates the unfathomable potential and value of "the whole person" and, under God, the harmony of all creation. When my personal alienation began to erode, a number of concepts, "discoveries" new to one who had never thought of nor been engaged by them before—I mean realities of the genial environment of intellect and spirit endemic to Saint John's—enticed me; they also caused some real apprehension because of their compelling character. Yet, these freighted "discoveries" emerged, as I would learn, from rooted, even sesquimillennial and older traditions.

Coincident with the time I began to revel in the foundations and breadth of a liberal arts education, I also began to perceive that Saint John's proffered much more as well, something approaching the unique. A short list of those earlier mentioned "discoveries," as I understood and was being enthused by them then, would read as follows. Almost physically shaken, I came to know:

- that liturgy (even the word was new to me) is an intrinsic part of an integral, non-compartmentalized life;
- that free intellectual inquiry and the love of God, like the harmony of local flora and fauna or the oils of a painting, are mutually supportive and designedly interactive, yet not simply compatible nor wholly separable in the quest for truth;
- that in the Rule's humane insights individual differences of persons are to be taken account of, even broadly cherished;
- that holiness, should anyone be moved towards it, centers not in the absence of faults but in creative love: one dwells on what to do, give, and be rather than on what to shun;
- that Catholicism, even the whole of Christianity, is not a philosophy or social system but a way of life that finds expression not in law, however lofty, but in a Person.[1]

1. This list is in fact extended, for these and other items I mention throughout were parts of a rationale that coalesced and urged, still with a certain disquiet, my eventual decision.

For me to discern such realities, philosophical, theological, and practical life realities, meant more than a personal sea-change of viewpoint. At seventeen, I had been totally innocent of such concepts before encountering and being encountered by them here. Much more engaging even then was the experience of seeing such concepts actually guiding the lives of monks and laymen who were my savants. That fact was not open to easy sophistic or theoretical rejection, and it became a good deal more for me than any mere, albeit powerful, process of osmosis. On this topic, more later.

Of course, a distaff side of things was present then as it is now. Not unlike today's omnipresent personal temptation for many citizens to avoid inconvenience at any cost (such seems to be a besetting '80s "sin") I found in those first college years that a temptation toward a corrosive cynicism is present over time to some religious. That temptation was born, I thought then, of one's own maturing grasp of seemingly fixed personal problems or by frequently meeting the frustrating inertia of a disparate group of other persons from whom one expected more. Thus, as a fledgling student I became aware that religious themselves may be subject to these same realities even as they also meet them in others' family life or in the Church. But I think, as Twain observed about guiding motifs of examined lives, my "discoveries"—some may incline to see them as mere chestnuts—are, indeed, chestnuts and not chestnuts. I am comfortable in knowing they are not chestnuts when they become one's own, on original assimilation; they support convictions that perdure, endure. Liberating and still captivating in their nuances, they are after time's testing still revelatory. And even in my incomplete listing, they maintain their appeal to me in the face of controversy and shifting fashions resident at Saint John's and in the history of any period.

Sometime during my sophomore year when I became reconciled to being here, I noticed the beguiling power of the place heightened as I grew in consciousness of the activities, apostolates, and historical worship and work that emanate from Saint John's. What I perceived germinally as an early '50s undergraduate, reverence of tradition made appealing by innovation and new knowledge, as a monk I see growing or changing to ever fuller proportions. Saint John's, as any living organism that is part of a whole, has been and is a part of what seem, now more clearly to me, to be the significant, lasting, deeply exciting movements in Christian, specifically Catholic, life in this century.[2]

I refer to the renewal of the liturgy and its sanctifying functions; the rediscovery of the living Word of God in the Scriptures; the burgeoning ecumenical activity and outreach—and the successive realization of all these individual movements in underlining the distinct yet mutual ministries of all Catholics, ordained and non-ordained, in vibrant Church life. In more recent times as a consequence, I have sometimes suggested to theology students such theses topics that could delineate the interdependence and synergistic relationships of these still arresting twentieth-century movements. A parade example of this is the 1989 founding of the Episcopal Diocese of Minnesota House of Prayer on the campus.

Further, I would hazard the opinion that these movements find, variously, some initiation or confirmation in a keystone early '40s ecclesial document, Pope Pius XII's encyclical *Divino Afflante Spiritu,* a writing I came to appreciate in the middle '50s. That seminal collection of directives officially, decisively moved the Church away from its tendency toward biblical fundamentalism and brought it, in some instances unwillingly still, into the twentieth-century intellectual and spiritual mainstream. While *DAS* dealt specifically with matters of scriptural interpretation and the true, full locus of the Word of God in Catholic life, in its suggestive implications and intellectual cast it seems to me to have augured notably for the subsequent full-blown developments that occurred at Vatican Council II in the early '60s. Of course, as one perceives about that council's documents and continuing Church life, the historian in me knows it is still too soon to make absolute or definitive judgments about the reception and lasting implementation of such deliberations after but a few tumultuous decades. However, to experience personally Saint John's engagement in a number of these movements[3] well before Vatican II and its aftermath was a heady, formative adventure I should detail somewhat now.

---

2. Sometime in my collegiate junior year I recognized that the seeds of increasing attraction to monastic life here, many as ancient as Christianity and undeniably compelling, were present well before I ever set foot on the campus.

3. My experience of such movements varied, both as a lay student and later as a monk.

Over time in summers, a number of Saint John's confreres and I participated as staff members and auditors in Saint John's exhilarating outreach programs of the '50s and '60s, local movements "with all deliberate speed" to use a memorable presidential line of those days—in view of some hierarchical apprehension. The Scriptural Institute for all clergy and the also precedent-setting Mental Health Institute in Pastoral Psychology for all clergy were innovative workshops lasting together and in tandem from 1954 through the early '70s. They encouraged recognized world leaders in these disciplines together with clergy of many denominations to come to Saint John's for separate, intensive weeks of learning together. Fortunately like other such here, these institutes were successful seeding efforts and had a telling role in spawning and abetting similar ecumenical, on-going national, and international seminars elsewhere. For myself personally, the message was once again that no one can be seriously involved in such activities or even live where they occur and not be, as with prayer, meditation, and religious praxis, formed by them. Something again of a *lex orandi, lex credendi* non-chestnut.

Additionally, besides the very well-known national and worldwide liturgical conferences, some initially here for the United States and now ubiquitous; the unimpeachable international influence of the publishing efforts of our local Liturgical Press; the manysplendored work of the Hill Monastic Manuscript Library; and the now twenty-one-year-old Institute for Ecumenical and Cultural Research here, lesser known, even deliberately unpublicized gatherings of Lutheran and Catholic seminarians and professors here beginning in the later '50s gave undeniable credence and regional impact to dialogues between differing but sturdy stances of faith with substantive intellectual inquiry. The effects of this latter work, itself now formally in abeyance yet somewhat detailed in the first, companion volume of this series, are still filtering into the churches as those seminarians reach mature pastoral positions and reflection. Especially while I was personally connected with such activities here, I felt the strong sense of human interdependence that is so characteristic of monks' moving through Saint John's history.

I mention these highly selective instances of striking formative activity at Saint John's for several reasons: (1) because we can take justifiable local pride in them and (2) because as a working archaeologist and antiquarian, I know that the past explains much about the present and gives, perhaps, a glimpse of an exciting future. In fact, not to be clearly informed of the past, one cannot know intimately the present nor make semi-intelligible projections of a shrouded future.[4]

Curiously, we monks who live at Saint John's tend regularly to take for granted what visitors—those who, along with the university itself and the fact that abbey confreres continue to be educated around the world, help to keep the place relatively free of parochialism and local tunnel-vision—always remark: the many beauties of Saint John's and the apparently communicable serenity of persons here, their inner mien and its external manifestations in architectural and visual expressions of their thought and values. Voiced often also is the fact of the comforting human scale of the place, rather like a small-town enclave, in its nineteenth-century European complexes that exist agreeably alongside twentieth-century projections.

The older woodlands, lakes, and outercampus terrain clearly reflect the changes of four distinct seasons of birth and renewal, growth toward maturity, ripening to harvest, and final death-rest cycles. These notable changes cannot be hindered from affecting even casual observers resident here. Instead, in cumulative caché all of nature seems to contrive to form those who dwell here into, among other things, convinced, if armchair, horticulturalists and conservation-conscious preservationists. Surely for monastics, these realities and landscape additions are undergirded fittingly by the *Rule's* altogether familiar counsels for care of all things and thoughtful moderation in one's actions.

Over a number of years some of our especially alert visitors have noted that the occasional small, even misshaped tree, shrub, or other planting is patiently tended as, they have suggested, are young persons here. As if some monastic sons remember their parents' admonitions to "make something of themselves" in time and who

4. By analogy, I now know two theological commonplaces well through experience and training. A fully adult, personal act of faith may have a long incubation; a gift originally, it gains vitality through many directions of experience and openness to grace, especially through other persons. Similarly, by my senior year I saw dimly yet convincingly that the Providence of God in our lives is best grasped or known with some clarity only in retrospect.

then project that concept also to growing plantlife in the hope, as the poet says, of making "plough down sillion" shine. Judging from the few random passages in the *Rule,* could Benedict have had it in mind that the very naïveté and youth of the young should move more experienced sojourners to charity? Certainly, it is patent that the practice of careful maintenance of living things applies also to property and inert objects such as the buildings and grounds of Saint John's generally; it also seems to include discrete items like the regularly polished brass spigots of the lavaboes in the sparely used lower chapels' area or the customary re-pointing of long-inoperative chimneys. Perhaps such attentive action derives from the *Rule*'s understandable and piously extended religious mentality.

But whatever is the case, the fact is indisputable that the *sine qua non loci* of formation at Saint John's are persons: monks, faculty, staff members, present and former students, close friends, and anyone who has lived and worked here over time. Historically, Benedictines have a custom of not publicly nor in a broadcast way especially honoring confreres while they are alive. On the whole that seems a wise practice, and I will not break the rather firm custom. Here, some words of Mr. Stephen Humphrey, a master teacher lionized in theory by generations of his students and faculty members, come to mind: "I beg you not to celebrate me while I'm alive; you can feel free to do anything you wish after I'm gone." The university acknowledged his wish but, some time after his death, named the theater in the renovated auditorium in his honor. Similarly, I want to speak of one monk confrere, lately deceased, who epitomizes for me what I believe others, monastics or not, have come to know of the power of human agency and example in seeking to be true sons and daughters of God. There are others presently living here who would also serve my purpose well. [5]

Fr. Dunstan Tucker was accomplished at passing over or straightening out a number of my unexamined assumptions and biases, even some that sporadically resurface in more mature years. Formed himself by his family, the many such avenues available at Saint John's, and by his tenure as a commander in the navy, his first counsel to me as a college student was that humility was far removed from humiliation, but that when the latter came, to act like

5. The diverse wealth of possibilities will be evident in this series of volumes.

spartina grass at the seashore: filter out the salt and be nourished by the water. A few years later, yet on the same topic, he noted pointedly that authentic "crosses" enough come to a monk or Christian and there is no need to go looking for them—as he sent me looking back to considered reflection of the *Rule's* trenchant fourth step to humility (7:35-43).

I have no doubt of Dunstan's conviction that the key to a holy monastic life is contingent on a monk's learning in all things to give himself away—to myriad opportunities for the common weal, community service, and for the world—so often did he mention it.

His was a particular gift for helping the young of any chronological age. Who (certainly not me until we talked about it) would have thought wisely that young people who know little about the concept of delayed gratification may "have to go to the limit before the idea of limit begins to make sense"? That phrase of Jaroslav Pelikan I heard recently, but it is a sensical view Dunstan had spoken in but slightly different words much earlier. Another of his observations allowed me to feel the hook gently: "Young people generally, through no fault of their own, mind you, usually have no real sense of the swiftness of time nor of its limits." At the time he was remarking that the vulnerability felt by young people at not being in command can be a good, even if that is seen only as a need to be open to grace. His naval experience and monastic life in combination?

Dunstan's own physical visage and sometimes courtly demeanor roundly suggested that Gilbert and Sullivan's "aspect stern and gloomy stride" has no place in monastic life, except perhaps when an egregious call on the baseball diamond occurs, demanding it. At times I imagined I heard echoes of my own Irish forebears speaking when he mentioned that a person should prepare in times of prosperity for times of adversity. And that when especially in the nearly pure democracy of monastic chapter meetings wherein everyone has the right of equal voice and equal vote, he opined that occasional flashes of silence add greatly to the conversation. On this occasion he summarized the point in a Whitehead-like way, something tantamount to "a clear voice is best only when it is matched by a like kind of prior thought."

That Father Dunstan was a man of considerable identification with sports of all kinds initially made it eye-opening for me to realize he was, above all, a Benedictine scholar of the classical mold and a deeply spiritual person. An *image sportif* he used when we talked about our monastic commitment was that "the rules and integrity of the game we monks have freely joined in, hold," despite what he felt some academics' persistent penchant—to manipulate meaning with language—might suggest.

My lasting impression of Dunstan is of a humane confrere who never did anything for no reason, a facet of personality and way of acting that appeals to me even if that appeal lingers too often only on the edges of action. Not surprisingly for me or probably others, he embodied a fullness of the word for one of the gifts of the Holy Spirit I had not well understood before our contact, "benignity." And I am wholly grateful that he let me discover early on that we shared some of the same nagging doubts, alongside difficulties with personally unruly tempers.

At those times when we were simply relaxing together, musing first perhaps about the risible aspects of community life, he once rather puckishly quoted the line about patriotism being the last refuge of the scoundrel; he allowed that people who believe that are innocent of the possibilities of community life. Occasionally, the talk that flowed from our experiences of the rich diversity of many male monastics living cheek by jowl twenty-four hours a day would launch us into a brief game of sorts, call it "question and answer." Quite possibly we did this to establish that we both knew the necessity for humor about oneself and community life situations that can elicit unplanned responses.

Q: What in our common life is the shortest millisecond of time? *A:* The time between the moment a freshly unwrapped bar of soap is placed in the common dish and when someone has already gouged a hole in it to clean his nails. Or *Q.:* (the same); *A.:* The time between the Monday morning delivery of a personal subscription to a *Time* or *Newsweek* magazine into one's open-sided mailbox and when someone has borrowed it until Thursday. Or *Q.:* (the same); *A.:* The time between the arrival of the daily paper, morning or evening edition, and when someone has already worked the crossword . . . poorly.

As the daily round moves forward in monasteries, such combinations of *Q.* and *A.* situations in a common life with other monks whose human nature, equally brittle, palsied, and ill-equipped by itself, seem endless. They may be indications that in some version of the physical law of entropy applied to human concourse, some things do not fall into desuetude, ever. But for those friends of religious life who desire to witness miracles, an unerring, peerless miracle, daily, in often mundane monastic life is present to everyone: the largely genial, continued learning and praying together of many variously gifted persons who, through the mysteries of God's benign grace and frequently marshalled goodwill, opt freely to live amicably and productively together over lifetimes. From my experience, I would guess with Dunstan's agreement, elemental frailties are most united in the most insurgent and intractable of all forces: human nature. At very least, I suspect there will always be evident wide variations in the perceptions of "right ways of doing things" in monastic community spaces.

Nevertheless, Dunstan was expertly optimistic about other monks' ability to change or to strive for an ideal. He favored quoting a hymn from our sung prayer: "The love of God is broader than the measure of [any] man's mind." And he did succeed in urging me to understand myself to a workable degree; a semblance of monastic insight prevails. He was almost apologetic in some of his proposals, except for a two-edged stance that may be his hallmark. First, he was unswerving in his view of an individual's inner monastic life and the matter of external status. Returning to the point with unsettling frequency, he believed a monk should never, if for no reason other than his own mental balance and spiritual peace, seek self-aggrandizing positions or positions of status; they may be asked of him. If such a request is made, then he supported a vigorous, affirmative response. Second, he spoke fervently in warning against a nemesis, the "tyranny of the key": "Keys that open or lock things you must avoid, for their possession not only alienates others, but can do constricting, appalling, near-fatal things to their bearers." Not to make too fine a point of it, that clear two-part counsel has remained with me through time like a bothersome fiber of celery wedged between my teeth.

Even in years of retirement from teaching and administration, Dunstan was a major model among many of how to do it, a paradigm for me and others. Nearly always participating in recreation, at table and in community prayer, his civility and restraint in speech or action that referenced other confreres nonetheless permitted him to be open to others as they asked it or looked to be in need of it. I recall his spontaneous leaving off from his desired retirement occupation with matters Dantean when I, and I supposed others as well, interrupted his focused attention to working out a matter of interpretation or academic moment. A confrere uncommonly able to maintain balance and unflagging perspective himself, he made it seem that he was the one interested in what was at the top of another person's mind. Near total deafness plagued him in his last years, but he learned to be gracious about that, too, embarrassment though it was. Although he would never use such terminology, Dunstan was one who practiced spoken and exemplary psychological reality therapy in his own life for others.

J. F. Powers' profoundly and properly praised novel *Wheat That Springeth Green* contains a deft, flawless critique of "Dreck," the chaff in the Church's life and in all human converse that never "springs green."[6] Father Dunstan, not realizing he was such an authentic "kernel," would have said: "Well done!" Similarly, I would say that I am warmly grateful to Dunstan and think of him more often than not.

As I continue to be graced by all Saint John's is and offers, only a little is mentioned in this piece. There is nothing, for but two examples, of the many opportunities for extensive education nor of official individual help and considerations given frequently. Yet, I return to Tevye and Golde's song and its review of all the instances of mutual love and service to and for each other. Their conclusion about the results of their arranged marriage is mine. After all the years together, unfeigned love of Saint John's may well be "nice to know." It is, in any case, the clear human key and signature to my entering the monastery after graduation from the college. My brother Fran seems to have known it from the beginning.

6. James Farl Powers is one of Saint John's current writers-in-residence. His wife, Betty Wahl Powers, died recently; she was a novelist also and contributed a crisp, elegant essay to the first volume of the series.

ALFRED H . DEUTSCH

A FEW YEARS AGO WHEN I WAS DOING SOME
idle work in the abbey archives, actually not idle for I had been
looking into the files that abbey chronicler Fr. Alexius Hoffman
had left behind—there were hundreds of them—I first became impressed with the sense of belonging in all of his writing. I had been
reading the series of blue notebooks which ostensibly were the diaries of the first abbey chronicler but revealed themselves also as
the autobiography of a monk.

As a chronicler he noted every bit of detail which happened day
to day in the abbey. Some little thing had been changed: there was
a notice of it with the due date. A visitor came to campus: Alexius
had all the relevant data in the book. The abbot had gone to a meeting: one learned of it.

Various conclusions could have been drawn: he was a snoopy
and nosey old man; he was a busybody for whom everyone's business became his own; he was the abbey gossip. Shortly all those
nasty thoughts disappeared, and I recalled from my academic training the importance of the medieval chroniclers who left in their
little jottings the history of the medieval monasteries.

In the course of this browsing, I discovered that the archives contained a number of similar diaries, none as elaborate and detailed
as that of Alexius. Others tended to be rather personal diaries. Finally, when the archivist showed me a little brochure which had

been one of the hundreds of little things that Alexius had created, my eyes opened wide. This was simply a do-it-yourself tour guide around the campus. Today we name buildings but we name very few spots. Chapel Island still remains Chapel Island; Mount Carmel is still Mount Carmel to a few. Today the abbey and university need a signage committee: in those days they knew the names.

To memory came the childish explorations into the world that lay around them and the remembrance of making things one's own by giving them a new name. Those early monks forged names which have been forgotten in the past ten decades. Which of today's monks has heard of Bunker Hill? of Adrianople? which can tell you what are the British Isles?

The brochure is entitled "In and around Saint John's University." It begins at the Great Northern Railway Station in Collegeville, a hamlet with a few houses but with streets that are named after the eminent monks who had preceded Alexius. Here in Ruskin prose that smells of *Sesames and Lilies*, the reader boards the U-Bus, a carriage drawn by two horses, is driven down The New Road for some time until he comes to the top of a long hill. "At what appears to be the terminus, the road seems to be guarded by two medieval watch towers, and indeed one is a watch tower." In orderly fashion the booklet guides one through the quadrangle, to the outside and the view of the adjacent buildings.

If the visitor has not yet tired, he is led to the Watab bottoms where in a fish hatchery "tens of thousands of diminutive wrigglers dart about in the limpid element in the troughs." Nearby is the Hydraulic Ram which pumps water which is "absolutely pure, always fresh." He sees the barns, the conservatory, and finally arrives on the front side of the university, where immediately he is set to a walk "around the beat." Along the beat he sees Bunker Hill, the Saint John Berchmans grotto and shrine, Boniface Bay, Caesar's Bay, Meyer's Bay, Doctor's Island, Meridian Park, Our Lady of the Lake Shrine, Adrianople, Poplar Alley. At the cemetery the tour ends.

In those days when land was generous and boundless, the solo monk could hack out a bit of wilderness, give it a name, care for it, experiment with it, nurture it. One monk got curious about telegraphy, and Alexius will record the date it was first used. Another was interested in fruit culture and produces a new species of fruit called the pearapple. A few trees still remain, the most noticeable on the west shore of the Sagatagan. Or he plays with grape varieties and produces a new species of grapes which are adaptable to Minnesota climate and soil. Fr. Angelo Zankl remembers the efforts to dam a section of the Sagatagan in order to make a trout pond.

In 1927 when I first set foot on the Campus—the transportation from the Great Northern depot had changed from the pair of horses to a probably home-made bus which the students called the cracker-box—the advertisements for the institution name Saint John's as located "in the heart of a landscape paradise." Then was my introduction to the monks who in a vague way began to instill my boyhood with a sense of place more than the landscape did.

Many of the places and things still existed as they had in the 1908 brochure of Father Alexius. From a four square block of city around Saint Bernard's Parish in Saint Paul, my world had expanded to an estate which embraced 2,800 acres (figures have varied from 2,400 to 2,800). Early I had accepted the jargon of the place and would proudly tell the occasional visitor that we had 2,800 acres of property in this place. A large part of it was closed off to the students in those days, for the shops were across the road which now is the service road to the kitchen. Across the road was the infirmary which one would be allowed to enter to visit the nurse.

Yet the sense of ownership of all this was not consciously roused, not as it was in the mind of one of the younger monks in the abbey who told me that "the day I came to prep school I joined the monastery." My sense of ownership had to wait until I had completed the novitiate which was the entrée to the abbey. Very clearly in my mind is etched that first day of freedom when I could move around the grounds without the accompaniment of twelve other novices and a *socius.* I could go to the bookstore and get a pipe and a pound of Union Leader. Somewhere on that first day of freedom I met Fr. Oliver Kapsner who greeted me: "Congratulations. Yesterday you were a pauper; today you are a shareholder in a five-million-dollar corporation."

The pride of place must have been working, again unconsciously, in 1970 when I had been writing *Bruised Reeds.* In chapter 3 entitled "Let the Monks Support Themselves," Abbot Martin—who is Abbot Alcuin Deutsch very thinly disguised—taps tobacco for his after breakfast smoke. Outside his window the brothers are turning the earth in preparation for the elaborate flowers beds which will be his office view for the summer. In the huge basswood trees the bees are swarming over the new blooms to bring their secretions to the hives and frames that other brothers had set out. These sights and sounds "roused an unconscious feeling of proprietary satisfaction." He flicks some dust from the window sill which had been crafted in the abbey carpenter shop. He muses to himself that "self-sufficiency should have been added to the Benedictine motto of *Ora et labora.*"

A tap on the door of the office reminds him that one of the junior monks is ready to take him on his customary summer morning walks around the grounds and shops. One of the brothers is mixing the materials to spray the apple orchards; another is pulling a steer to the butcher shop; another is moving along with the beekeeper's netting over his head. The carpenter shop is screaming with the noise of home-cut maple becoming boards for flooring. The cows are mulling around after the morning milking:

> Abbot Martin beamed with the glory of the morning and with the manorial benevolence of a medieval commendam Abbot anticipating the benefits of all that he surveyed—3600 acres of forest land from which, through the labor of the monks, some farmland had been cut, forest which yielded the oak that went from the kiln through the plane and thence into the carpenter shop, which produced the oak paneling that framed the walls of his office.[1]

When the tower clock struck eight, the junior monk—Alfred himself thinly disguised—returns the abbot to his office. There the abbot reflects on some of the economic aspects of the American system:

> In his view of his office, he was Lord Abbot over a large group of monks, responsible to God for their progress in the "school of the Lord's service"; he was also responsible to God for the 3600 acres of land the monastery owned; he parceled out roles for the monks to fill and reminded them frequently to handle all things like the sacred vessels of the altar.[2]

1. Alfred Deutsch, *Bruised Reeds and Other Stories* (Collegeville: Saint John's University Press, 1971) 23.
2. *Ibid.* 23.

How much that sense of place had been stirred by some business of the monastic chapter of a year earlier is at this moment unknown. A chapter meeting of immense significance had taken place on February 25, 1969, which may prove in the long historical view of Saint John's to have been a major turning point. For some months previous university and monastic officials, jointly and separately, had been feverishly considering what has come to be known as the Hatch Act. That act threatened the importance of being a "religious" university, consequences of which might well destroy the tax-free status of this and any Catholic university; impede any kind of substantial fund drives (government aid and perhaps more).

In that year the university had already been functioning for about nine years with the aid of lay persons, known as an associate board. Then president of the university, Fr. Colman Barry set up a committee, with the legal aid of Fred and Kevin Hughes, to foster a plan which could above other considerations "safeguard the purposes of the Saint John's community in conducting educational apostolates, and to indicate how the control of Saint John's University could be shared without being compromised" (minutes of the chapter, February 25, 1969).

It developed into being the longest uninterrupted chapter meeting in the history of the abbey. The issue requiring a vote was to give approval to a new set of statutes for the university. Memory, even without the chapter notes which I had by my side when I wrote this, recalls clearly that Abbot Baldwin Dworschak was ready to call the question on the motion when Fr. Jeremy Murphy objected to the vote call. He then requested that all laymen present at this meeting be asked to leave.

Then for well over an hour Father Jeremy read to the tired members of the chapter a statement that he had carefully prepared, opposing approval of the newly devised statutes. He began after stating his qualifications as a layman, lawyer, priest-professor, and member of the chapter. In the subsequent hour, through careful analysis of the charter which had established the university and of the proposed statutes, he convinced the monks that an affirmative answer to the motion before the chapter would transfer control of the university from the abbey to a lay board. The majority voted with Jeremy against the motion.

This was a period in our history when business of the university had been more and more shared with lay associates, when the university faculty was shifting noticeably in the proportion between lay persons and monastic personnel. Though the issue was rarely, if ever, formally discussed openly, the tension had remained and still remains under the surface as a sort of power struggle. When as a result of the Hatch Act many Catholic universities had separately incorporated their universities, by this action Saint John's Abbey retained control of the university. Now called the Board of Regents, the laymen of the board have consistently acted as they had since the first establishment of an associate board.

Abbot Baldwin had well stated the function of that associate board in a letter of February 19 addressed to all the voting members of the monastic chapter. He had stated "that there had been no pressure from the outside for this move, and certainly not from the Associate Board who wish to help us in the way we think best. This Associate Board has been very helpful to us in the past nine years, and perhaps we should give them more opportunity now to help us even more. . . ." (Minutes of February 25 chapter). I understand that the present Board of Regents has never changed the spirit of that first Board of Associates.

Nonetheless, though there is no tension in the Board of Regents, there is occasional tension within the faculties, and only occasionally one hears the outburst of a monk that the lay persons want to run us monks out of the university.

One of the noticeable consequences of the establishment of the Board of Associates was a change in the budgeting process. On the corporation books the university has since become a separate section of the corporate financial statement. Funds for the operation of the university, some invested funds, and such things now become the function of the Board of Regents to create and distribute. Theoretically, the abbey chapter retains its control of the university through its right to approve and amend the budget prepared for the university.

Hence once a year the monastic chapter has been summoned to give its approval of the proposed university budget. It took some time and some years for the monks in the chapter to become accustomed to this fact and to learn some of the jargon built into talking about budgets. To this day most of us voting members of the chapter are quite honestly financially illiterate, and hence we place our trust in the members of the monastery who represent the university interest.

In the course of this learning process, I can still see a frustrated Fr. Gervase Soukup rising in the chapter house and trying to explain some of the intricacies of the process in language that could be understood by us illiterates ("in one of the shoe boxes under the bed of the bursar is a fund for . . ."). And we came to understand something about vested funds in the picture of shoe boxes. And in this learning process there was always a voice rising loudly in the chapter declaiming the "they" which was taking away our money. So Gervase would again patiently explain that "there is no they and no we. We are we, and they are we." How many times he had said that in the many years when he was to the abbey the voice of the business office only his guardian angel has counted.

End of a short version of what is a long story. It was in the following year that I wrote the first half of *Bruised Reeds*. Though Abbot Martin (Alcuin) had never had to worry about boards and others sharing his authority, it must have ingrained itself into me as I drew his image. The chapter on his morning walk with the young monk Jerome concluded with thoughts on the voiced self-subsistence which the abbot has talked about, and the closing words of the abbot to the young Jerome were these: "Some day, young man, we may have to give up our self-sufficiency. But as long as I am abbot we will continue to produce our own milk, grow our own vegetables, slaughter our own meat and fill our containers with our own honey."

But young Jerome, hurrying to his class at 8:10, had questions for himself:

> Was the Abbot deliberately ignoring some of the facts of a twentieth-century economic system? Was he unaware of the two semi-trucks that pulled up to the potato cellar each October and loaded the bins in the storage cellar, of the Belduc feed truck that each month unloaded sacks of feed at the dairy barns, of the Armour truck that weekly brought sausage for the student and monastery dining rooms . . . . Was it possible that he didn't know that the mill was now for the most part idle and that the flour used in the secret-recipe bread the monks boasted about was mixed at and purchased from a flour mill in a nearby town?[3]

3. *Ibid.* 24.

All of these events and persons, all forming over the years in an unconscious tapestry, came to a conscious head by 1981. That January I had written and delivered a conference to the novices on one of their monthly days of reflection. It was untitled at that time but since has taken the name of "On a Sense of Belonging." I might have delivered that finished essay to Father Colman for this volume.

This is how it opened:

> One of the greatest revelations that I have had in my monastic career came in the late '60s when I first discovered that I had had a problem of identity without having been aware of it. I should not have been surprised because I have always been psychologically quite naive and had to learn what was meant by an identity crisis. . . . Since those years I have often asked myself about one phase of the identity question "How Do I Belong?"

The talk developed into a discourse on a sense of stewardship, a new word which worked its way into monastic jargon in the early '80s. Chiefly during the regime of Abbot Jerome Theisen this view of the 3,600? 2,400? acres which had been granted us in the act of incorporation over a century ago has colored much of the operations in and around the monastery holdings. The abbey archives could reveal the minutes of chapters in which we argued about the use of the land that surround these buildings. We have arrived at the stage now when projects for the care of the property receive overwhelming support. Most recent of these events, which has gained much recognition, has been the setting aside of many of these acres in a wetlands project that every monk feels is his own. Instead of walking around the beat, monks are more likely to watch the shaping of that area, easily seen from I-94, where egrets now find a home, where wood ducks are willing to settle, where blue-birds again feel welcomed.

All of the above events came full circle about this same time, while I had been writing a biographical sketch of Fr. Alexius Hoffman, whose memoirs and journals manifest intimate knowledge of all the details of the monastery. For years I had been reciting at least once a month with all the monks psalm 48 as just another of the four to five psalms which are the usual portion of morning and evening prayer. But on this one morning of grace the psalm

hit me with the force of an epiphany when it came to the climactic
lines:

> Walk through Zion, walk all around it;
> count the number of its towers, Review
> all its ramparts, Examine its castles,
> that you may tell the next generation
> that such is our God . . . .

The slight change I had to make by substituting Saint John's
for "our God" gave to me that sense of identity, belonging, and
power that the Hebrew poet voiced when from his vantage point
he looked with button-bursting pride on all that his God had blessed
him with.

Br. Louis Blenkner

I AM BEGINNING TO WRITE THESE REFLECTIONS on August 24, 1989, the feast of the Apostle Bartholomew, alias Nathanael. The gospel reading for this day's Eucharistic celebration is from the first chapter of John. Philip, the hometown friend of Peter and Andrew, had just found Nathanael and told him, "We have found Jesus, son of Joseph, from Nazareth." In a somewhat smart-alecky response, Nathanael asks: "Can anything good come from Nazareth?"

Nazareth, after all, had no prior claim to fame. It was not the birthplace of priest, prophet, or prince. No bloody battles had been fought here to the shame or glory of Israel. It could not boast of a stately structure like Solomon's temple in Jerusalem or Solomon's stables at Megiddo. Nazareth was just another hick town in Galilee, as insignificant as such minuscule Minnesota municipalities as, say, Pemberton and Janesville, where I grew up between one and sixteen, and Collegeville where I matured between sixteen and sixty.

Looking at a map of Minnesota and barely being able to see the name of Collegeville in tiny five-point type may cause one to wonder: "Can anything good come from Collegeville?" Indeed, what sense can one make out of a place that small? Many a visitor and tourist has had the same reaction as an Irish publisher and his wife had when I drove them down to the railroad tracks south of I-94, pointed proudly to the station sign that announced

"COLLEGEVILLE," and said: "Ta da! This is it!" They were genuinely disappointed. Not even one cafe, filling station, auto body shop, grocery store, or stoplight. Not even a stray dog slinking across the gravel street. Shades of Lake Wobegon. All the more reason to wonder: "Can anything good come from Collegeville?"

The answer to that question is the same short and sweet reply that Philip gave Nathanael after the latter's cocky question, namely: "Come and see!"

I came and saw Collegeville for the first time in September 1945 when I enrolled as a junior at the Saint John's Preparatory School. I thought I wanted to be a priest. A visiting missionary, Fr. Oliver Munie, O.M.I., had given a parish mission at Saint Ann's Church in my hometown of Janesville, and when I told him I wanted to be a priest he suggested I go to a minor seminary to start the study of Latin. My pastor, Msgr. Francis English, suggested three prep schools I might attend, and Saint John's of Collegeville was one of them. It was the only name I recognized, thanks to a newspaper picture of the seven Theisen boys of Wadena, dressed as Mass servers in their black cassocks and lace surplices. Three of them, the picture blurb said, were attending Saint John's. One of them, Robert, now Father Wilfred, came to be my classmate and confrere through prep school, college, novitiate, clericate, and on through to this day. In that case, one picture was worth a thousand words.

A thousand pictures flash through my mind as I recall all I saw at Saint John's in the years that followed. I saw a school surging with new life as World War II veterans came to the college. Saint John's grew by leaps and buildings. For example, during my first year in prep school, both preps and collegians ate together family style at one sitting in the refectory. It wasn't long before we had pushed the adjacent print shop to the wall and then through the wall to another location entirely to make room for more eager eaters. Army surplus barracks were installed on campus to provide living space until more substantial buildings could be erected. A combination classroom and snack bar was placed between the gym and Devil's Tower. Leo Lauer, one of the few laymen on campus in those days, managed the snack bar. When I heard it said: "Linger longer in Leo Lauer's Lunchroom," I was attracted to alliteration and have been hooked on it ever since.

From the beginning I liked what I saw at Saint John's. I saw a lot of Benedictine monks as teachers, prefects, counselors, and craftsmen. I liked to watch the monks process reverently and silently, save for a few groaning floor boards and squeaky shoes, into the church for Saturday evening Benediction. Those were the days, as someone said later, when to speak of "exposing the Blessed Sacrament" did not mean writing a critical commentary on the Eucharist.

I began to see that Saint John's was more than a place to "come and see." It was a place to "come and stay." The college chaplain, Fr. Lancelot Atsch, helped me sort out my options between the diocesan priesthood and monastic life. But it was a layman, the inestimable Steve Humphrey, who better than anyone else helped me see that Saint John's offered a wide and rich array of opportunities to use my God-given talents. Saint John's had missions as far away as the Bahamas, Puerto Rico, Mexico, Japan, and Kentucky, and parishes as nearby as Avon and Albany. Saint John's had a prep school, a college, and a seminary in which to teach.

Monsignor English, for all his good intentions, made my decision easier when he took me on a tour of the Winona Diocese one summer day and drove through his former parishes in the little towns of Wykoff and Fountain. I wasn't sure anything good for me could come from such places. I realized I was getting a sense for the place called Collegeville that same summer when I started feeling lonesome for Saint John's. Maybe Saint John's was becoming more than just a place. It was starting to become home, as in "there's no place like home."

home

Home it became in the hot summer of 1949 when I entered the novitiate. There were seventeen of us crowded into a common dormitory and a common study hall, for this was the era of mass migrations from the Secular City to a variety of Seven Storey Mountains. Our novice master was Fr. Cosmas Dahlheimer, a gentle man of God who aptly fit Saint Benedict's job description of that office, namely, "a senior chosen for his skill in winning souls . . . to look after the novices with careful attention" (the *Rule,* 58:6). He did his best to "set down nothing harsh, nothing burdensome" while remaining realistic enough to prepare us for that "little strictness in order to amend faults and to safeguard love" (Prologue: 46–47). He gave us a vision of monastic life solidly based on one primary principle, namely, Benedictine balance. *Ora et labora,* worship and work, was our simple scheme of daily living. We needed a good measure of both to survive and thrive.

Slowly but surely it became apparent that my sense of place was dependent upon my seeing Saint John's as both a place of sense and a place of presence.

A place of sense involves the common sense that Saint Benedict demands of cenobites, that strongest kind (*fortissimum genus*) of monks "who belong to a monastery, where they serve under a rule and an abbot" (the *Rule* 1:13, 2). Time and again I have marvelled at and been grateful for the durability of the Collegeville common sense, the community's good sense of what has been the truly right and just action to take.

Hearing horror stories from men and women religious of other communities about what went on in their houses in the name of initial and ongoing formation has made me continually and increasingly thankful that Saint John's store of common sense is plentiful. Unlike a certain community of men I heard about recently, we never felt it necessary to assemble a local or general chapter to debate whether monks should be allowed to wear pajamas rather than their habits to bed as prescribed by Saint Benedict fifteen centuries ago (the *Rule* 22:5). We have had our fair share of community characters over the decades, thank God for them, but community crackpots intent on imposing their idiosyncrasies, whims, and quirks on everyone else have been mercifully scarce, easily identifiable, and sedulously ignored, thank God also for that. Saint John's has been a place of common sense. We do not panic easily. We don't even frighten easily!

Saint John's also has been for me a place of presence, particularly a place of the presence of God. In his key chapter seven on humility, Saint Benedict sets his ladder of life on the firm foundation of belief in God's presence: "We must believe that God is always with us" (the *Rule* 7:23). My favorite name for God is Emmanuel which means: "God is with us" (Isa 7:14; 8:10). Like the patriarch Jacob who had a dream of a stairway to the stars with angels going up and down on it and the Lord standing beside him, I have every reason to repeat his powerful profession of God's presence:

"Truly, the LORD is in this spot, although I did not know it!"
In solemn wonder he cried out: "How awesome is this shrine! This
is nothing else but an abode of God, and that is the gateway to
heaven" (Gen 28:16-17).

It has not been difficult to know that God is present in our massive concrete monument to Emmanuel, the abbey church. In a place
that has as awesome and inspiring a worship space as Saint John's
does, there is nothing tentative or timid about our sense of God's
presence. It is not always so easy, however, to remember and realize
that God is also and especially present within me and within everyone I live with, work with, pray and play with. There lies the truly
"solemn wonder" that makes life a marvel.

Much of the marvel of my forty-four years at Saint John's is
connected with the presence of the people I have known. The great
majority of these men and women have been loving, caring, cooperative, wholesome, good-humored, and helpful folks, a long line of
confreres, colleagues, and friends who have been for me the ongoing incarnation of God's love made flesh and dwelling with me.
There are also a few who would qualify for the title of "Spherical
S.O.B."—a person who is an S.O.B. no matter which way you
look at him. So there are those who are the salt of the earth and
those who are salt in the wounds.

Whatever wounds I carry have come mainly from the administrative assignments I was given. And most of these wounds, let
me say, were self-inflicted. As dean of men of the college from
1959–63, I played the "sheriff of Collegeville County" at a time
when the disciplinary concept of *in loco parentis* was becoming as
outmoded as a sling shot. But there were rules to be made and
enforced.

Lights on freshman floors were turned off at 11 p.m. Candles
were lit at 11:15 p.m.! Students were expected and encouraged
to go to Mass several times during the week. A few preferred, it
seemed, to pray in the privacy of their lockers. Students signed
out and signed in when they left and returned to campus. Only
seniors could have cars on campus. Bermuda shorts were not allowed in the student dining room. Class absences were recorded
and reported to my office. Fr. Boniface Axtman, a previous dean
of men, had to tell a student assembly: "Too many of you have
too many grandmothers and grandfathers who are dying and be-

ing buried so you can go home on weekends." My own favorite phrase was "Boozers are losers. Abstainers are gainers." And to prove it, the Welfare Committee met almost weekly to consider cases of excessive drinking and to give so many three- and five-day suspensions that eventually the group's name was changed to "The Farewell Committee." Eventually I went from being called "The Green Dean" during my initial year to being known as "Lurkin' Durken, the Sneakin' Deacon" during my last year at that job. Others obviously enjoy alliteration, too.

As novice master from 1963–69, I was in charge of the spiritual formation of new monks at the time when the whole Church was being reformed by Vatican Council II. Catholics, especially men and women religious, were becoming novices again to learn how to live in a Church that had suddenly decided to put an end to the old defensive siege mentality and to open up the windows to let in some fresh air and light. Welcome to the Church in the Modern World.

Monastic life was modernized. Two of the biggest and best improvements made by Vatican II were the change from Latin to English in our community prayer (no longer did we have to wonder what the hell it meant to pray *Buccinate in Neomenia tuba* [Ps 81:4]) and the full integration of the brothers into the community. No longer did the youngest clerical novice outrank the oldest brother. No longer were there separate novitiates for clerical novices and brother novices. No longer were deceased brothers buried in their own section of the community cemetery (segregation to the very end). Come to think of it, there were a few times when common sense had failed us.

Other changes were noticeable. More younger monks left the community before making solemn vows. Some left after final vows and others after ordination. I remembered what my novice master had said: "Don't worry about the ones who leave. It's the ones who stay who will give you trouble." Novices asked more questions in and outside of class. We discontinued the daily public recitation of the Rosary. We served "near beer" (2 percent) at a novitiate picnic. The last group of neophytes I instructed wore buttons under their scapulars that proclaimed: "Novice Power."

The two years (1969–71) that followed my term as novice master were both "the best of times and the worst of times." Teaching full time at Luther College in Decorah, Iowa, was the best of times as I saw ecumenism at work among my colleagues and students. I had a hand in improving Lutheran-Catholic relations the first time I led the daily chapel service. It was the birthday of Pope Paul VI. So I asked the congregation to sing "Happy Birthday" to the pope. They did so—a little tentatively. And Martin Luther probably took another turn in his grave.

The worst of times came the following year when I volunteered to assist at Saint Anselm's Church in the Bronx. I was asked by the pastor, Fr. Timothy Kelly, to direct the religious education program for hundreds of black and Puerto Rican children who came like locust clouds on "Terrible Tuesdays," "Wicked Wednesdays," and "Suffering Sundays" to be prepared for confession, Communion, and/or confirmation. Given the fact that the names of these three sacraments begin and end with almost the same sounds, I could appreciate the little girl who one day said to me: "My mother wants to know when I get the white thing on my tongue." I left Saint Anselm's humbled by a good dose of culture shock and in admiration of the many confreres who had over the years worked and prayed in that difficult vineyard.

For the next seven years (1971–78) I continued to see the greater Saint John's and its place in the Church when I was asked to be the abbey's personnel director. I visited confreres from Naytahwaush to Nassau, from Ponsford to Puerto Rico, from Bottineau to the Bronx. I remember my trip to Bottineau, North Dakota, because that was the time I stopped at a smalltown gas station when my tank was almost empty only to learn that the pumps at this station were also empty. The memory of the Bronx is mixed with that of the chapter meeting when the community had the common sense to realize we could no longer competently staff a faraway, big-city parish. Not enough confreres were willing to say: "Here I am; send me" when the Lord asked: "Whom shall I send? Who will go for us?" (Isa 6:8). The vote to give this parish to the New York Archdiocese was like getting the first olive out of a jar. After that, subsequent transfers came easier and with some regularity.

My visits with confreres working in our pastoral apostolate gave me a firsthand view of a dimension of Saint John's influence that can too often and too easily be overlooked or taken for granted. Benedictine monks had originally come to Collegeville to serve the spiritual needs of Catholic settlers. Those pastoral pioneers had gone forth from Collegeville to hundreds of parishes in the Upper Midwest and beyond to preach and teach the Good News of Jesus. Their continued efforts are a tribute to the spirit of generosity and faithfulness that marks them as apostles who, like Jesus, have come not to be served but to serve.

In the summer of 1978 I was named director of The Liturgical Press and began a decade of challenging work that gave me a still wider view of the Saint John's outreach. I experienced just how much mightier the pen is than the sword. The far-reaching influence that Saint John's has had on the liturgical and biblical apostolates has yet to be adequately recognized and recorded. A solid Collegeville Connection in this country and around the world has been created and sustained by such publications as *Worship* magazine, the *Old and New Testament Reading Guides*, the *Short Breviary*, the Heinisch-Heidt books on the history and theology of the Old Testament, Pius Parsch's *The Church's Year of Grace*, the best-selling *Of Sacraments and Sacrifice* by Clifford Howell, S.J., the weekday and Sunday missalette, the *Bible and Liturgy Sunday Bulletin*, the award-winning series of seven books on *Alternative Futures for Worship*, and the increasingly popular Little Rock Scripture Study Program.

The following example of The Press' outreach boggles my mind: Each and every week some 320,000 copies of the *Bible and Liturgy Sunday Bulletin* are used in parishes from North Pole, Alaska, to Our Lady's Church in Nassau, Bahamas. That comes to a total of 16,640,000 copies per year!

Despite the national and international attention that The Liturgical Press brings to Collegeville through its current list of some seven hundred titles—not to mention the substantial surplus income that the sale of these titles generates for the abbey's operations—it still happens that speakers and writers who list the ongoing accomplishments of the Collegeville campus too often manage to omit The Liturgical Press as though it were Saint John's best kept secret. Over the years I suspect that Saint John's maple syrup operation has gotten more and better media coverage than our worldwide publishing efforts.

While local media people and some corporation leaders were learning these last few years not only where The Liturgical Press was on campus but also what it does, the work of directing The

Press remained for me as stimulating as it was rewarding. Much of the challenge and reward came from and through the people I was privileged to work with, people like the general manager, John Dwyer of happy memory, and the energetic team of managers, namely, Mark Twomey, Luther Dale, and Brad Vogt, and all the other people from the display room to the shipping room and every station in between who made it possible to run a multi-million dollar business without getting run over by an ulcer or a heart attack.

As I finish writing these reflections on the eve of Labor Day, I realize that it is a lot of working and praying people who make this place of Collegeville so precious and special. Surely Saint John's would not be the same place if someone took away the lakes and the loons, the Pine Curtain and the bell tower. But Saint John's would be no place at all if there were no people—people such as the abbots, priors, presidents and prefects, deans and directors who have helped to give Saint John's its unique stamp of excellence; people like confreres, colleagues and confessors who are able to tolerate a fair amount of foolishness for the sake of brotherly love and the hope of eventual conversion; couples like Dean and Joleen, Jack and Rita, Bob and Dorothy who remind us monks that we are not the only ones who have to be faithful to an earlier commitment; women like Dolores and Elaine, Colleen and Ida, Eva and Esther who remind us day by day that "it is not good for the man to be alone" (Gen 2:18); and former students like Gar and Michael, Dianna and Denise who keep the truths we teach alive in a new generation. It is people who make it possible for me to repeat what Peter said when he saw Jesus transfigured: "Master, it is good that we are here" (Luke 9:33).

BALDWIN W. DWORSCHAK

B·EFORE BEGINNING THIS ESSAY, I HAD TO DE-
cide what "sense of place" means. "Sense" means a capacity, a
consciousness of something deeper than what appears on the surface. "Place" is expressive of a location calling forth a certain mood
or a mode of behavior. The definition, then, could be: a capacity
to appreciate, to be conscious of something deeper about a place
which entails a certain emotion and a fitting mode of behavior.

On April 23, 1953, the monastic community chose Marcel Breuer
to prepare a comprehensive architectural plan for the second century of Saint John's Abbey and University. Breuer's response was:

> Before I can begin I need to know much about your way of life.
> Having read Fr. Colman Barry's *Worship And Work,* the story of
> your first one-hundred years in this place, also the *Rule* of Benedict
> and much more, I need to know how deeply you have involved your-
> selves in this place and its way of life; I need to understand the
> spirit and how those who live here now are committed to it while
> those who died sanctified it.
>
> I think of your plan as an effort to rediscover and rededicate your-
> selves to the profound purpose abiding in this place, deeply rooted
> in the past and deeply imbedded in the present, as Professor Au-
> gust Krey has portrayed Saint John's in his essay "Monte Cassi-
> no, Metten and Minnesota."
>
> What I see before me is a community of men deliberately ori-
> ented towards God, guided at all times by a *Rule* of life which sets

it down as a necessary condition to live a life of "worship and work."
This immediately holds my attention because for a great majority
of persons this orientation is unknown, unrecognized. I can see that
for you a sense of life, its ultimate meaning, translates readily into
a sense of place that looks far beyond what is here. The glory of
what is here I presume is meant to lift one often and easily to what
is to be.

We asked Breuer in 1952: "Can you as architect help us build
structures that in turn will remind us constantly that contemporary
Benedictines, in these troubled times, have something to say to the
Church, to the world-at-large?" It is my intention to search for
Breuer's answers in various direct and indirect statements to be
found in what he published, but mostly in what he said to our
monastic community.

When Breuer agreed to be the architect of the comprehensive
campus plan at Saint John's, he soon became aware that his relationship with us would be unique. His client would not be a single
person nor a small committee but a community of men whose lives
were regulated by centuries of tradition and a rule set down 1,500
years ago.

On January 14, 1955, Fr. Cloud Meinberg wrote to Marcel
Breuer:

> The main point I would like to make in this letter is that I feel the
> interior details of the monastery as they appear presently in your
> drawings, lack, in part, positive monastic character. That is, of
> course, a hard thing to define. The old interiors at the Cloisters
> Museum in New York clearly have it, but in a medieval mold. We
> do not seek the medieval mold. Modern commercial interiors are
> and look contemporary. They may even be simple and well
> designed, but this alone does not make them monastic."

Father Cloud, deeply devoted to monastic life and always ready
to contribute his talents as a trained architect, frequently corresponded with Breuer, who welcomed Father Cloud's sincere efforts to be helpful.

Breuer's answer on January 27 is typical of his concern to grasp
the full meaning of and to create the appropriate setting in which
we as a monastic community could live our vow to "the monastic
way of life." Breuer wrote:

That you are unhappy about the interior details of the Monastery is worrying me, frankly, because we have put a lot of energy and time into clarifying these details. Knowing your very great interest in this project, and your point of view about architecture, may I suggest that we talk about these things without prejudice and try to find a solution that is mutually satisfactory. I would be very grateful . . . to know and see clearly where my responsibilities lie.

In a letter of more detail Breuer wrote:

I found that Saint John's has a hearty regard for technical perfection. This is why we tried to keep all details technically up to date though as simple as possible. Of course, it would be more than satisfactory for all of us if these details could have also definite monastic character. This is what was my aim.

Here we see Breuer expressing a certain fear that he might not succeed in helping us to communicate to all who come here a real sense of place that speaks forth as a witness of faith.

When we invited Marcel Breuer to design buildings for us, we asked him to serve our community by pulling the community well beyond its practical intentions so as to serve its most profound needs, namely, to give, architecturally, a true and lasting expression of the life that it represents. The buildings we created together was a new thing, expressing not just the style of the architect but also the spirit of the community.

Breuer's relationship as architect with such a client was almost immediately the subject of comment by interested observers. For example, Whitney Stoddard, professor of the history of art at Williams College, came to Saint John's with the request to capture the "story" and to share his findings with others in his book *Adventure in Architecture, Building the New Saint John's* (New York: Longmans Green, 1958). The blurb told what he had to offer:

Here, in words and pictures, is the most exciting story since the building of the great medieval churches in Europe, the grand plan in which the monastic community in Collegeville, Minnesota, and a world-famous architect, Marcel Breuer, have embarked. . . . Each building must be planned to meet the challenge of the community summed up in a letter to the competing architects: "The Benedictine tradition at its best challenges us to think boldly and to cast our ideals in forms which will be valid for centuries to come, shaping them with all the genius of present-day materials and techniques.'' Functional and artistic success in such a building program depends upon the sensitivity of both patron and architect and the cooperative spirit that is engendered between them. The partnership between the community and Breuer has proved to be as productive as that of any of the great church builders of the Middle Ages. . . . This spirit of cooperation has impressed architects all over the world.

One of the architects that Stoddard referred to could have been Bernard Jacob, a fellow of the American Institute of Architects, who came to Saint John's in 1981 and wrote as follows in the Minneapolis *Tribune* of March 14, 1981:

My 90-minute pilgrimage from the Twin Cities (to Collegeville) was very rewarding. In unequivocal and dramatic ways the language that is architecture transmits the story of a community, of the spirit of a place, of high accomplishments in design and construction and of the evolving and changing priorities of the church and religious life of our times.

Great works of architecture are a result of a coalescence in time and space. One part of the recipe is a great architect, the other is a demanding, far-seeing, sensitive and clear-minded patron, and the third is the symbiosis between them.

This occurred in Collegeville, Minnesota, when Saint John's Abbey selected Marcel Breuer to develop a comprehensive master plan for the next hundred years. In a way Breuer was prepared for this challenge; he had designed many family dwellings and in doing so had shown a warmth and sensitivity to family and locale.

Though the new buildings at Saint John's did not initiate a new style of architecture, they do represent the apotheosis of modern architecture made subservient to the humanism, the aspirations of a religious community—in the process and by the dramatization of its ideals—transcended them in form and expression. This is the gift of architecture.

The aim of the master plan for the future of Saint John's monastic community, so clearly stated in the abbot's letter, was handsomely fulfilled, and the church stands as an important and meaningful example of religious architecture in this century. This accomplishment is laden with responsibility, however, as with any great work of art, the responsibility for its care, its integrity, its meaning, and above all the clear expression of its sole purpose—to remind those who enter and those who pass by of Christ, and to renew his spirit among us.

Still another note of encouragement and affirmation came from the visit of Roger G. Kennedy, director of the National Museum of American History of the Smithsonian Institution, author of *American Churches*. He begins his introduction thus:

> This is a book about religious buildings, but its central idea is that the content, not the container, makes a building religious...what counts is the degree to which it reinforces religious feelings and actions. . . . More than anything else we want to know how these buildings have provided for people to assemble for the purpose of coming into a closer relationship to a Mystery. . . . One of the glories of architecture is that it offers multifarious testimony to the boundless variety of his revelations.

A little further on Kennedy makes reference to Breuer: "Breuer not only designed a church; he was asked to provide a plan for the next century's construction. New forms developed in this way offer a new crystallization of the needs of the community for solace, stimulus and reaffirmation."

In words that echo Bernard Jacob, Kennedy writes:

> Great churches represent a harmony between the artist and the community—and at the same time an extension of the liturgy. The entire building becomes an altar, set in the midst of the community. . . . We can miss the full benefit and joy of this kind of participation if we do not feel kinship with the architect, and we fail if we do not understand we are engaged in a *Sacred* activity, touched by the Spirit of Mystery that intervenes in every moment of our lives.

To have a sense of place is to lay claim to a place, not merely of possession, but more so of responsibility; this transforms simple ownership into reality. Whatever I see in this place calls me to account. It may rebuke me for neglecting its message: this is a holy place, a friendly place, a place of hospitality, a place of prayer, of peace, a place of final preparation for eternity. This is a place of healing, of growth, of reconciliation, of natural beauty, of silence, and all this is sacramental.

This is a place to pay tribute to those from whom we learn how best to live our own lives.

One has a sense of place when he or she knows it is the right place for him or her. All through life we are tempted to think that the right place for us is somewhere else we have not yet found. It is interesting to know and tempting to wonder if in our lifetime we fail to find the right place because we have forgotten what we have set out to find.

In one way or another we pray every day that our monastery becomes what Cardinal Basil Hume, O.S.B., called "an affirmation of God." It is here that each one writes, not always in words, the story of his inward journey, of the discoveries he made along the way, and how these inspired a fresh and deeper understanding of his relationship with *the living* God.

When Marcel Breuer died on July 1, 1981, it was not difficult to speak in grateful memory in the name of the community of Saint John's to whose sense of place he had contributed what many thought were his best efforts as an architect and friend.

In my homily on July 3 in the abbey church, I said:

> When we at Saint John's come together, in the presence of God, to celebrate his saving deeds, we are greatly helped by the setting, the environment, in which we find ourselves. It is not accidental that the setting is so helpful, so friendly to the liturgy, and that it contributes to the awe, the mystery, the reverence, the thanksgiving, the praise which the liturgy calls for.
>
> We will always be grateful to those who did so much to help us realize that this building is none other than the house of God and the gate to heaven. We are especially grateful to Marcel Breuer who designed this church, this altar, as well as the rest of the furnishings. We thank God for him. If a community has with great care selected a competent and skilled person as architect for its church, it will receive from him a design which will stimulate and inspire as well as serve the needs of the community for a space or a building for praying, singing, for listening and speaking, for active participation—where the mysteries of God are recalled and celebrated in human history.
>
> During the four-hour rite of consecration of this church and this altar by Bishop Bartholome, perhaps no one followed the ceremonies more intently than Marcel Breuer as he sat in the front row of the balcony. I saw him only briefly that day, and his parting words were, "All I can say, Father Abbot, is that this is the first building I have designed and the first object I have designed which has been made so sacred, or, as you would say, consecrated to God. I am more deeply moved by this than I can tell you."

Mr. Breuer was always grateful when he heard or read that this church fulfilled our expectations liturgically and contributed much to the prayer life of the monastic community and that of the students. In 1961, not long after the consecration of the church, Breuer was invited to speak at the Walker Art Center about the church. In part he said: "Plans and details of the Saint John's Abbey Church were based upon a meticulously re-examined liturgical tradition. To crystalize this tradition was a vital contribution of the devoted monastic community at Saint John's to the building. Although the church may be a new sensation to the eye, its architectural concepts resemble those of religious buildings in the Middle Ages. . . . Church architecture at its best is always identical with the logic of the enclosure. I merely put a shell around the sacred space designed by the monastic community. How much we will be affected by the building, how much it will signify its reverent purpose will depend on the courage it manifests in facing the ancient task: to render the enclosed space a part of infinite space."

What does the client, in this case the monastic community, say to the architect about to embark on designing a church? (There are a number of things the client does not say: what should be the style of architecture, what materials should be used, etc. In these matters the architect is the expert.) What the architect wants to know is what the building is for. The church has a spiritual purpose, not entirely invisible; but the material serves the spiritual. A good architect will look to the client (community) for an understanding of the character and purpose of the liturgical assembly. With that kind of rapport, it is the architect's task to design the building, using contemporary materials and modes of construction.

What we told Mr. Breuer, in general, was the following: the Catholic church should be a cheerful place, one where the atmosphere is that of joy and confidence, because the prayer offered there is one of victory. Christ has triumphed over sin; life has come from the cross and the resurrection. In other words, the church should display a sense of faith and hope. The church should be flooded with light because light is the symbol of faith and of the supernatural life coming from Christ the Light of the world.

We told Breuer that the Twin Towers had, since 1879, been a kind of symbol of Saint John's Abbey and University and that we would like to have the new church proclaim itself with a suitable tower housing the same five bells that had sounded the hours for a hundred years. What Breuer designed was a dramatic bell-banner whose supports shelter the main entrance and which bears within it a large cross that hovers high above the surrounding campus and countryside.

Breuer knew that he would have to be faithful both to what we asked of him and, at the same time, to his own instincts and talents. He said on one occasion: "As I understand you (the monastic community), the church must have a more powerful presence on campus than most buildings do; and more than most buildings it should remind everyone that a skilled hand was at work here." Thus he realized his own responsibility as architect.

The kind of fidelity with which Breuer responded to our deeper spiritual needs, in designing both the monastery and the church, was possible only because of a *profound relationship* which came to exist between Breuer as architect and the monastic community. It is this relationship which became the object of much interest and which has been pointed out and praised again and again.

The latest example of the significance of this relationship was an article by an architect, Bernard Jacob, who wrote: "The evolution of the design of the Saint John's Abbey Church, from first sketches to the finally erected building, is a fascinating record of that rare symbiosis between architect and client that produces extraordinary results. The building is unlike anything Breuer had designed before and probably better than anything he designed thereafter" (Minneapolis *Tribune*, March 14, 1981).

Whatever the final reckoning of Breuer the architect, he will assuredly be given as his own best eulogy, what he himself wrote: "Man comes and goes. The building, the street, the town remain. To build, in final appraisal is not to play a role, not to take a vote, not to give an opinion: It is a passion, a basic one, the bread we eat. The final significance of architecture is surely *beyond* pure form, beyond pure use, beyond just a roof over our head, beyond just human sentiment, beyond just the product of the marketplace." In that he summed up what was most true of the man and the movement which his death so clearly terminates.

What is our debt to Marcel Breuer? We owe him a lasting remembrance for the service he rendered to us as a religious community. We, as a religious community, represent in a special way the Church as a servant to the world. We have a commitment to be a sign, a witness and an instrument of the reign of God.

That commitment must be reflected and implemented not only in the individual lives of its members but also in the choices the community makes.

I believe one of the most important choices we made as a community was our choice of Marcel Breuer as architect of the place where we come every day to renew our faith and our vision; where we celebrate what is most personally ours and what is most nobly human; where our actions witness the great deeds God has done and where we confirm our covenant with him who is our God. With such vision can this place where we gather daily be anything less than a vehicle to meet the Lord and to encounter one another?

Frs. Benno Watrin and Demetrius Hagmann

ARNO A. GUSTIN

ESSAYS "FROM THE INSIDE" FOR THIS VOLUME
of *A Sense of Place* help in tracing the roots of our Benedictine beginnings as well as parts of our story in this century. Saint Benedict could not have had the dreams he dreamt nor the visions he
saw apart from the Gospel. His faith in God, first nurtured at Subiaco and Monte Cassino in southern Italy, flowered and ripened
into action with the passing of the years and with the changing needs
of the human family through the centuries. This faith traditional-
ly has found expression in "a search for God." Thomas Merton
caught the spirit of this search in his *Contemplation in a World of Action*. One of Merton's former novices at Gethsemane Abbey,
Ernesto Cardenal, summed up an aspect of the global pilgrimage
of peoples and races in the explanation of the contemplative community he had founded at Solentiname, off the shores of Nicara-
gua. He wrote:

> Contemplation means union with God. We soon became aware that
> this union with God brought us before all else into union with the
> peasants, very poor and very abandoned. . . . Contemplation also
> brought us to the revolution. It had to be that way. If not, it would
> have been fake contemplation.[1]

1. *The Gospel in Solentiname* (Maryknoll, N.Y.: Orbis Books, 1977) I, 267.

Similarly, Cardinal Basil Hume, a former Benedictine abbot at Ampleforth Abbey in England, reflects that our task is "to hand on to others the things that we have contemplated."

A generation ago we did not speak about contemplation as readily as we do now. By definition to contemplate is to look at or to study thoughtfully. Scripture always has been a bottomless source for both contemplative thought and action. The *Rule* as a thoroughly biblical document is often as revolutionary as the Gospel itself in providing a vision beyond the trivial concerns of a possessive world. Benedict says in chapter 73 of the *Rule:* "What page, what passage of the inspired books of the Old and New Testaments is not the truest of guides for human life?"

Biblical guides are constants in our daily lives. Despite all distractions they help us to be present and available to others. Presence was one of Fr. Walter Reger's distinctive contributions to Saint John's. I remember seeing him "listening" to students, in his first-floor Benet Hall room, during late evening hours fully asleep at his desk. Such great variety prevailed over the years. Frs. Matthew Kiess and Bede Michel tended their chemistry labs; Fr. Aldrich Huhne, his shop; Emerson Hynes '37, fielded questions in the corridors after class sessions as both he and the students had to move to the next destination; and Steve Humphrey '29 developed into an elder "Mr. Chips" for both students and the younger members of the lay faculty; Fr. Conrad Diekmann as a fellow graduate student at the University of Minnesota lived in constant and seasonal—"today the lake must be breaking up"—homesickness for the lake, trees, trails and community of Saint John's; Fr. Adelard Thuente, during his colorful lectures in the former prefects' room after meals, honed his rendition of the chicken as nothing more, down the long evolutionary process, than "a snake with feathers." And Brother Ambrose! He served as night watchman for years, at times slept on isolated corridor floors as sleep came, collected old tennis shoes after the close of school as fillers for the holes he had dug for young trees planted on the slopes where the library now stands. He wore shoes that had not outlived their usefulness regardless of color combinations. He practiced heroic poverty.

Sometimes when we allow our own brokenness to touch the lives of others, the Lord will make us creative. Saint John's graduates have told us again and again, often years after leaving, that the formation that took place here had become the rock of their lives: the impact of place, fellow students, faculty and eccentricities.

This is the context for much of the essay that follows. We began with the pivotal decision on the number of students we were to admit at the college level. Given the circumstances, the decision happened with considerable suspense and pain under the pressure of the influx of GIs after World War II. Saint John's had had a more or less general understanding that the college enrollment was to be held at about four hundred students. However, when the veterans of the war began to come back in numbers, especially from January 1946 on, Fr. Martin Schirber, dean, and I as the members of the admissions committee responsible for day-to-day decisions, found ourselves unable to hold the line. We sensed that neither the circumstances of the post-war years nor the prevailing spirit of the Saint John's Abbey and college community could yield to a simple legalism: "We have a policy of no more than four hundred students in college." How can you say this to men who, worldwide, frequently had laid their lives on the line?

A creative tension confronted us, and 1946 became an epochal year. The "sanctions" of facility limitations had to be removed. We were forced to look beyond Benet Hall and the fourth-floor dorms of the main building for student housing. Flynntown, Saint Joseph, Avon, Saint Cloud, and a scattering of other places in the area had to be resorted to for emergency help. On campus we did as much "staging" (interim use) as a limited number of lounges or just open spaces would allow. Multiple-room occupancies and double-decking became the norm. When Fr. Boniface Axtman walked into all of this as dean of men in charge also of housing, he remarked in his quaint way: "If only they could count!" Nevertheless, he had a sleight of hand talent for assigning as many as one hundred students to transitional beds. Despite all, the wrenching time for the closing of registrations always came too soon both for young men who had planned on Saint John's and us. In this general context, forty-five or so years later, there is a delightful humanity about a sentence in the 1948–49 catalog: "Married students are not subject to on-campus regulations."

1946 stands out as the decisive year. Saint John's had not yet made a formal policy commitment on the number of college students. We rolled with the stress of the day. As I recall, Fr. Vincent Flynn, then president of the College of Saint Thomas, had suggested that barracks buildings for the housing of college students, veterans, were available for the asking. Abbot Alcuin Deutsch, then also president of the university, hesitated however for some weeks to give his consent to the acquisition of such barracks. Finally, on the last day the offer of the government could be honored, he gave his okay to the barracks. We learned later that some alumni, notably Fred Hughes '31, Judge Ed Devitt '34, and Herb Adrian '29, had a determining voice in this decision. A new era, clearly, had come into being: without loss of identity, outside voices had begun to play a more telling role in the future of Saint John's. When, after his retirement, we asked Abbot Alcuin why he had given us such a hard time during the housing episode, he replied that all along he had held the conviction that a student body of more than four hundred entailed the loss of the Benedictine community ideal. This had been the most difficult decision of his life.

An article in *The Record* of June 20, 1946 says all too simply: "Army Barracks to Accommodate 80 Fall Students." To this day I'm fully convinced that the date given is not accurate. The summer had seemed endless. Still another report of August 29 under the heading, "Fall Students Invade Campus in Full Force," dramatizes the housing situation: "The biggest problem confronting the administration today is finding room for 760 collegians and 230 preps . . . every conceivable adjustment is being made to allot every bit of available space. . . ." It claims that "rooms" were being furnished in the gymnasium and auditorium, and it repeats the off-campus emergency listings. Sheer euphemism! The rooms in the gym were the dirt floor area downstairs and the loft; the handball court, if I remember correctly, served for desks and study space. Beds were not made too regularly. Foxholes had been neither that genial nor secure. The barracks, it must be added, were late in coming; and when they went into use the fellows "rearranged" them. They were located where the present Saint Mary's parking lot is, beyond the old handball courts which gave way shortly after to Saint Mary's Hall, and a patch of no-man's-land, weeds, to the west. Other adjustments had to be made as well.

To cope with the "mad rush" to the dining hall at noon, "when

800 students try to crowd into the refectory," a second shift became necessary. The print shop, the present Walter Reger Room, had already been converted into a Prep dining facility. We were simply caught downstream. During an after-meal visit to the kitchen, we found the wonderful Sister Jordana, under pressure from the student influx, standing by her oven with tears streaming down her face. A moment of poignant and exquisite silence followed. The Black Franciscans, as they were known, had served the entire Saint John's community for many years. Family style meals, competitive waiters on the run for seconds, had been the custom. The sisters had become a respected unit within the larger community, greatly and lastingly appreciated.

Similarly, worship arrangements had to be changed: simultaneous services had to be held in the upper and lower church, now the bookstore, with prep and lower classmen downstairs and the Anselmites, college priesthood students, on the gospel side upstairs. And lest the academic be overlooked, *The Record* of September 1946 mentioned that the program of studies, by way of "another innovation," included theology for lay leaders. In those days we talked about leaders rather than men and women as people. Alumni groups reacted warmly to theology as a study for lay persons.

After the end of the war, discussions of college and university professionals often centered on what the veterans would be like as students, or, for the more timid, what will they do to us? Our experiences at Saint John's, I think generally, were good, very positive. These were banner years. Often the inductees had been "boys" when they left. They came back men from the global battlefields. Their perspectives of life and death often had matured radically. They knew why they had returned to college, and time seemed late. We found, in marginal cases by admissions standards (status symbols), that former high school and college records meant very little. We learned a difficult lesson about young people: they are never to be written off because they goofed or lacked maturity along the way. There is no magic about prognostic instruments, even about the Miller Analogies. Not that we should not work at it, but who can pinpoint the depth and promise in life of another person? Students who were given a second chance not only completed their college studies, but some went on to graduate studies as well and later moved into community and professional life as standouts. I do not recall any outright failures. College is a starting point, not an end in itself. The mistakes we made were on the side of having been too severe.

From January to April 1946, GIs drifted in as they were released from the services. Someone always seemed to be standing at the counter in the office of the registrar, which was then also the admissions office. In our darker moments we were tempted to think that the word on our open-door policy, seven days a week, had spread too far. Fr. William "Okey" O'Donnell, then dean of the College of Saint Thomas, remarked jokingly one day: "When they come on Sundays, we send them to Saint John's." He died in May 1974, one of the most selfless persons we ever had the privilege of working with. We were unable ever to say: "You should've been here in January!" The members of the faculty, without a dissenting voice, lived through it all. Applicants who came in March, for example, were registered in two instead of the regular load of five courses. Courses which normally require much reading were given the preference. I'm inclined to think that we still have not caught up with one of the greatest secrets of learning, in school and throughout life, namely reading. Perhaps some of the wisdom of Fr. Claude Sons had seeped through to us. Sometime during his junior or senior year in college, he had written inside the front cover of his history of philosophy textbook: "Don't let your classes interfere with your education!" This proved more than words. While others of his class were busy cramming for exams, as a smiling study hall classmate observed several years later, Claude made screeching catgut noises as he strung tennis rackets or continued to read, cover to cover, *The Catholic Encyclopedia*. We are never wholly on our own.

The abbey and the college community took the years immediately after World War II in stride. Both teaching and administrative loads became excessive at times, and the growth in the number of faculty members and compensation hardly kept pace. In 1945–46 the college had an enrollment of 434 students, and about 180 of these came at the beginning of the second semester. During the summer of 1946 there were 163 students, very unusual for those times. The 1946–47 registrations grew to 793 students; in 1947–48, 935. The faculty of Saint John's and all who were part of the academic community pitched in heroically. These will always remain memorable years. The students, mostly, were mature men, and the faculty responded to them with generosity; the world outside, nevertheless, remained in focus.

Emerson Hynes '37 is an example of the manner in which both he and the college responded. When in 1958 the newly elected Minnesota Senator Eugene McCarthy '35 asked this highly gifted and esteemed teacher to become a member of his senate staff, Hynes' first reaction was that this could not happen. He never had any occupation other than teaching, his classes in ethics and sociology were always overflowing, he knew the local grocer by name as well as the other people in the neighborhood of his rural Collegeville home. Rural life ran in his veins. Emerson and his wife Arlene had no other dreams for themselves and their large and growing family. Even after twenty years, life seemed just started. He shared his misgivings with a number of us, who, though fully aware of his anguish and our possible loss, urged him with one voice to accept, not only as a challenge but as an obligation. This man of established human and social concerns, great talent, and singular integrity simply had to become an active presence on the levels of national and world affairs. We granted him an indefinite leave of absence with the option to return whenever free to do so. He died in Washington in 1971. Many of us have always considered him a contemporary Saint Thomas More.

The decision to keep growing and changing with the increase of student needs became a matter of destiny. As the barracks and later Mary Hall and off-campus arrangements came into practice, the things of old faded into history. In broad outline, the sites of the flour mill and chicken coop now serve Tommy Hall, and the new art building (the latter under construction in late 1989); a part of the large barn and dairy farm area is now occupied by four student residences, with space reserved for still another as well as for the projected student union (Saint Joe Hall and the pottery annex are on the way out); and the clay tennis court area, where, in the quip of Ralph Williams, "We played on one court and ate on the others," is now the home of the Alcuin Library and the Hill Monastic Manuscript Library.

The passing of the dairy farm, understandably, caused much pain. It signaled the transition from the traditional monastic self-sufficiency of the first one hundred years to a substantially greater dependence on outside sources for food and services. Unknown even in the later '40s, the magnificent one-hundred-year plan which grew out of community needs and planning and the genius of Marcel Breuer, waited restlessly in the wings. All this is epitomized in the former Twin Towers and the new Banner.

In regard to faculty compensation, something of substance was worked out as early as the mid-1950s. As we collectively were able to catch our breath, faculty compensation and related matters were given thorough study and action. Institutional growth and new needs had much to do with what happened. In 1945–46 there were six lay faculty members. In 1957 there were seventy-three full-time faculty members, nineteen laymen, ten part-time members, including "the visiting teachers from the College of Saint Benedict." The military science faculty had their own procedures for compensation, promotion, etc. Other university employees had to be brought into full consideration. Our archives particularly for the '50s contain a surprising amount of information on faculty salaries, insurance, and related topics; also, the general college and university concerns with policies and practices on employment are reflected in the Saint John's committee reports and decisions. Two or three paragraphs here can hardly do justice to the discussions and developments over a period of several years. The elements of policy never fall together at a given moment. Individuals, representatives of groups, and several committees worked together. The committee on Rank and Tenure, the Faculty Reorganization (North Central Association) Committee, and the Faculty Committee elected by members of the lay faculty, kept working. Fr. Martin Schirber served as a key resource person. The committee reports and minutes speak for themselves.

The Rank and Tenure Committee reports of April 2 and 12, 1955 summarize much of what had been achieved at these dates: qualifications for appointment and promotion, faculty services, contracts for services, faculty salaries, tenure, retirement, vacations, leave of absence, attendance at meetings of learned societies, faculty privileges, faculty housing, professional and social organizations, public relations. The minutes of October 30, 1957 dealt with a number of significant details: lay members of the faculty, as well as nonresident employees, are covered by federal old age and survivor's insurance, and by a group insurance plan covering health, accident, and hospitalization. The latter plan was developed by a faculty committee in cooperation with Travelers Insurance Company to meet special circumstances of both academic and non-academic employees of the university. Father Martin states: "Saint John's also has a retirement program for all male and non-academic employees which is designed to supplement the retirement benefits under the Social Security program. The entire cost of this program is borne by the university." Persons who are members of the Order of St. Benedict received equivalent benefits.

The passage above, "a retirement program for all male and non-academic employees," did include women in the various non-academic services of the university. Mrs. Frances Pond who had worked here during the summer months as an academic secretary as early as 1955 (students served during the year), became the first full-time secretary in the late '50s, an "Abraham" of the women secretaries.

The Benedictine way of life is ultimately centered in God and people. For an educational institution this includes students, their families, and friends. Hence it is a shock to page through 1945–46 issues of *The Record.* Here again were the faces, so bright and young, of Johnnies who had given their lives in the service of their country and for peace throughout the world. Can we forget so quickly? The headlines of forty-five years ago are still devastating: "Gold Star List Grows," "Alumni Make Supreme Sacrifice," "Deaths on the Foreign Fronts Reach 57," and "Johnnies Who Won't Come Home." Each becomes a wordless story, paints an imaginary picture that can neither be fenced in by time nor space: a sense of place has global connotations, and more. "Who has cupped in his hand the waters of the sea, and marked off the heavens with a span?" (Isa 40:12). God never allows lives to be wiped out as an end in itself; the reward is always greater than the gift. We knew these men as students and members of the larger Saint John's community. We knew them by name. The nature of their continuing presence among us will always defy description.

A word about one or the other is in place. Pat Murphy '43 had one of the finest minds of any student to walk this campus—he wrote Socratic dialogues. Jim Boyd '43, once a colorful broken-field halfback, flew off on a lone mission in the vast Southwest Pacific and never returned; and Ed Welte '43, a Navy surgeon. Some of these men left wives and children. The Gold Star Lounge and the listings on the huge memorial board ("They served America and Saint John's") are faint reminders of men who gave their lives in good faith, men who died as men.

Passing observations about two Saint John's personalities are, indeed, in order. A February 8, 1946 *Record* notice about Miss Sabina Diederichs, the resident and highly regarded campus nurse for years, mentions that she had been hospitalized. And an occasional visit to the abbey-parish cemetery brings us to the grave of Coach Joe Benda. He died of an incurable illness in 1949. Joe had imparted his Knute Rockne spirit to some of the men who flew the vast expanses of the Pacific, some never to be seen again. He himself went as an intrepid warrior to the end.

Saint Benedict's words, following years of contemplative prayer, grow in significance by the day. The deserts of our lives may be the kitchen, anywhere along the way, or old age, where, Fr. Carroll Stuhlmueller in speaking of the declining days of Moses, muses strikingly: "Adults never find it easy to shed themselves of dignity and ambition, of power and influence, to change and become like little children!"[2] This is a beautiful way of saying that to be maturely human is to be contemplative.

A delightful happening in this connection: Dr. John LaLonde '52, now a prominent surgeon at the United Hospital in Grand Forks, and James "Jake" Leinen '51, had been friends at Saint John's. Twenty-five or so years later John found Jake by the Bismarck Holiday Inn swimming pool, in trunks and back to the entrance, in dead earnest doing (he had been a popular mimic in college) one of Father Boniface's assembly talks, with punch lines such as "Stealing is not allowed!" John's gleeful response: "Only a Johnny could have done that!"

A story by Mary Vineyard comes even closer to timelessness. A three-year-old had begged his parents for a few moments alone with his newborn brother, and when he thought himself alone he moved up to the crib with "Quick, tell me where you come from . . . and tell me about God. I'm beginning to forget."[3]

"I'm beginning to forget" reflects both a search for God and serves as a reminder about who we are and what our human limi-

2. "Biblical Meditations for Ordinary Time, Weeks 10–22" (Mahwah, N.J.: Paulist Press, 1984) 182.

3. Richard Rohr, "Radical Grace" (July–August, 1989) 8.

tations are. Implied here is a theme the psalms keep repeating: blessed are those who trust in God. This contrasts head-on with the obsessive quest for security through nuclear arms, military might, and, during the last few years in the U.S., star wars and the stealth bomber. This quest has been called a course of "terminal materialism," inevitably the road to self-destruction. Fr. Richard Rohr, following his sermons and talks throughout the country, generally finds people commenting, "Nice talk, Father, but you know in the real world . . . ." He reflects wearily, "Man's capacity to disguise his own darkness seems limitless." The price is too high. Jose Miranda, one of the many voices that have not been heard, documents the fact that millions of children "die each year from simple malnutrition."[4] The billions of dollars that have been and are being invested in instruments of security and war should be diverted to housing, employment, and the conditions of peace. Our Gold Stars, followed to this very day by countless men and women and children, have given their lives in the battle for freedom, justice, and peace. We have no debt other than to renew our faith in God, to undergo a change of heart, and to foster a spirit of reconciliation made concrete in what we are doing and can do.

As for the Bismarck swimming pool scene, its symbolic meaning may well have been more a matter of Collegeville spiritual osmosis than of outright intention: be still, listen, cut the self-talk in your heart. This is how we understand the words of Sr. Joan Chittister about contemplation as "an immersion into the mind of God and the life of Christ to such an extent that the way you live your own life can never again be quite the same."[5] This life in Christ is a walking in faith alongside people. It finds its vitality in the building of God's Kingdom where widows, orphans, and all members of the human family may come to fullness of life.

In this all-embracing perspective there is a captivating contrast between the students who sought to continue their education forty-five years ago and the millions who are unemployed, starving and homeless, or enslaved by the trivial. There are tides in giving and in receiving. To offer people only what is human or material, as

---

4. *Communism in the Bible* (Maryknoll, N.Y.: Orbis Books, 1982) 73.
5. *Sojourners*, June–July (Washington, 1989) 14–19.

Jacques Maritain observed years ago, is to betray them. Miriam Therese Winter adds a beautiful insight:

> The Liturgy is not over because it is the liturgy
> of life and there are lessons yet to learn . . .
> how to discern the incarnate Word in the dailyness
> all around me, still learning how to pray the perfect prayer.[6]

Where are we going, and what should our mission be today? Listen—*Obsculta!* the *Rule* insists.

In closing, I like sky and water. They have a kinship with the human heart, mutely reflecting its inner depths. And both are always there for us who room on the east side of the Breuer wing of the monastery. Lake Sagatagan takes on many of the moods of life: complete calm, sparkling brilliance in the sun, the shimmering golden moon path, the drabness of cloudy days, the restlessness and fury of windy days. And the expanse of the sky. Thank God that there is so much of it! Childhood memories linger on. As a native Dakotan the hypnotic charm of the great open spaces, the sloping valleys and hills framing the lonesome thereness of the buttes, with floating clouds in the boundless sky—all remind one of the eternal with people on pilgrimage.

We of this generation have been blessed, we may say consecrated, through the gifts to us and all humanity of great men and women, refreshingly selfless persons like Pope John XXIII and how the Lord made this man into an embodiment of God's love for us all. His "I am your brother Joseph" (Gen 45:3) is a text for persons and nations. Often we seem to be just catching on, ever so haltingly, to the truth of this great saying, a magnificent word meant by God to be addressed to every man, woman, and child.

Happily, person-to-person relationships and our sharing in all things created have both natural and spiritual dimensions. At the time of the death of Pope John, Dr. Edgar Carlson, then president of Gustavus Adolphus College, remarked with complete sincerity: "No death in my experience has touched and moved me more deeply as a personal loss than that of Pope John." And during August 1989 a fatal plane crash in Ethiopia claimed the lives of Congressman Mickey Leland and fourteen fellow workers, including Patrice Johnson, his chief of staff. Jesse Jackson tells how

6. Rohr, 2.

the congressman had fought for the approval of the House Select Committee on World Hunger. He had answered opposition charges about the waste of money and the suggestions that he devote his energies to problems at home with, "I am as much a citizen of the world as I am of America." He died as chairman of the Select Committee in search of help for the otherwise helpless. Similarly, Patrice Johnson is said to have traveled the "fast track" for some years in behalf of the needy and homeless. I'm not surprised, for I vividly remember her mother, Josie, from a conference on social problems she, Ed Henry, and I attended during the late '50s at Itasca State Park. Later Mrs. Johnson became the first Black regent of the University of Minnesota.

Be it John XXIII, Archbishop Oscar Romero, the Saint John's Gold Stars, or the countless heroes and martyrs of our time, there often is evidence of a singular grasp and awareness of God's presence, redemptive and ongoing in all of human history. It never has been, never could have been, by force of the obsessive drive of those intent on the pasteurizing of doctrine. The farewell message of Jesus (John 12:24) keeps snowballing: "I solemnly assure you unless the grain of wheat falls to the earth and dies, it remains just a grain of wheat. But if it dies, it produces much fruit." Awesome beyond words, Eucharist.

Fr. Otto Weber and friends

S INCE THERE SEEMS TO BE SOME HAZINESS AS TO
how the Hill Monastic Manuscript Microfilming Project was conceived and begun, I, who was in the deal from its start, will try
to give a clear and complete picture of how the project was born
and evolved.[1]

The real architect for the project is Fr. Colman Barry. Shortly
after he was selected to be the president of Saint John's University
in 1964, he contacted me, working in the library then at Saint Vincent Archabbey and College, to inquire (''coax'' could perhaps
be the more correct word) whether I would be willing to supervise
the microfilming of medieval manuscripts in European Benedictine monasteries. Since he concluded from our telephone conversation that I would be available for such an assignment, he next
brought the idea to the attention of Abbot Baldwin Dworschak,
who agreed that that would be an excellent undertaking for Saint
John's.[2]

Father Colman had come to his grandiose idea from the example
set by the Vatican Library. In 1951 this library arranged with the

1. Cf. with adaptations Oliver L. Kapsner, ''History of the Manuscript Microfilm Project,'' *The Scriptorium* XXV (Christmas 1986) 71–90.

2. Cf. Colman J. Barry, ''Preserving Manuscripts of Our Religious and Cultural Traditions,'' *Studies in Catholic History in Honor of John Tracy Ellis,* N. H.
Minnich, R. B. Eno, and R. F. Trisco, eds. (Wilmington: Michael Glazier, 1985)
417–39.

Jesuits from Saint Louis University in Missouri to have its precious manuscript collection put on microfilm. Father Colman maintained that, since the Vatican Library had shown the way, the Benedictines should follow its good example and photograph all old manuscripts still preserved in Benedictine monasteries in Europe which have enjoyed an unbroken existence since the Middle Ages.

Actually, it was also a Benedictine who conceived the idea to microfilm the Vatican Library, namely, the late Cardinal Anselmo Albareda, who was at the time prefect of the Vatican Library. He was also the Vatican librarian during World War II and came to realize firsthand that their whole library collection could be blown to smithereens in a matter of hours, thanks to the destructive clout of modern warfare.

The story goes that Albareda arranged the deal with an American Jesuit from the Gregorianum at some afternoon coffee sessions in Rome. The Jesuits in turn approached the Knights of Columbus to fund the project and received a grant of $500,000. Operating with six cameras and Jesuit brothers serving as cameramen, the work ended after five years when the fund was used up and thirty thousand Vatican manuscripts had been put on microfilm. That constituted not quite one half of the extensive Vatican manuscript collection.

That is some of the background of how Father Colman arrived at the idea of undertaking a Benedictine manuscript microfilm project. Actually, he only knew that the Vatican Library project was done, but was hardly informed as to the complexity involved in carrying out the work. I got busy making an estimate, first of how many medieval manuscripts actually were preserved in European Benedictine monasteries. Fortunately, Paul Oskar Kristeller, a distinguished Columbia professor, had toured European libraries, including monasteries, in order to make an estimate of extant medieval manuscript collections. In 1960 he published the first edition of his results in a volume entitled *Latin Manuscript Books before 1600; a List of the Printed Catalogs and Unpublished Inventories of Extant Collections.*

From that book I estimated that the three major Benedictine libraries in Italy, three in Switzerland, and eleven in Austria possessed a total of from twelve thousand to fifteen thousand old manuscripts. I also knew that the only firm in this country engaged in major microfilm work was University Microfilms Inc. in Ann Arbor, Michigan. I wrote to its director, Eugene B. Power, mentioning what we had in mind and requested a meeting with him during Easter Week of 1964 when the Catholic Library Association would hold its annual convention in Detroit.

At the meeting he impressed me that he was in full command of such work, and I also saw how smoothly his firm functioned. He suggested that the work be done with two cameras, while camera operators would be trained in the country where we were stationed. University Microfilms would do the microfilming.

Myself, or somebody like me, would have to be on hand to make the proper arrangements with each monastery for moving in and seeing to it that a convenient, separate room which could be darkened was provided. That person would be in charge of getting the manuscripts and returning the manuscripts undamaged to the respective library every day. I would also have to prepare a typed sheet or card which was to be photographed ahead of every film. This sheet would identify the manuscript by its proper library signature and contain a summary of its contents. Then, for University Microfilms, I would also keep an eye on the cameramen so they did careful work and wouldn't loaf; send the films to some firm in the country to be developed; see that the cameramen carefully inspect the developed film on the reader and compare it against the original manuscript; pay the cameramen their salaries and cover occasional expenses from a bank account which University Microfilms would establish in each European country; get the developed negatives packed and shipped to Ann Arbor where they are stored in temperature-and-humidity controlled vaults. Two positive copies of the films would be made, one for Saint John's and one for the respective Austrian library.

The charge for all this would be $.04 per original negative, which would cover all overseas expenses: films, developing, shipping, salaries, van or small truck, and occasional expenses. Positive copies of the film would cost about $.01 per exposure. The charges for positive copies are actually computed by film footage. That seemed fair. At The Catholic University of America in Washington, where I had been a catalogue librarian ten years previously, they also did some microfilming, mostly magazine articles, and charged $.03 per exposure.

During July 1964 the American Library Association met in Saint Louis. I attended the meeting and also visited the Pius XII Memorial Library at Saint Louis University. The Jesuit librarian was very gracious, showed me the microfilm collection of the Vatican Library manuscripts, and even offered to let us use their portable cameras. But University Microfilms only use mounted cameras and a solid table for doing the work. Again I had learned something.

In July I returned to Saint John's. Abbot Baldwin had written in April to fifteen Benedictine monasteries in Italy, Switzerland, and Austria, presenting our project to them and requesting permission to photograph their manuscripts. In explaining the purpose of our project to the European abbots, Abbot Baldwin's letter stressed two main reasons for our action, namely: (1) to secure the preservation of all hand-written or manuscript books dating prior to 1600 still extant in Benedictine libraries and (2) to make these resources available under certain conditions to all scholars in a single center in the United States. So far only one had answered, and that seemed to be a kind of half-hearted response from the Archabbey of Monte Cassino, motherhouse of Benedictines worldwide. I went to a confrere who was well versed in Italian for help in obtaining a clear idea of the letter. He also had the impression that, while the Monte Cassino librarian did give his consent, he also seemed to hint that he would rather not be bothered.[3]

3. The restrictions were actually much more prohibitive. Cf. Archives of Saint John's Abbey, Thommaso Leccisotti to Baldwin Dworschak, Monte Cassino, March 9, 1964:

As the archivist in charge of the manuscripts, I have been asked by the Rev.mo P. Abate of Monte Cassino to write you.

The proposal to have the Cassinese codices reproduced in microfilm, excluding however the right of printing and publishing the collected material, is acceptable under the following preliminary conditions.

1) For centuries the codices formed part of the archives; hence they are not clearly distinguished and separated from strictly archival material. The photographing would have to be limited to those manuscripts which, according to our judgment, do not belong to this latter category; everything that has the character of an archival document remains excluded.

2) Since our contribution, both in quantity and in quality, is very notable and not similar to that of other monasteries, it seems to us that we must ask for a mutual favor, namely, that you deposit also at our abbey a copy of all the reproductions of codices made in the various libraries.

These are the conditions that it will be opportune to establish before the Father in charge prepares to come here.

The next step was to get the project funded, as it was obvious that we would need considerable financial support for such an undertaking. Father Colman and Abbot Baldwin thought that the Hill Family Foundation of Saint Paul should be approached, and I was asked to draft an estimate of the expense involved. Eugene Power had given me an idea of how many exposures each cameraman is expected to do per day. On that basis, and with a charge of $.04 per original exposure and about $.01 per exposure for positive copies, I estimated that the project would cost about $40,000 per year. The Hill Family Foundation granted Abbot Baldwin, Fathers Arno Gustin, Colman, and myself an interview and, to our surprise, was immediately impressed with such a noble cultural venture. Mr. A. A. Heckman, executive director, who presided at the meeting and sparked it, wanted to know how long it would take to finish the job. I judged that it would take four years to photograph the twelve thousand or so medieval manuscripts in the fifteen Benedictine libraries.

The Hill Foundation agreed to support the project for two years at a time, and said the first check would be forthcoming that fall (1964). At a subsequent meeting at Saint John's, Fr. Florian Muggli, abbey treasurer at that time, asked whether the $40,000 included a salary for me. When I said that it didn't, Abbot Baldwin remarked that if the Hill Family Foundation could be so generous, then Saint John's should be disposed to provide a field director for the project *gratis*. Actually, as it turned out, if I had been salaried as a foreigner, I could have stayed only six months in Austria. This highly socialized republic takes precautions that all its citizens are guaranteed a job.

I then contacted some medieval scholars in our country to obtain their opinions about the project and whether we should do selective photographing, and if selective, how to select which manuscripts to photograph. I wrote to Harvard and Yale Universities and medieval institutes in the United States and Canada, ten altogether. They all approved highly of the project and said we should not do selective photographing but should photograph everything up to the year 1600 as that is the accepted standard for considering a document a medieval manuscript. Saint Louis University had done selective photographing at the Vatican Library and scholars in this country were complaining of gaps.

Then came August 1964—still no further responses from the Benedictine monasteries in Europe apart from the tenuous acceptance from Monte Cassino. This made me wonder whether the project was at all possible. Fr. Odo Zimmermann was visiting then at Saint John's from our foundation, Abadia Del Tepeyac, in Mexico. He mentioned that they had needed a librarian at their monastery and school. But when he brought the matter to Abbot Baldwin, the abbot decided against the idea and wanted me to go to Europe anyhow and give it a try. So, *ex obedientia,* I made plans to proceed.

I wrote to Monte Cassino that I was coming. When I arrived on October 5, 1964, I explained to the librarian just what it all meant; namely, that we would work with two cameras operated by laymen and that the job would take about five or six months. Monte Cassino had a good-sized manuscript collection despite depletions suffered during the reign of commendatory abbots in the fourteenth and fifteenth centuries. The next day he laid down three conditions: (1) we could not bring laymen into the monastery because of the previous bombing; (2) we could not work there a long time; (3) he wanted a copy of everything that we would microfilm in Europe. Any of those three conditions would have made it impossible for us to do our job at Monte Cassino, let alone the three nullifying factors taken together. I also learned later that we could not have operated at Monte Cassino anyhow, as the Italian government would not have allowed it. That government had ruled that all microfilming of manuscripts and archive material must be done by the government or under its control and that the state provides private institutions with the proper equipment if such work is to be done. That is precisely what happened at the abbeys of Subiaco and Cava, each of which had a smaller manuscript collection. Each had a large mounted camera from the state and a developing room, and each photographed its manuscripts for us (Subiaco 300, Cava 60). They did this after two years, though the quality of their filming does not compare favorably with the work we did. The abbey of Montevergine, which had only twenty manuscripts but was also equipped with a mounted camera and a developing room (it had a precious archives) also agreed to provide us microfilm copies of its manuscripts, but never did so.

When nothing was accomplished at Monte Cassino, I decided to try my luck in Switzerland. On the way I stopped in Rome for a few days. There, through the courtesy of Fr. Ulric Beste, I met Abbot Benno Gut of Einsiedeln Archabbey, who was attending the Vatican Council. Our project appealed to him, and he wrote to his librarian, granting us permission to begin the project at Einsiedeln. But even before my departure from Rome, I received a letter from the Einsiedeln librarian informing me that we could not photograph their manuscripts. He added politely that I was welcome to come for a visit, but not for microfilming. A few days later I arrived at Einsiedeln. The guestmaster at Einsiedeln was a fine man, something like our Fr. Fabian Wegleitner, and liked our project. He put me in contact by phone with the librarian, a monsignor, at Saint Gall, a former famous Benedictine abbey. The monastery was dissolved in 1849, but the library remained intact and became the property of the Catholic Church in the Canton of Saint Gall.

The monsignor received me politely and let me see some of their precious manuscripts, including the famous codex 914, probably the oldest existing copy of the *Regula Sancti Benedicti* (it is probably a copy of the copy which Charlemagne had made of the original copy in Monte Cassino) but he also informed me that we could not photograph their manuscripts. He said that they did not need us since they had their own equipment and for some years were photographing their own manuscripts as needed. Later I learned that he also photographed Einsiedeln manuscripts when requested to do so.

At Engelberg both the abbot and the librarian said they would go along with our project if other Swiss Benedictine libraries would do so. There I also learned that there was an association of religious libraries in Switzerland (Benedictine, Dominican, Franciscan, Jesuit) which had their annual convention two months before my arrival. At this meeting the association had decided to reject our offer. In Rome the Einsiedeln abbot had not yet known about this decision.

In Switzerland I experienced the second setback for our project. I decided to continue my exploratory visits in Austria with actually little hope of success since nobody from Austria had answered Abbot Baldwin's letter. I had the feeling that by Christmas or shortly after I would be on my return journey to the States, empty-handed.

From Einsiedeln I wrote to the Benedictine abbeys in Austria, mentioning just when I planned to visit each abbey to discuss our offer. I allowed three days for travel and a visit to each abbey, beginning the trip on November 15 and planning to be back at Einsiedeln by December 20 to rest and spend Christmas. As at the four abbeys in Italy and the three in Switzerland, it was the same story at all but two of the ten Austrian abbeys which I visited. They are located in characteristic Benedictine fashion off the beaten path, and my traveling was all done via public transportation in the late fall and early winter months. How often did I stand in the rain or drizzle or even snow waiting for bus connections. But I made it—and survived.

My first stop in Austria was at Saint Peter's Archabbey in Salzburg. The abbot was most gracious and felt favorably inclined towards our project but hinted that not all Austrian abbeys felt the same way. In fact, he said that two abbeys had telephoned him to inform me that I need not come there at all. But he signed a written agreement to indicate his willingness. Lambach Abbey was the next stop. There the abbot had just been deposed, and there was no librarian; hence, not much could be accomplished.

The next stop was Kremsmünster Abbey. When I arrived, the porter immediately told me that the abbot wanted to speak to me on the phone, whereupon I was set for the next treat of bad news. But his first words on the phone were: *Willkommen in Kremsmünster. Sie werden in Kremsmünster anfangen* ("Welcome to Kremsmünster. You will begin your work here"). Brother, what a day that was for me, to hear such good news with my own ears. The abbot, Albert Bruckmayr, was newly elected four months previously. In Rome he had been a classmate of Fr. Vitus Bucher. He said that after all that Saint John,'s had done for them during the hard years after World War I, it just would not be right to turn Saint John's down now. Here I also learned that during the general chapter of the Austrian Benedictine Congregation in the summer of 1964, Abbot Baldwin's offer was considered and was turned down. Ironically, the instigator for this unfavorable decision was the librarian from Kremsmünster, who had recently attended a convention in Munich where the director of the mighty Bayerische Staatsbibliothek had thundered against fulfilling requests coming from other countries to photograph whole portions of their manuscript collections.

So the assembled Austrian abbots simply said that if the librarians don't want it, that's it. Ever so fortunately, the aged abbot president of the Austrian Congregation neglected to inform Abbot Baldwin of this decision. If he had done so, I would not have left for Europe.

When Abbot Albert informed their librarian of his decision to let us begin our work at Kremsmünster, the librarian turned about completely and was totally cooperative. He even went out of his way to improve the reading of the agreement which I was presenting for signing, making a few minor modifications, and rendering the German more elegant. He then also duplicated enough copies for my use during the rest of my trip. Next, he asked why we planned to contact only Benedictine monasteries in Austria? Why not also the Austrian Cistercian, Augustinian, and Premonstratensian abbeys? I told him that I had no objection whatever if that could be arranged. So the next day he himself accompanied me to Sankt Florian, a famous Augustinian abbey thirty miles away that possessed an excellent manuscript collection. And a contract was signed at Sankt Florian.

The sky was beginning to clear before me. Three monasteries had signed the agreement. Now negotiations were considerably easier. First, Michaelbeuern signed, then Seitenstetten, then Melk, then Göttweig (the abbot of Göttweig was also the new administrator of Lambach, so he signed for Lambach). From Göttweig the Cistercian abbey of Zwettl lay to the north, and another Cistercian abbey, Lilienfeld, to the south, both of which signed. I met a Cistercian monk at Lambach who also encouraged me to visit the Cistercian abbeys in Austria, gave me their names, locations, and directions for reaching them conveniently on my visitation tour of the Benedictine abbeys. Then I was off to Schottenstift in Vienna, which signed the agreement. There too the librarian was most gracious to me. One day he accompanied me to Klosterneuburg of Augustinian canons ten miles north of Vienna, which signed the agreement.

The following day he accompanied me to the Cistercian abbey of Heiligenkreuz, twenty miles south of Vienna, which signed. Only here the abbot, who had a reputation as a stickler, required that I obtain a letter for him from my abbot showing that I was duly authorized to do this work. The Austrian Benedictine abbots had all received such notification beforehand. From Vienna I went way down to the Benedictine Abbey of Saint Paul in Lavanttal in Kärnten. At first, the abbot hesitated but then did sign the agreement.

Then came my last stop, Admont, where the librarian was vehemently opposed to our project. The kind abbot called a meeting of the Small Chapter to which I was invited to explain our offer. The meeting ended with the signing of the agreement.

Now I could return to Einsiedeln on December 20 to relax a bit and to enjoy Christmas. What a Christmas gift I had in my bag: fifteen Austrian abbeys had signed the agreement: ten Benedictine, three Cistercian, two Augustinian. And the big break had come when least expected. I immediately reported what I had brought together to Eugene Power at University Microfilms; the firm would not move in anywhere to operate unless the prospects looked good. Things sounded good enough to him, and I met him in Vienna in late January. We hired a car to drive out to Kremsmünster, one hundred miles from Vienna, so he could make an on-the-spot check of the manuscript collection, possible working facilities, and the nature of available electric power. He felt that it could be done. Incidentally, he was ever so pleased with the hospitality which he experienced at Kremsmünster. From Vienna we also drove to nearby Klosterneuburg, which again impressed him favorably.

Eugene Power returned to Ann Arbor to get things organized and to prepare the shipment of equipment. When all was ready, Power said, he would provide one cameraman to come from England where University Microfilms has a branch. I was to look for another promising candidate in Austria, a person fairly young, reliable, and not inclined to be nervous.

I located such a person through the American consulate. He turned out to be tops and stayed with us through the seven years of my stay in Austria. The man from England—he was really a German who had drifted to England—was dismissed after six months because he did not do good work and did not improve. We engaged another Austrian who stayed with us for four years. He was succeeded by another Austrian. A candidate can readily be trained on the job to do this type of photographing. He need not have previously been an expert cameraman. Local talent also know where and how to get supplies in Austrian shops, as such needs pop up constantly when one works daily with mechanical equipment.

The shipment from Ann Arbor arrived in Vienna in early April 1965. After some bickering with the customs people—a usual experience whenever we brought in new equipment, especially a camera—everything was cleared and the shipment was transported to Kremsmünster where it was set up for operation. A temporary drawback there which usually occurred whenever we moved to another abbey was to get hooked up with sufficient electric current. Our two cameras each operated with four 300-watt lamps. In other words, we needed *Stark Strom* (high voltage). In order to get this, we had to lead a 100-foot cable from the kitchen and through the windows to our level. To obtain the properly adjusted operating electric current, we had to transport a heavy transformer, which took two men to lift. In addition, two men were needed to move the eight-foot metal mast on which the mounted cameras were raised and lowered for proper focusing. Likewise, it took two men to carry the tables.

When I first toured the Austrian abbeys, several abbots mentioned that, in any case, our camera team should not include women, as that could not be allowed in monasteries. In my very first letter to Eugene Power, I fortunately did not forget to mention that factor. This remark disturbed Mr. Power considerably, so much so, that he phoned Einsiedeln to inform me that we must be able to use women because in Ann Arbor they employ only women to do the photographing. That is also very likely the reason why he was unable to supply initially a competent cameraman from England. When he visited us in Austria two years later and saw how we had to transport heavy equipment at each move and how the camera operators had to carry heavy manuscripts every day (sometimes for a block or two and up stairways), I asked him whether he still thought it would have worked with women as camera operators. He promptly replied: "Not at all."

After a few more precious lessons during the first days of operation at Kremsmünster, things functioned well during the seven years I was in charge. I personally typed all the inventory cards for about four hours each day, usually with cold hands and under poor light, selected the illuminated pages which were to be photographed separately at the end as color films, and supervised the work in general, keeping an eye on the cameramen so that they did their work and did not damage any precious manuscripts. It was also necessary to inspect the developed negatives and to send shipments of the developed films to Ann Arbor.

Sometimes two cameramen could live in monastery guest quarters, but usually they had to look about for living quarters outside at reasonable rates. Except for one occasion I always lived in a monastery, but it wasn't a luxury to live out of a suitcase for seven years. There were plenty of headaches working with people, old books, and mechanical equipment. While I survived it all, I don't think I would care to go through it again. Yet some of my good confreres think I had seven years of vacation in Europe.

I stayed on as supervisor of the microfilm project overseas for seven years instead of the contemplated three or four years. By that time, instead of the estimated 12,000 or so manuscripts to be photographed, we had photographed 28,000 manuscripts. This output came not only from fifteen libraries, but from forty-two manuscript collections, large and small, namely: twenty-eight monasteries (twelve Benedictine, five Cistercian, four Augustinian, two Premonstratensian, three Franciscan, one Dominican, one Mechitarist), and fourteen non-monastic libraries (three diocesan, two university, six state or municipal, one castle, and two private). When the microfilm team had their three week vacations during the summer, I cruised about arranging for contracts with libraries which had not yet been contacted. When I departed in 1971, in my seventieth year as a pilgrim on this planet, there were still a half-dozen libraries in Austria with which I had reached agreement. These were for Fr. Urban Steiner, my successor, to take care of. He merely had to continue the work, as the system was all set up and functioning. I was very happy when Father Urban was assigned to take my place. He was the right age (upper thirties), had excellent training in library science, and had one year of experience in cataloging manuscripts in the Hill Monastic Microfilm Library at Saint John's.

A word about expenses. The original Hill Family Foundation grant was $40,000 per year for overseas operations, the amount we had requested. After a year of operation, we saw that this was not enough. Reasons: our annual output was 20 percent greater than I had originally estimated, hence another $10,000 per year was needed. University Microfilms from the start was charging $.05 per original exposure, whereas they had told me it would be $.04, which made an additional $8,000 per year necessary. We also did color filming, which had not been included in my original estimate. Eugene Power got the idea to do color filming when he saw the medieval manuscripts at Kremsmünster. This cost $23,000 per year. Actually, this is an inexpensive way of getting pretty good copies of beautiful illuminations in the manuscripts at about $.15 per exposure.

When I was called back to Saint John's in 1966 for the Alcuin Library dedication and to make a personal report to the Hill Family Foundation at their invitation, I requested an increase in the grant and explained why. The increase to $60,000 per year was readily granted. That remained the annual Hill Family Foundation grant year after year, and it was always sufficient. The overseas' operation never dipped into the red, although there never was much left over for other purposes.[4]

Saint John's Abbey paid for my personal expenses, which averaged $700 per year: $600 for room and board in the monasteries and $100 for other expenses. Twice, in 1966 and 1968, I was called back to the States to report to the Hill Family Foundation; the plane fare was $650, a total of $1,300 for these two years. That is the complete story of the first overseas microfilm operations.

A word must also be said about the operation at Saint John's. *Ab initio* there was probably little thought that the microfilm collection would expand to present proportions and eventually constitute a new library in its own name. When I first returned from Austria in 1966, the films were simply stored in a small seminar room on the library's second level. Few thought that there should be extensive facilities for consulting the films. The new library was already under construction when the microfilm project was conceived. By chance I met Fr. Paulin (Michael) Blecker in the library. He from the beginning had shown an interest in the project, and I mentioned to him the pitiful way in which the films were being stored. He asked me to come with him to the basement of the library, where he showed me to larger adjoining rooms not being used for much (I believe they were intended for the education

4. The Hill Family Foundation contributed $1,750,000 in direct support to the project from 1964-1984. Cf. Colman Barry, *ibid.*, 421.

department). Since after another year the seminar room on the second level would already be crowded with stored films, I called the abbot's and president's attention to these available rooms in the basement of the library for the microfilm collection.

About the same time (June 1966) Dr. Julian G. Plante was engaged as curator of the new microfilm collection. Some time after my return to Europe, the films were moved to the two basement rooms in the library where, before many years, the situation again became crowded not only with films and reference works but also with people. Catalogers, scholars, and visitors were falling over each other. Even the approach via a long stairway was awkward and uninviting, especially for elderly scholars, and there was no public elevator in the library. This situation was solved by the new Bush Center. It is readily approachable and has space to house three times the present microfilm collection and three times the present number of reference books, besides providing adequate facilities for catalogers and for scholars to do their work.

Perhaps it is not out of place to tell how this early surprise structure known as the Bush Center came about. I myself never dreamt that such an event would happen during my lifetime. In 1973 the microfilm library thought it appropriate to honor my seventieth birthday with a festschrift entitled *Translatio Studii: Manuscript and Library Studies Honoring Oliver L. Kapsner OSB*, edited by Julian Plante. The expression *translatio studii* means the preservation and handing down of culture. The presentation was made at a dinner where, in expressing my appreciation, I also mentioned that all this was made possible through the service of Al Heckman, who arranged the Hill Family Foundation donations needed for founding and continuing this project. Then when it was his turn to say a few words, he first thanked me for my kind words and then calmly added: "And here is another $100,000 as an addition to the original Bush Foundation Grant of $500,000 to erect a separate building for the bulging microfilm collection." The Bush Center, designed by Marcel Breuer, as his last building at Saint John's, today houses the expanding manuscript collection in distinctive and functional accommodations.

Who would ever have dreamt in 1964 that the microfilm collection for medieval manuscripts would grow to its present proportions? There are well over 73,000 manuscripts from complete collections in Austria, Spain, Portugal, England, Germany, Ethiopia, and Malta. In addition, copies of individual manuscripts were also obtained by purchase or exchange from libraries in France, Italy, Hungary, Belgium, Netherlands, Sweden, Russia, and Israel. It is the largest medieval manuscript collection on microfilm in the world. The Saint Louis University microfilm collection contains 30,000 Vatican manuscripts (no color films) from the fifth century to the nineteenth century. Ours are from the sixth century to 1600, besides papyri dated from before Christ, and contains some 60,000 color films.

There are libraries, like the British Library—formerly the British Museum—and the Bibliotheque Nationale in Paris, which have perhaps 40,000 manuscripts, but not nearly all are "medieval" manuscripts. The Austrian Nationalbibliothek in Vienna also has 34,000 manuscripts, which makes it the fourth largest manuscript collection in Europe, but only 14,000 were medieval manuscripts when we cataloged that collection.

In his December 28, 1976 report on the financial statement of Saint John's Abbey and University, the corporate treasurer valued the book holdings of the Alcuin Library at $1,379,877 and the microfilm collection in the Hill Monastic Manuscript Library, built up during only a decade, at $982,316. Incidentally, the Alcuin Library and its book collection were not handed to Saint John's on a platter as were the microfilm collection and the Bush Center— the Hill and Bush grants alone total over $2,000,000. There have also been many grants from a continually developing number of foundations and friends. The Hill Monastic Manuscript Library contains in one convenient center the precious medieval manuscripts or earliest books of some one hundred European libraries, along with the facilities to study and use precious material which will never go out of date but will increase in value as the years and centuries roll by.

The microfilm collection housed at Saint John's has value even if it is not as yet completely cataloged. While photographing the manuscript collections in Austria, we also photographed unpublished handwritten catalogs as well as catalogs which were only on cards. These were later made available in xeroxed book form by University Microfilms. While they are indeed a help, they still are not a substitute for a good integrated catalog job done on the spot where the films are kept. But such cataloging is not an easy task. It demands language skills, especially Latin, a good knowledge of medieval culture, theology, Scripture, and the humanities, and powers of concentration and of exercising infinite patience.

The 73,000 microfilmed manuscripts—meaning so many bound volumes—contain over 200,000 separate titles or items which must be cataloged separately. By comparison, the 300,000 books in the Alcuin Library consist of about 170,000 distinct items or titles. A twenty-volume encyclopedia, for example, is one item or title. The manuscript cataloger must do original cataloging every *incipit* of the way. He does not have the convenience of a title page, a table of contents, printed Library of Congress cards, or some other source of printed cards to work with. It will be an excellent ministry awaiting Saint John's monks of the future. I gave forty-one years of my monastic career to library work, the bulk of which was devoted to doing a cataloging job which begged to be done. The career began one month after completing the novitiate in July 1923 when Abbot Alcuin Deutsch, like myself, out for a morning stroll after breakfast, called me: "Father Oliver, come here. I want you to work in the library." And thereon hangs the tale.

Within the brief space of twenty years, there have been major changes in the names of institutions involved in this microfilm project; namely, the original Monastic Manuscript Microfilm Library is now the Hill Monastic Manuscript Library; the Hill Family Foundation—actually the Louis W. and Maud Hill Family Foundation—now is the Northwest Area Foundation; University Microfilms in Ann Arbor, now is the University Microfilms International. Unchanged remain the names of: Al Heckman, Oliver Kapsner, and Julian Plante.

T HERE IS A SENSE OF PLACE ABOUT SAINT
John's, but it is not circumscribed by cloister walls or the university campus; it extends to the immediate neighborhood. This sense
of place cannot but permeate and be permeated by Stearns County,
Minnesota. Since I was born and raised in this county, there is
for me a double connection and, perhaps, a vantage point from
which to reflect on the relationship that binds this monastic family
to the community in which it resides.

The historical relationship between abbey and county is as obvious as it is profound. Like the German immigrants whom they
were to serve, the early monks of Saint John's came to Minnesota
to live and to work. They followed and to a certain extent led German Catholic immigration up the Mississippi and into the Sauk
River Valley. There the abbey and the county grew together.

A monastery moving into an area that is already developed will
by virtue of the Benedictine character of rootedness inevitably be
tied to that local community. But when this interplay is central to
the origin of both communities, something uniquely important takes
place. While the relationship can be modified, enhanced, ignored,
or even resisted, this bond remains.

It is impossible to overestimate the connection between Saint
John's Abbey and University and the development of the Church
in Stearns County. Currently, sixty-four parishes exist in the
county, and two out of every three were founded from Saint John's.
Almost half continued to be served by the abbey until after the es-

tablishment of the diocese of Saint Cloud in 1889; for sixteen of them the connection extended into the twentieth century. The ubiquitous and beneficial presence of monastic women from the Convent of Saint Benedict in Saint Joseph helped to reinforce the Benedictine character of these parishes and the Stearns County presence.

I grew up in a Benedictine parish. As a result I inevitably viewed the Church through Benedictine eyes. There was a difference, I believe, though this was not often articulated and only dimly understood. It was Father Luke, for example, and not Father Fink, and somehow that was significant. There was a feeling of greater closeness to a parochial clergy whose own home was nearby.

The Benedictine character of the parish was evident in the liturgy. The publications of The Liturgical Press were taken for granted and produced a link with Saint John's. The dialogue Mass was fostered in those early days of the Liturgical Movement with appropriate booklets. Other publications of The Press provided the text and music for the more common Gregorian chant Masses and promoted devotions and instructions in Catholic doctrine. Through these means there was a conscious awareness of the closeness of Saint John's.

The Benedictines not only came to Stearns County with the immigrants; for many years they replenished their numbers to a considerable degree from the families of the local area. The abbey was not, to be sure, an exclusively Stearns County institution. From the beginning there was significant recruitment from elsewhere, but in the early period the Stearns County flavor was unmistakable.

Thus, an early list of monks that did not include the lay brothers showed that in 1893 seven out of twenty-two American monks were born in or near Stearns County. All but one of the seven had entered the community within the preceding six years. An undetermined number of the fifty-six foreign-born monks would have been members of area immigrant families as well. A quarter century later in 1915, a similar list indicated that Stearns County natives who had entered the community in the preceding twenty-five years represented 38 percent of the total American-born entrants in the same period. By 1940, Stearns County was accounting for almost two professions a year. However, the average annual profession rate for community members from outside the county was now numbering almost four, and the gap was beginning to widen.

Saint John's was obviously a strong force in the early secondary and post-secondary education in the area. Over 20 percent of the students enrolling at Saint John's in its first century came from Stearns County and adjacent areas. A similar, though somewhat larger, percentage of students hailed from outside Minnesota. Attendance from Stearns County kept pace throughout the period with the rapidly increasing enrollments in the school generally.

Stearns County residents continued to make up a significant part of the student body of Saint John's Preparatory. Throughout the first century the emphasis on providing an education for young men in the local area who were considering the priesthood was especially strong. As college became more and more a reality for residents of Stearns County, an attraction to Saint John's was evident, especially when commuting to classes was sometimes feasible.

Historically, then, there is an obvious connection between Saint John's and the local community. This relationship was strong and generally positive. How has this continued?

Thirteen parishes in Stearns County remain in the charge of Benedictines. A link to Saint John's in these parishes is still apparent as is a strong commitment on the part of the monastery to the area pastoral apostolate. The pastors manifest a high degree of community involvement. Furthermore, monks in the ministry training program regularly serve in nearby Benedictine parishes. With regard to the local Collegeville parish, the lease of land for the Collegeville parish center is evidence of a positive relationship.

During my years in the clericate, as the six-year formation program for monks preparing for the priesthood was then called, a day-long tour of a number of Stearns County parishes staffed by Saint John's took place every six years. Clerics, as a result, got a sense of the history of Saint John's involvement in this apostolate and became acquainted with the parishes for which they might one day be working.

Such an introduction was deemed useful and its relatively minimal character underscored in a paradoxical manner the loosening of the connections between abbey and county. The tour was made once in six years so all could get a view of Stearns County parishes in their clericate experience. This already reveals a certain isolation. In addition, the numbers of those for whom this excursion was needed was becoming greater. Nowadays, indeed, such tours are not done at all, though novices regularly visit some of the parishes.

At mid-century the composition of the Saint John's community underwent a significant change. The period from 1940–65 manifested phenomenal growth, and the greatest proportion of that increase came from outside Stearns County. Its natives were still joining the community at the rate of over one per year (down from the average two per year of the previous quarter century), but at the same time more than seven were coming annually from elsewhere in Minnesota and the United States. Stearns County accounted for only 14 percent of the entrants from that period. Part of this decrease is attributable to a relative population decline in the county, but regardless of the reason, the Stearns County character of the community had weakened.

The period after the conclusion of Vatican Council II in 1965 was a turbulent time at Saint John's and elsewhere in the Church. In view of all the variables, generalization about any single aspect is risky. Nonetheless, the 1989 list of the Saint John's monks shows just five entrants from Stearns County in the preceding twenty-four years, representing only 7 percent of all Americans coming into the community. The latter group, now numbering sixty-eight and accounting for an average profession rate of slightly under three per year, had also greatly declined in that period.

By the '60s the composition of the student body at Saint John's University was also beginning to change. Enrollment from Minnesota outside Stearns County and from other states was increasing spectacularly. The 1970 graduating class, numbering 318 students, showed forty residents of Stearns County, more than half of whom were from Saint Cloud. This represented an increase of more than 40 percent over the average rate in the '50s, but now this number comprised only 12.5 percent of the entire class.

The class of 1980 still had forty-two seniors from Stearns County, about 13 percent of the entire senior class. However, growth had peaked. The two latest graduating classes of 1988 and 1989 showed an average of just thirty-two residents of Stearns County, half from Saint Cloud, which amounted to only 8 percent of the whole. While students from the county were declining in numbers, those from other areas of Minnesota or from other states and countries were increasing by 18 and 46 percent respectively.

Factors for such a change include escalating cost and the immense widening of the college pool. The metropolitan areas of Minnesota and more far-flung regions now bear the brunt of recruiting efforts. In addition, the legitimate desire of many students to go further away for college impedes successful recruiting in the local area. In any case, a Stearns county "base" seems to have eroded.

There are currently an abundance of non-curricular activities at Saint John's. Some of them draw well from the area. One activity of recent origin, the Saint John's Boys' Choir, exercises an impact locally. The growing reputation of this group reflects favorably on Saint John's and Stearns County, from where most of the participants come. Since this organization is associated most directly with Saint John's Abbey and not specifically with one of its schools, the positive interrelationship between abbey and local community is exemplified.

Saint John's Abbey and its satellite operations have a powerful presence in Stearns County. Still the identification of Saint John's with the local area seems to have been modified. There is a diminished recognition that the immediate area and the abbey are engaged in a common purpose. Saint John's is, I think, more detached from its local roots at the present time.

A variety of circumstances have contributed to this result. The very size of the house is daunting for Stearns County circumstances. When the effective elimination of a Stearns County base in the membership of the community is added, an occasion for alienation is presented. Equally significant in this connection is the extent of the property which Saint John's holds. It is by far the largest estate in the county, and its tax-exempt status could be considered a drain on the resources of the county.

A monastery, by a stated desire to withdraw from the world to go about its professed business of religion, is separate from the larger society. A paradoxical tension in a Benedictine monastic institution sets it apart from its surroundings at the same time that it seeks to sink roots. A necessary distance characterizes a monastery, but this is often counteracted by an evident involvement in local affairs through pastoral concerns and other activities that have meaning for the local community. When, however, this detachment is combined with size, a noticeably cosmopolitan membership, perceived wealth, tax-exempt status, and a focus of activity that is not in the first instance directed to the local community, the opportunity for seeming to be alienated arises. Being an outsider in a rural community is a heavy burden to carry.

Obviously, there are reasons of social utility which justify tax-exempt status for various religious and secular enterprises. Furthermore, in seeking to become self-sufficient in certain areas of fire protection, utilities, maintenance, and security, Saint John's has been endeavoring to make its own contribution to the area, helping thereby to share the burden. Nonetheless, it should be a concern of us monks, rooted in this place, sharing our resources with our neighbors, to ask the questions seriously regarding ourselves and our activities: How does our being here enhance opportunities for those who share our sense of place? How sensitively do we exercise our influence? What meaning does this have for our employees, most of whom, as residents of Stearns County, are also our neighbors?

Neighborliness does exist at Saint John's. We are attempting a positive outreach. We have concerns for local charities. There is a willingness to cooperate on an equal basis with the town board on matters of mutual concern. One example would be our proposal to present payment in lieu of taxes for the recent paving of a township road abutting our property.

Our land-management policy of recent years reflects a keen sense of stewardship and a concern for the preservation of resources that can rightly be considered a local patrimony. It represents the preservation of place, not only for Saint John's but for the locality as well. Policy regarding access to the trails, use of the lakes, forest management, and development of the wetlands all are based in some measure on the utilization of such resources by area residents. We are trying to be a good neighbor. Perhaps we can do more.

Any institution may encounter some difficulty relating to its own neighborhood, especially a rural or small-town one. But since we are a group which professes community and stability, our relation with the surrounding area must be strongly positive. There should be an awareness that a potential for alienation exists. As a result, we need to be consciously committed to enhance Saint John's place in the local community. A strong sense of place which includes the local area provides the context and the inspiration to make progress.

EMERIC A. LAWRENCE

Y EARLIEST MEMORIES OF SAINT JOHN'S
go back to the academic year 1922-23, the year that John V.
McNally won four varsity letters: in football, basketball, track, and
baseball. I can still see him pitching on the old baseball field, now
occupied by the church banner and science center. That was John's
last year at Saint John's until he returned—after an interval of
twenty-five years of great success as a professional football player
and coach—to finish his degree and graduate in 1949. We young
Johnnies continued to hear about him and were aware that we were
in on the beginnings of the Johnny Blood legend.

Benet Hall had just been built, and the south end of the old gym
was partitioned off as an area where we members of the Junior
Hall could play our league basketball games. Sabina Diederichs,
R.N., reigned in the infirmary, now Greg Hall, where she took
care of our physical ills. By the end of my first year at Saint John's,
I felt I had found my future home.

In those days all the profs were monks except for Ed Flynn, athletic director and chief of mandatory physical education periods
(we called them "physical torture") several times a week. A house
had been built for him and his family across the Watab, and when
other houses were added for the workers and their families, it all
became "Flynntown."

Most of the profs, notably Frs. Placidus, Isidore, James, Hilary
("Toby"), and Polycarp were, of course, "characters." Father

Placidus still wore the long white beard that was customary in the abbey's early days, and I can't remember if he ever answered our question, "Is it under or over the blanket when you go to sleep?" He regularly heard confessions every evening after supper, and the questions he used to ask occasioned lots of enjoyment: "Did you mean it?" "How many times?" "Vat is dis necking bizness?"

Father Placid taught Latin and Greek, and it was not his fault that, much to my regret in later years, I never learned to read Greek. I still remember how, when the tower bell rang at 11:00, he would bow his head for a moment of quiet. When we asked why he did that, he said, "I pray the *Ultima.*" "Teach it to us," we asked, and he did. After that, every day when the clock struck 11:00, we all prayed together:

Ultima in mortis hora,	At death's last hour,
Filium pro nobis ora,	to your Son pray for us,
Bonam mortem impetra,	a good death ask for us,
Virgo Mater Domina.	You who are Virgin, Mother, and our Lady.

For many years now the entire community sings the *Ultima* as our *Au revoir* to a departed confrere as he is lowered into his grave. And I suspect that it is the favorite night prayer of some of the monks.

There were ten of us in our 1928–1929 novitiate, and we were fortunate in having the holy, wonderfully kind, and wise old monk Fr. Athanasius Meyer as our novice master. He taught us the *Rule,* Benedictine history, and the psalms. Several of us were cigarette smokers, and it wasn't easy to quit "cold turkey." The cheap, dry cigars that the Father Master gave us on Sundays were probably meant to encourage us to give up smoking entirely.

"I hear you liked to dance," the master remarked to me one day in a private conference. I reluctantly admitted that I did, but wasn't very good at it (the Charleston was the rage in those days). "Well, that's something I never learned to do," he said.

We used to begin morning choir at 4:30, with Prime, Terce, Sext, and None, with the conventual Mass and the entire monastic community present. After that the priests would descend to the basement chapels in the old church for their private Masses, while the abbot celebrated the clerics' Mass upstairs at the main altar for those clerics who did not have to serve downstairs.

The ungodly hour of 4:30 was not conducive to attentive praying of the psalms. At the *Gloria* after every psalm, we rose and bowed low; more than once Fr. Martin Schirber went to sleep at the bottom of his bow, and I would have to lift him up. If one came late to choir or if he missed a preceding hour, he had to "kneel out" in the middle of the choir for a short period.

First profession in 1929 introduced us to the clericate, now known as the juniorate, with its variety of seasonal activities. We lived in the Junior Hall over the kitchen, the hall where I had spent my first two years of prep school. In addition to the Saint John's clerics, there were others from Conception Abbey, Saint Bede's Abbey, and colorful Fr. Canisius Blummel, a German-born cleric from Saint Joseph's Abbey in Louisiana. I remember his telling me in the early '30s about his fears for the future of Germany under the leadership of Hitler, who was just coming into power. But the story about Canisius I best remember was his indignant remark to a Saint Bede's cleric who slept next to him in the dorm. After seeing the cleric strip down completely before putting on his pajamas, Canisius broke into the night silence with the remark: "I did not join ze monasteerie to zee ze bare arse of my confrerrre."

To preside over such a mixture of young monks from so many different monasteries, Abbot Alcuin appointed a patient and much respected English professor and World War I military chaplain, Fr. Sylvester Harter. After a couple of years, he was succeeded by Fr. Christopher Bayer, also librarian and guestmaster, whose weekly *Culpa* talks consisted mainly of the single theme: "You got to obey the rules and regulations." Then came Fr. Godfrey Diekmann, fresh from his studies in Rome, and, as I remember, we all thought he was a bit too young. But his *Culpa* conferences had more substance than we were accustomed to.

Our philosophy and theology courses left a lot to be desired. Our class did not have Fr. Virgil Michel in philosophy, but we heard from the class ahead of us that we didn't miss much. I wondered, because the philosophy professor we had (a monk from another abbey) had studied at Sant' Anselmo in Rome under Fr. Joseph Gredt, O.S.B. If philosophy ever did have any fascination for our young minds, our professor had no idea how to uncover it. We did have a good Introduction to Scripture course from Fr. Basil

Stegmann, and that was the last worthwhile formal Scripture course I remember having had.

In dogmatic theology Fr. Alexius Hoffmann tried to make Tanquerey's Latin textbook interesting, but after beginning class with a few minutes of introduction in Latin, he gave up and launched out into stories and meditative reflections in English, which was all right with us. In fact, it was a kind of a liberal education, for Father Alexius was one of the best-read Christian humanists I ever knew. Besides, Fr. Ulric Beste had convinced the clerics and seminarians that his class in moral theology was the only essential course we would need "in order to solve cases in the confessional." So we spent almost all our time studying for "Doc" Ulric's tests. A year ago I discovered my old Sabetti-Barrett textbook in a storage box and did a little paging through it. When I saw the margins filled with hand-written notes, Doc Ulric's voice came back to me from the distant past: *Habemus notam hac de re.*

Summers were special. We fulfilled the *labora* part of the Benedictine motto by building stone walls that are still standing in their solid beauty after nearly sixty years. Abbot Alcuin had an obsession with stone walls, and before long we nicknamed him "Stonewall Alky." The cleric workboss didn't trust me to lay the stones, so I teamed up with old Max Schmoeller and mixed the cement or the "mud" as we called it. I shall always cherish the compliment Max gave me after one sweaty session: "Dat Emeric is a gut man." After all these years that continues to warm my heart every time I look at the wall enclosing the monastery garden.

Summer was also a favorite time for reading—both light and serious. Most of the light pleasure was provided by P. G. Wodehouse's stories about history's most competent butler Jeeves and his light-headed employer Bertie Wooster. Wodehouse was so popular in our group that he influenced the writing style of some of us, notably Father Martin.

On the serious side we had Sigrid Undset whose stories of medieval Christianity in Norway were not only fascinating in style and content but contributed a lot to our pre-ecumenical mindset. Undset was a convert to Catholicism, and both her subject matter and her reputation as a serious writer bolstered our feeling of the superiority of Roman Catholicism over any Protestant denomination. In my last move back to the abbey in 1988, I discovered a typed article by Undset entitled "Why I became a Catholic." My name is written at the top in the handwriting of Dr. Harris Kaasa of Luther College, one of the dearest friends I ever had.

There were other authors who contributed to our Catholic superiority complex, notably the English converts G. K. Chesterton, Hilaire Belloc, and Christopher Hollis. I can't remember which of them was responsible for the story that so delighted us about the English Catholic who had lost his faith. When asked if he was going to join one of the Protestant denominations, he replied: "I told you I lost my faith, not my mind!" It was a story that helped shape the sneaking feeling some of us had that a Protestant was insincere and dishonest or he wasn't quite "all there." It was a feeling that quickly vanished from my mind when I joined the faculty of Luther College in the fall of 1967. But I'm getting ahead of myself.

The early '30s also witnessed the blooming of Fulton J. Sheen, not so much then as a radio or television speaker as an author of popular theology books. His *The Divine Romance, The Eternal Galilean,* and others with their poetic insights gave me a taste for the richness of theology that Tanquerey's scholastic theses never knew. But Sheen ran into trouble when he wrote *The Mystical Body of Christ.* Maybe there was too much poetry in it and not enough solid theology. In any case Fr. Virgil Michel ripped it to shreds in a two-page review in *Orate Fratres.*

During those years both the abbey and the school benefited from visits of Maisie Ward and Frank Sheed. The latter intrigued us with vivid accounts of his street preaching in London's Hyde Park; also we learned from Dorothy Day and Peter Maurin, founders of the Catholic Worker movement, who were undoubtedly attracted by Virgil Michel's Social Institute weekends. I can still remember how beautiful Dorothy Day looked in her black and red checkered dress. On the other hand, there was the Baroness Catherine de Hueck of Friendship House in Harlem in whom dynamism and enthusiasm made up for her lack of physical beauty.

Before leaving this period I must not forget the importance for a rounded education that we acquired from the daily table reading at both dinner and supper in the monastery refectory. It featured a variety of books, both "lite" and "medium lite." But the *pièce de résistance* for years was *The History of the Popes* by Ludwig

Pastor. Every pope—or anti-pope—through the centuries was covered, or uncovered, in great detail, and many of the lives were shocking, to put it mildly. I still wonder how good Catholics must have felt, living under such awful leadership. Only in later years did the values of such reading dawn on me, the greatest one being that the Church had to be of divine origin in order to survive its all-too-human top leadership. Another related value: if one doesn't like a present pope, be patient: none of them lasts forever.

Another memory of early years at Collegeville was the popularity of handball among the monks. When I came here there were brick handball courts, later replaced by tennis courts, on the site of the present Alcuin Library. Mary Hall now rises up over an area once occupied by half a dozen cement courts. It seemed to us young students that playing handball was an essential part of life at Saint John's, so naturally we played too. The monks, obedient to the will of Abbot Alcuin, always played in their habits. Whenever Fr. Polycarp Hansen played, he attracted a crowd of spectators. I don't know if his being a mathematician had anything to do with it, but he always made more "killers" than anyone else (when the ball hit the wall just above the floor, it was a "killer").

Yes, the monks played in old cassocks or religious habits—handball, softball, tennis, touchball. The abbot had a thing about the religious habit. For him it identified the monk; it reminded him that he was a monk always and everywhere. It seems that the abbot was convinced that a monastery was on its way to decline and eventual disintegration when monks gave up wearing the habit.

My story would be incomplete without mention of Fr. Clarus Graves, who was responsible for my first academic career as a French professor. He had studied French and Spanish at Columbia University in New York and at the Sorbonne in Paris. He returned with an M.A. in 1925, brimming with fresh ideas about teaching languages. It didn't take long for his reputation as a dynamic teacher and a generous marker to spread, a prof made to order for a not too industrious student like Tony Lawrence. I began my French studies with him in 1926. Father Clarus used what came to be known as the "direct method," which involved a lot of repetition and personal involvement on the part of the students. No textbook satisfied him, so he wrote his own—not only in French, but also in Spanish, German, and Latin. The first words one saw on opening a Clarus Graves' language book was *Repetitio est mater studiorum*.

Teaching languages could not exhaust Father Clarus' energy, so in the evenings he directed dramatic productions. His Lenten plays *Everyman* and *The Great Theatre of the World* attracted large crowds. One spectator was so touched after seeing one of the plays that he rushed out to find a priest to hear his confession.

Father Clarus went to Mexico twice, first in 1944 to help the monks of Saint Benedict's Abbey, Atchison, to teach in their Tepeyac school; he went back again in 1946 for three years as prior of Saint John's own foundation. He returned to Saint John's and was named prior in 1951, and he also returned to his first love of teaching French in the college. He died in his sleep in 1964, and I can still see the consternation in his students' faces when I took over his class and told them that Father Clarus had died. Clarus was one of the most talented and selfless monks I have ever known.

I took three years of French from Father Clarus, and when it became apparent that he would need another teacher to help him Fr. Walter Reger arranged to have me study at Laval University in Quebec during the 1936–37 school year. The following summer Father Martin was to attend Harvard, and he urged me to join him there, which I did. I liked it so much that I asked Abbot Alcuin to allow me to stay on for my M.A. degree. He granted my request, and I continued at Harvard for the 1937–38 school year. I think my informing him that three of my professors were Catholic, including the well-known Louis J. A. Mercier, helped along a favorable decision. It was the vast amount of reading in both literature and history that Mercier required, along with that country's power to turn out numbers of great saints, that turned me into an unashamed Francophile.

Armed with the M. A. degree, I returned to Saint John's in August 1938. Life here in the last years of the '30s was conditioned greatly by the growing disarray in Europe caused by Hitler's increasing belligerency, culminating in his invasion of Poland and the outbreak of war in 1939. Soon American troops began mobilizing and chaplains were enlisting.

At that time the idea came to me of writing "meditations" on the Sunday liturgies for our students, and before long we started sending the mimeographed bulletins called "The Week with

Christ'' (the name chosen for the meditations) to hundreds of chaplains around the world. The ''we'' who did the mailing included Jim Barry (now Father Colman) and Tom O'Neill (now Father Virgil).

Soon monks started volunteering, and by the end of the first semester of 1942, I handed over ''The Week with Christ'' to Fr. Baldwin Dworschak and went off to chaplain school at Harvard. I used to say that I became a chaplain in order to get to France, but after sixteen months at Big Spring, Texas, I spent the rest of the war on the islands of Attu and Shemya at the end of the Aleutian chain.

I returned to Collegeville in June 1946 to the turmoil of a college bulging with returning GIs and incredibly inadequate housing conditions. Abbot Alcuin never did want a big college, and the GI ''invasion'' surely made him unhappy. But at the very last moment, under great pressure from Dean Martin Schirber and Registrar Arno Gustin, he reluctantly signed the paper which permitted the building of five barracks on what is now the Mary Hall parking lot, along with a ''snack-shack'' in front of the old science hall and a special hall next to it for ''dayhops.'' These buildings were all free gifts from the government. From then on for the next fourteen years, fate and Father Martin decreed that dayhops were to be my special and happy preoccupation. Many of them, after all these years, remain very special friends.

The basement of Saint Mary's Hall, completed in 1951, became the new dayhop study hall, and my office was located between the study hall and the cafeteria. I don't know how it started, but that office soon became a gathering place for confreres such as Father Martin, Godfrey, Eleutherius, Arno, any guests that Father Martin wanted to get rid of, also and especially lay profs Steve Humphrey, Emerson Hynes, Frank Schoffman, and assorted others who enjoyed a cup of instant coffee and interesting conversation, which didn't have to be planned. It was invariably or alternately witty, serious, and often political. Guests included Senator Hubert Humphrey and Governor Orville Freeman, the former Communist Grace Carlson, who had returned to the Church and who has become a Benedictine Oblate of Saint John's and my life-long friend.

Fr. James Minette, an alumnus and parish priest in Saint Cloud, was a regular weekly participant in our discussions. When he returned in February 1990 for a visit after twenty-five years of missionary work in Venezuela, he told me that those gatherings were like a liberal education for him.

Our own Gene McCarthy was a frequent visitor. I recall that we all thought it was unwise for Gene to run for the senate after several terms in the house, but he ran and won and then came to Saint John's to convince Emerson Hynes to move to Washington to work in his office. We were all saddened when Emerson accepted the offer. Our coffee hour was never quite the same without him.

I can't remember how or when I became interested in "Specialized Catholic Action." In the late '40s I had read about Canon (later Cardinal) Joseph Cardijn of Belgium and his having founded a specialized Catholic Action movement for young workers called *Jeunesse Chrétienne Ouvrière,* shortened to *Jocist,* with the purpose of inspiring young workers to improve working conditions in factories. The movement quickly spread to France and its technique, "Observe, Judge, Act" was applied to the student milieu, where it was known as the *Jécists (Jeunesse Etudiante Chrétienne).* I visited their national offices in 1950 when I used my GI bill of rights funds to attend summer school at the Sorbonne.

That visit increased my enthusiasm for YCS (Young Christian Students), which we had already started at Saint John's as early as 1947. Meetings consisted of a discussion of a gospel selection, followed by further discussion in the course of which we observed a situation or attitude among students, made a judgment on it, and then decided on a course of action. Observe, Judge, Act. An overall goal of YCS was to try to convince students that a genuine Catholic education consisted not only in preparing for a future profession but in becoming a well-rounded, fully educated and cultured person. I think, I hope, that Saint John's has become a better college as a result of a decade of student Catholic Action. I know that it enriched the lives of hundreds of its members and my own, too.

A special personal benefit for me was that YCS brought the friendship of one of the finest, most innovative priests I have ever known, Fr. Louis Putz, C.S.C., of Notre Dame. I also became a friend of that special group of Chicago priests whose liturgical, social, and spiritual ideals had been shaped by their seminary rector, the legendary Msgr. Reynold Hillenbrand, who in turn had been greatly influenced by Virgil Michel.

YCS sort of faded away by the end of the '50s and was no longer in existence when I returned from a year at the Lumen Vitae Catechetical Institute in Brussels and a glorious year of translating in Paris (1960–62). I don't know if YCS is still operating, but I believe that the Christian Family Movement (CFM), specialized Catholic Action for married couples, is still in existence.

The '60s was not a particularly happy decade for me after my return from Europe, mainly because I wasn't much of a success as the student chaplain that our new president, Fr. Colman Barry, asked me to become (1963–67). Then came President E. W. Farwell's visit to Saint John's in the spring of 1967 and the agreement between him and Father Colman for an exchange of professors between Luther College and Saint John's. I was very uneasy when Colman asked me to become the first Benedictine at that Lutheran college, and I remember spending the whole summer studying Lutheran theology. We used to say that Colman had so many ideas that some of them were bound to turn out well. For me the exchange was one of the best of them all.

A new era in my life opened that fall. It covered eight years in two Lutheran colleges; Luther in Decorah, Iowa, and Concordia in Moorhead, Minnesota. I can't begin to describe what the experience meant to me. From my first day at a Luther faculty meeting, I was made to feel at home. Nor did it take long for that old joke ("I told you I lost my faith, not my mind") to lose its humor for me. I came to know my colleagues in the religion department as rigorously honest, sincere, and well-trained theologians (all with doctorates in theology or Scripture from American and European universities) who were convinced Lutherans who indeed had not "lost their minds."

I was deeply impressed by the conviction, shared by all the faculty, that they were teaching at "a Church college," a conviction that set them apart from state colleges and from non-denominational private colleges. The tradition of breaking into the class schedule for forty minutes each morning for "chapel" also impressed me. The service consisted of a hymn, a Scripture reading, a short "chapel talk" by a faculty member, not necessarily the chaplain or a member of the religion department, and a final hymn. I have a large file of chapel talks that I gave both at Luther and at Concordia. I recall gently scolding President Joseph Knutson at my first talk at Concordia for not having a statue of Martin Luther on campus, as was the case at Luther. Concordia now has one, but I'm not sure I'm responsible for it.

Neither I nor my students were happy about my first religion courses at Luther. They wanted answers to questions like the veneration of saints, especially the Virgin Mary, celibacy, indulgences, etc., whereas I felt they needed a well-rounded course in Catholic theology. It wasn't until we began using *A New Catechism,* popularly known as "The Dutch Catechism," that both they and I were satisfied. For me it is still the best, most thorough and spiritual theology book I have ever studied.

I also presided over discussion sections in the "Core Program" that gave freshmen an excellent foundation for a complete liberal arts education, and I never studied so hard in my life.

Carved on the cornerstone of most of the buildings on each campus are the words of Martin Luther's motto *Soli Deo Gloria*—"To God alone belongs the Glory." It was a motto that for me wasn't terribly different from our own Benedictine *Ut in Omnibus Glorificetur Deus*—"That God may be glorified in all things."

"Now They Take Me For Granted" was the title of an article I wrote towards the end of my experience of teaching at these Lutheran colleges, but, and this needs to be emphasized, not at the expense of a loss of loyalty to my true home and first love, Saint John's. It's funny about the human heart, how it can expand to enclose many fidelities without the loss of the essential first love. It never took me long, on my return for vacations, to fall back into the familiar monastic routine. But it is always a pleasure to return to the Luther campus for a visit. In May 1989 I was there briefly and received a lot of good Lutheran hugs.

If I have written more warmly about Luther College than about Concordia, it is probably because I spent six years at Luther and only two at Concordia. I liked Concordia, despite the fact that it was an old Minnesota Intercollegiate Athletic Conference rival, and I had many good friends there. Besides, Moorhead was just across the Red River from family in Fargo, and I was also able to live with confreres at Saint Joseph's parish in Moorhead.

What impressed me deeply about both colleges (and perhaps made me a little envious) was the musical tradition (inherited from Martin Luther?) both colleges enjoyed. Concordia attracts thousands to its yearly Advent-Christmas concerts, and the chief Advent event at Luther is the production of Handel's *Messiah,* sung by about two thousand students, alumni, and townspeople. This tradition is almost a century old. Both colleges have half a dozen or more choirs, orchestras, and bands.

I believe that the Luther College professors who came here to teach also have fond feelings about Saint John's, and I suspect that Abbot Jerome (when he was plain Fr. Jerry Theisen) and Frs. Daniel Durken and Zachary Williams shared at least some of my enthusiasm for the experience, even though each was there only one year. Living close to and celebrating Mass at Saint Benedict's Church in Decorah and having our meals with the good pastors, Frs. Al White and Ed Lechtenberg, did a lot to make us feel at home. And I have been told that our Benedictine presence did much to remove ancient antagonisms between Lutherans and Catholics.

Finally, my "life with the Lutherans" provided me with an obsession for ecumenism, for unity among Christians, along with an abhorrence of any kind of destructive divisiveness. Christ's prayer "That all may be one . . . ." means everything to me; and that's a grace that, next to God, I owe to Buck Farwell and Colman Barry. I have no optimistic illusions that unity among Christians will come soon. But this unity has to have priority in the prayers of all Christian Churches. In *Understanding Our Neighbor's Faith* (1974) I wrote that we must pray that

> all Christian hearts be changed and made ready for what God desires. . . . If Jesus desired unity, if he prayed for unity, so must the Christian. But unity will not come unless we do more than talk about it; we must work for it, remove the obstacles within ourselves, pray, suffer, be willing to die for it. The great French theologian and ecumenist Yves Congar, O.P., once said: "We must pass through the doors of ecumenism on our knees."

After the 1975 school year at Luther College, Abbot John Eidenschink asked me to return to Minnesota. My first assignment was a short three months as chaplain at Saint Mary's Hospital, Detroit Lakes. Then I began twelve and a half happy years as chaplain at Saint Scholastica's Priory in Duluth. I loved being there, but again, I knew where my true home was. Abbot Jerome called me back to the monastery in 1988, and now I feel so much a part of the place that I hate to leave. The Duluth sisters know how I feel about them, so I'm not going to write anything here. Besides, the editor wants me to say something about my books.

I have already mentioned *The Week With Christ.* It became a book and was first published by Fides in 1950. They chose not to print a second edition and relinquished publishing rights to The Liturgical Press, which published it in 1955 and 34,000 copies were sold. This was followed by *Meditating the Gospels* in 1957 and *Homilies for the Year* in 1965. Others followed, all published by The Liturgical Press, except *Each Month With Christ* (Helicon, 1961) and *Make Us Grow In Love,* which will be published in 1990 by Our Sunday Visitor.

With the exception of *A New Meditating the Gospels* (1977) and *Becoming A Mature Christian* (1979), the books were all on the Sunday and daily Masses of the seasons of the liturgical year. The three on Advent, Lent, and the Easter season have already been published, and the book on Ordinary Time, *The Holy Way,* will be published by The Liturgical Press in 1990.

Going back to my first efforts with *The Week With Christ,* I have always believed that the readings and psalms of every Mass, especially the seasonal ones, abound with spiritual riches, but they need to be discovered and meditated on. This is what I have tried to do.

I owe the original idea for *Meditating the Gospels* and *A New Meditating the Gospels* to the French theologian Fr. Louis Bouyer who once wrote:

> If it is truly God whom we seek, we have to seek him as a person. Martin Buber . . . has expressed this very adequately: ''A person is only sought as a person in dialogue. It is only in the 'I to Thou' relationship that the person remains personal for us. Someone of whom we get into the habit of speaking as 'he' is no longer a person for us.''

I also translated Fr. Eleutherius Winance's *The Communist Persuasion,* published by P.J. Kenedy & Sons in 1959. Monks from Saint-André Abbey in Belgium had made a foundation in Szechwan province in China in 1927, and in 1942 they moved to Chengtu. The Communists arrived in 1949, and monastic life and teaching became impossible. Some monks were imprisoned and others, among them Father Eleutherius, had to submit to a long program of brainwashing before being deported. In his book Father Eleutherius describes, analyzes, and interprets the brainwashing he had to endure and the suffering of the long journey to expulsion from the land these monks had learned to love.

The Communist Persuasion would be a fascinating book to read now in the aftermath of the uprising in Tiananmen Square and the bloody suppression of the students. Unfortunately the book is out of print. I often thought of Father Eleutherius during the uprising. He and his fellow monks now have a foundation at Valyermo, California, and they never lost hope of someday returning to China.

In my last letter to the sisters of Saint Scholastica's Priory after the celebration of the sixtieth anniversary of vows of our class on July 11, 1989, I wrote:

> It is people who have made and continue to make Saint John's a very special place, but the place itself is very important—the lake, cemetery, church, the old quad, and I must not forget Chapel Island. A few days after the July 11 celebration, I climbed up cemetery hill to visit old friends, including four classmates, and many former monks who contributed so much to my formation. Then the thought came to me that there are two poles on which our Benedictine community is built: the present community in continuity with the one up there on the hill whose members built what we now have and on whose shoulders and vision we now stand, carrying on what they so valiantly began. There is no separation between us: we are still one community.

If we haven't been sufficiently aware of that fact in the past and sufficiently grateful to our monastic forefathers, it is not too late to begin now to thank them—saints, sinners, and just ordinary monks, but God-seekers all, and now at last God-finders. Without their efforts and sacrifices, we would not be where we are today.

Maybe it would add to their Christian and liberal education and make them more aware of Benedictine values if we tried to make our students more conscious of the "treasure" that is buried under so many of those granite tombstones up there on the hill overlooking Lake Sagatagan.

NEAL HENRY LAWRENCE

From within the dark church
I could see the bright sunlight
and beckoning trees,
Yet I was still held in prayer,
Caught up in God's sweet presence. [1]

THE PEACE OF SAINT JOHN'S ABBEY IS PERMA-
nently impressed upon my soul, mind, and heart from my first
visit. Every time I return I recall that new world of a monastery
I first experienced. Even now when I come back to Saint Anselm's
Priory, I have a similar moment of peace, distinct from the teem-
ing city of Tokyo. The reason is in part due to the surroundings
of the two monasteries.

My first visit to Saint John's was in 1951 as a diplomat returning to Washington, D.C., for consultations at the Department of
State. At that time I was director of the U.S. Information Services
in our embassy in Taipei.

Flying to Minneapolis and taking the bus to Collegeville, I felt
transported back hundreds of years. Virgin forest engulfed the road,
a deer dashed from a thicket, and sunset could be seen through
the trees. The bus stopped in front of the old abbey church. Soon
I was welcomed in warm Benedictine fashion and began an unforgettable visit which ended years later in becoming a member of
the community and being sent to Saint Anselm's Priory in Tokyo,
a mission of the abbey.

The surroundings of the abbey and the priory resemble one another only in having churches of outstanding architectural beauty

1. Neal Henry Lawrence, *Rushing Amid Tears—Tanka Poems In English* (Tokyo:
Eichosha Shinsha Co., Ltd., 1983).

and in having gardens. Saint John's has woods where Indians used to live, fish, and hunt. In July the lawns are dew-sprinkled at dawn and swirls of pink clouds fill the sky at dusk. A rainbow of roses, petunias, bleeding hearts, and zinnias color the campus. Lake Sagatagan is a pearl of great price with its cool clear water and sunfish, walleyes, and bass. All changes with the seasons, brilliant colors in autumn, deep blankets of snow in winter with ice on the lake, and a great resurrection in the spring.

Saint Anselm's in contrast consists of a quadrangle formed by the church, Saint Theresa Chapel, the old wing of the monastery, and a new wing. The garden is a treasure, having been that of a banker before World War II with two ancient Japanese stone lanterns and huge rocks of unique shapes valued by the Japanese. It has trees, bushes, and flowers in all seasons: camellias in winter, wisteria and cherry blossoms in spring, gardenias in summer, and red maples in autumn. Snow comes but rarely and disappears quickly. On a clear day Mount Fuji can be seen.

Saint Anselm's is near Meguro Station on the Yamanote-Sen, a train which makes a circle in both directions around the city. Saint Anselm's is like an oasis and though the trains can be heard, the sound is soon unnoticed within the monastery. The surroundings of both Saint John's and Saint Anselm's give me the same feeling of peace.

I heard much of Saint John's and something of Saint Anselm's while I was serving abroad. Fr. Aldo Cadena, whom I met in Mexico in 1939, was studying at Saint John's for the priesthood. When he invited me to visit, my curiosity was considerable, being surprised to find him there and having no personal experience of a monastery. I thought monasteries were dark, gloomy, medieval places for retreat from the world. I was not a Catholic although I had long been attracted by the Church.

My vocation was a late one, as after graduation from Harvard College in 1929, I worked as an executive for the Lever Brothers Company until World War II when I volunteered for the navy. If it had not been for the war, I think that I would have continued there until retirement as I found that career challenging and rewarding. The war changed the course of my life as it did for millions. Neither Lever Brothers nor myself were the same. I was sent to the U.S. Naval Military Government School at Columbia University to study for the invasion of Formosa, China, Okinawa, or Japan. Military government was a natural for me as it represented the turn of the tide of battle.

Later in Okinawa, I made up my mind that I wanted to return to the Orient and that I wanted to do something to prevent the tragedy of war. Knowing that it would take time to find a proper niche, I went back to Columbia University and completed an M.A. in public law and government, largely in the field of international relations and law. Having applied for the foreign service in the U.S. Department of State, I received an appointment and was sent to Tokyo to be a member of the diplomatic section of General MacArthur's headquarters where I spent two years doing economic and political reporting.

Two diametrically opposed groups of people I had known in the Orient influenced me to become a priest, namely communists and missionaries. I experienced communism at close range in Japan and later in Malaysia. In the latter a hot war was going on, so I received first-hand knowledge of what the free world would face in this deadly enemy. It became evident to me that Christianity is our hope of preventing communists from attaining the world domination they desire. I felt I might play some role, though small, in stemming the onrush of communism. As for the missionaries, when young I regarded them as rather strange people. Some of them certainly are, but most are dedicated people, both Protestants and Catholics.

I shall never forget my first visit to Saint John's. I did not know of Saint Anselm's while in Tokyo since I was not a Catholic. I remember meeting Abbot Alcuin Deutsch, Frs. Paschal Botz, Fabian Wegleitner, and Ernest Kilzer, as well as some of the clerics and students. I was deeply moved by the kind welcome given me.

"The way to a man's heart is via his stomach," is an ancient axiom. Waiting for the bus to Minneapolis early one morning at the end of a visit, Abbot Alcuin came by, said "good morning," and talked about my visit. Then he asked me if I had breakfast to which I said no. Just at that moment Father Fabian came by and was told to take me to the refectory and see that I had a good breakfast. I did just that and keep the memory of it even until today. Whenever I visited Saint John's afterwards, someone always saw to it that food was available. The bread at Saint John's is one of the good memories of living there, even the commercial loaves which Fr. Walter Reger promoted to help the finances of the abbey. Father Walter was a consummate teacher and raconteur. He made Church history something alive and pertinent. Another spellbinder was Fr. Colman Barry, whose comments on historical events were often startling and always thought-provoking.

I returned four times before coming to prepare for the novitiate. On each occasion I found the same reception and each time peace and happiness among those seeking God unlike any I had known before. For me psychologically, I entered the Benedictines on February 15, 1953, when I became an oblate of Saint John's Abbey with permission of Abbot Baldwin Dworschak. Fr. Paul Marx, who was studying at The Catholic University of America, received my oblation at Saint Anselm's Priory in Washington. I chose Benedict as an additional name. The genesis of this ceremony traces back to July 1952 when I went to Saint John's to find out as much as I could about the Benedictine way of life and whether I could fit into it. I attended Office and Mass for nine days, meeting Abbot Baldwin for the first time. He deeply impressed upon me the basic importance of the Office recited in choir. This has always been recognized in Tokyo, but when it was attempted by Fr. Hildebrand Yaiser, the founder, it was in Latin. From 1978, under Prior Odo Haas, it has been a daily part of community activity in Japanese.

Abbot Baldwin also gave me my first clear idea of the worldwide nature of the Benedictines, highlighting those of Saint John's both in Minnesota and abroad. I learned of the missionary activities under Abbot Alcuin in Peking, Manila, the Bahamas, Puerto Rico, Mexico, Kentucky, and Japan. Saint Mark's in Kentucky was only about forty miles from where I was born, Clarksville, Tennessee. I did not feel ready to discuss the possibility of a vocation with him. I did however talk with Fathers Aldo and Paschal concerning my interest and received encouragement. Father Paschal later became one of my professors and has remained a friend and inspiration. Like my confreres, I have enjoyed eating the fish he caught, but never became enamored of that sport.

Before returning to Washington in 1952, I asked if there were anyone there from Saint John's and learned the name Fr. Paul Marx. I wanted to keep in touch with Saint John's and also wanted advice on becoming a Catholic. From that time on I went to daily Mass. At one of the first Masses I attended at Saint Matthew's Cathedral, a regular course of instruction was announced to be given by Fr. Ramon di Nardo. On matters which particularly bothered me, I got in touch with Father Paul.

In September 1952 I was conditionally baptized, which seemed unnecessary to me and still does, but Father di Nardo explained it as a requirement at the time. I felt I had already been baptized of my own conviction in the Methodist Church when I was fourteen years old. I recall Father di Nardo when discussing the time of baptism saying, "I really don't know how long you have been a Catholic." I myself have a feeling that I acted like a Catholic long before I formally became one.

Both Fathers di Nardo and Paul brought up the subject of the possibility of the religious life for me before I mentioned it, although I had the intention to discuss becoming a Benedictine with them as I had done previously at Saint John's. I had come to consider it a matter of timing. At Father Paul's suggestion I went to New York to see Abbot Baldwin who was there in November 1953 at Saint Anselm's Church in the Bronx, which was then staffed by Saint John's Benedictines.

Abbot Baldwin suggested that I come to Saint John's University for the second semester, saying I could brush up on my Latin and also let the community look at me at close quarters. I came as suggested and made application to the novitiate at the proper time. Until then I lived in Saint Joseph's Hall and experienced the long, cold, snowy Minnesota weather. I was grateful when I learned I was accepted for the novitiate in July 1954.

Other influences leading toward the religious life were the writings of Thomas Merton. Father Merton came to Saint John's for some of the Mental Health Institute sessions held in the summers. These sessions brought together leading psychiatrists and psychologists with Catholic priests, Protestant pastors, and Jewish rabbis for lectures and discussions about the mental problems facing modern society. Being assigned to administration, along with other confreres, we were hosts and involved in hospitality for the visitors. What I learned from listening to the lectures of experts was invaluable.

The Oblate and *Worship* made ideas clearer. I read much about the Masses and other phases of Catholicism. A publication called

Introibo, put together by seminarians at the Theological College of The Catholic University, led to a rather lively correspondence with one of the seminarians who extolled the life and work of diocesan priests. The publication was directed toward GIs who were trying to make up their minds what to do after getting out of the armed forces.

A number of others encouraged me during my visits to Saint John's, although some may not know it to this day. Father Fabian was one who always made me feel at home. I remember his greeting at the porter's office when I arrived in January for school after a bus ride through the icy countryside. His friendly "Welcome home!" and intercession with the German sisters for some of their delicious chili for dinner put him deep in my debt. Father Aldo was understanding of the problems of a late vocation, although mine was much later than his. Fr. Chrysostom Kim was a cordial member of the community and had a special interest in Japan, which he retains as the present pastor of Saint Anselm's.

The years of study passed quickly although not without pain. My first studies were Latin, psychology, and philosophy, the latter because studies at Harvard were considered lacking in Catholic scholars, such as Thomas Aquinas. The novitiate began with eighteen of us from a wide variety of backgrounds. It was a real retreat from the world. The only major news given us was the death of Stalin. A criticism of the novices was that we all thought we were Indian chiefs, meaning each had his own ways of doing things. By the end of the year, this tendency to independence was modified and we were a tribe of Indians who could better cooperate.

Before I entered the novitiate I knew a lawyer, the late Fr. Donald McGinnis, who had become a cleric, so I thought if he could do it, I could also. Bits of memories of the novitiate include popcorn and ice cream on Sundays and a bottle of Cold Spring beer on July 4. I also developed a dislike for string beans after having picked what must have been tons of them and for chicken after the yearly slaughter and cleaning.

Some pleasant memories are the daily walks in the forest and along the lake with the other novices in turn and later the clerics. I was rather surprised that as far as I know no one paid any attention to my mature age. Our senior novice, the late Fr. Otto Weber, a champion wrestler and all-round athlete, knocked the wind out of me playing touch football (what a touch). I did better at soccer, but Br. Diego Jiminez from Mexico ran circles around me. We also had a taste of other sports as swimming, volleyball, skiing and hockey.

When I was in college, it was rather fashionable to do physical labor. I worked during summers on the building of a dam for a hydroelectric project on the Ohio River at Louisville, Kentucky. At Saint John's I could use all the muscles I had acquired then in helping in some of the construction work on the new church. I am always glad to be able to say I helped build the church, including some work on the monumental stained glass window of Bruno Bak.

Gregorian chant attracted me from the beginning and is still one of the aspects of prayer which I try to promote. At the English Mass of Saint Anselm's international community, chant is sung on special feasts. During my study at Saint John's, which was before Vatican II and use of the vernacular, chant was emphasized.

While I was remembering novitiate times, a telephone call came from Saint Anselm's prior, Fr. Kieran Nolan, who was at Saint John's for meetings and home leave, saying that Fr. Conan Mawhorr, a member of my novitiate class, was seriously ill with cancer in Memphis, Tennessee.

With Father Conan I first met Fr. Hildebrand Yaiser, founder and prior of Saint Anselm's. He was at Saint John's seeking "men and money," which he needed to do all his life. Father Conan and I went to see him, indicating interest in missionary work in Japan. It was on this trip that Father Hildebrand made an appeal to the whole community of Saint John's which had the opposite effect from what he meant it to have. He said something like! "Saint John's should sacrifice and bleed for Saint Anselm's like a mother for her child." That did not go down well, yet Saint John's has made many sacrifices in order to help Saint Anselm's and its other missions. When I came to Tokyo, Father Hildebrand said he didn't remember meeting me. Further he told someone that he was disappointed that Abbot Baldwin sent him such an old person (I was fifty-two). He was not always the diplomat.

From the time I met Abbot Baldwin, I never hid the desire to be sent to Saint Anselm's. One of the main reasons for wishing to become a Benedictine at Saint John's was knowing of Saint Anselm's. However, Abbot Baldwin always told me the needs of the community came ahead of the wishes of an individual. I never ceased to hope, but did not know for certain until after ordination that he would send me. I had made solemn vows on July 11, 1958, and was sent to Tokyo on September 9, 1960, after a baptism of fire at Saint Mary's Hospital in Duluth, Minnesota, during the summer following ordination.

Besides seminary studies I was asked to teach in Saint John's University, not only because of my academic background but my experience in business and government. One of the characteristics of the Benedictines is to take advantage of talents the monks possess. I had never thought much about teaching, but despite my trepidation I had no objection, became enthusiastic and found it rewarding. I worked with Fr. Jeremy Murphy and Dr. Edward Henry in the political science department giving courses in international relations and American government.

I have done much teaching at universities from 1962–85 in Tokyo to help financially at Saint Anselm's, and it is a way of reaching Japanese young people. Foreigners are usually expected to teach their own language, but I also taught international politics, ethics, and Japanese poetry in translation. I used my own writings of tanka poems in English which I began writing in 1975. I still teach at Saint Anselm's Priory, including Bible classes, catechism, and lecture to groups of students from the English Speaking Societies of Tokyo University and the Tokyo University of Fisheries.

In 1984 Abbot Jerome Theisen gave Saint Anselm's community his vision of a Benedictine monastery in Japan, based on the *Rule*. We were already aware of the direction in which we should go, being guided by many conferences during his earlier visits to Japan. In 1983, on the tenth anniversary of STAIFA (Saint Anselm's International Friendship Association), he spoke of the international character of the Benedictines, saying both monks and nuns exist in most countries of the world. At the fifth anniversary in 1978, Abbot John Eidenschink had also encouraged STAIFA.

STAIFA is a special activity of the priory with which I have been involved since it grew out of a Bible class in 1973. During sixteen years the aims have included efforts toward world peace by promoting better understanding among all people regardless of race, color, religion, or sex.

Saint Anselm's Priory itself has an international character even though the numbers are small. For example, the four forefathers were of four nationalities: Fr. Hildebrand Yaiser, Swiss; Fr. Joseph Schmerbach, German; Fr. Aloysius Michels, American; and Fr. Emile Butrille, French, who was a member of Saint André in Belgium, began his Benedictine life at Solesmes Abbey in France and spent twenty-five years in Szechwan, China. Fathers Hildebrand and Joseph were members of Beuron Abbey in Germany. Father Emile came to Japan, where he always wanted to come, only after being driven out of China by the communists. Fr. Gabriel Furuta was born in the United States but raised in Japan and was the first priest to be ordained at Saint Anselm's. He later left the Benedictines and is now dean of general education at Kanda University of International Studies and a specialist in medieval theology. He has translated all the works of Saint Anselm into Japanese. Added to these cultural backgrounds were Fr. Bundo Soh, Korean, in 1984, and Otillien Abbot Odo Haas of Waegwan Benedictine Abbey in Korea, a monk of Muensterschwarzach in Germany. The latter became prior for five years at Saint Anselm's. Other priors have included Fr. Aloysius Michels, Br. James Zarr, a former Benedictine, and Fr. Patrick Okada, deceased, a Japanese-American who blended both cultures.

Abbot Jerome's vision was that each monastery accepts the basic features of the *Rule* but adapts and puts on native flesh. Saint Anselm's traditions are heterogeneous but are becoming homogeneous. I recall being asked a number of times by Father Hildebrand: "Is that the way they do it at Saint John's?" to which I said yes since I knew no other Benedictine way. The differences in traditions led to a richer monastic life, but they sometimes led to confusion and conflict. Now in 1989 with Japanese members, Fr. Peter Kawamura, subprior and assistant pastor, and Br. Marcellino Fusejima, seminarian, and present members more acquainted with Japanese custom and language, adaptation to the needs of the times and the demands of the culture and a sharing of traditions is improving. The influence of Saint John's has grown as all other monks are from Saint John's: Fr. Kieran Nolan, present prior; Br. Andrew Goltz, who has served as treasurer, nurse, cook and housekeeper; Br. Nicholas Thelen, plant manager; Fr. Finian McDonald (latest arrival), business manager and director of formation.

Saint Anselm's has had five priors since Father Hildebrand retired in 1975 and Archbishop Peter Seiichi Shirayanagi made him pastor emeritus. One might characterize Father Hildebrand as "the right prior and pastor for the times." I think he would have liked to have become the abbot of a large monastery somewhere outside Tokyo. He sought such a place and so did subsequent priors until Father Aloysius succeeded in obtaining Fujimi Benedictine Monastery, which had been a house of the Redemptorists. He is now the pastor of Fujimi Catholic Church of Saint Joseph, Naganoken. The monastery is being extensively used in summer and is being readied for use the year round.

Father Hildebrand obtained the support of Abbot Alcuin to establish the parish of Saint Anselm's in Tokyo and achieved this with remarkable success. Fortunately he wrote a diary and later wrote his memoirs. Written in German, the diary has been translated into Japanese by Akio Yanase, a parishioner, and published in Tokyo in 1989. Noteworthy excerpts have been translated into English in 1984 by Fr. Gall Fell of Saint John's under the title "The Long Yesterday—Fifty Years As a Benedictine Missionary in Japan."

The last line in Father Hildebrand's diary is: "Have I come to understand Japan? Maybe yes. Maybe no. But one thing is sure. I have come to love Japan." That love continued until his death in 1983. He was born in 1901 and came to Japan to establish a new Beuronese foundation in 1931, but World War II brought an end to that. He became an attaché at the Swiss Embassy to visit prisoner of war camps and detention centers for foreign missionaries and nuns. He succeeded in having many repatriated and their conditions improved. Before the war he taught at the seminary and became editor of *Phos Christi*, which promoted the liturgy, including the vernacular and the adaptation of Japanese customs.

Fr. Joseph Schmerbach was also a Beuronese monk who lived in Japan during World War II. He was head of the kindergarten at Saint Anselm's for twenty years and was decorated by the late Emperor Showa for his outstanding contribution to education. He was also noted for his work in preparing couples for marriage.

Although I did not arrive in Tokyo until 1960, I became involved with Saint Anselm's in 1958, handling the publication at Saint John's of a newsletter to English-speaking friends and benefactors.

This meant much correspondence with Father Hildebrand. The newsletters were mostly continuous until Christmas, 1982, and contained highlights of developments in Tokyo during that time. In 1983, the newsletter was merged with the Saint John's Abbey *Quarterly*. In writing for this, correspondence with Fr. Alfred Deutsch provided lively comment on events at the abbey as background. His editing kept us aware of the interest in Saint Anselm's.

As I write now in 1989, the comparison between 1958 and 1989 is dramatic. Father Hildebrand wrote in the newsletter of 1958 that under the kindly wing of Saint John's Abbey, Saint Anselm's Priory and Parish was started in an old factory building with nine faithful in 1947 and had grown to a parish of 1,350, including 200 foreigners. Since that time, two parishes have been carved out of Saint Anselm's: Our Lady of Edo (Himonya of the Salesians) and Our Lady of the Martyrs (Takanawa of the Scheut Mission Society). Saint Anselm's now has about 1,000 Japanese members and 200 foreigners.

Saint Anselm's Church, consecrated in 1956, the parish hall and kindergarten, and one wing of the monastery were designed by Antonin Raymond, an American architect who came to Japan with Frank Lloyd Wright to build the Imperial Hotel which withstood the Great Earthquake of 1923. The clashes between this architect and Father Hildebrand furnished table conversation over the years, some episodes repeated over and over, at times likely with embellishments.

Raymond in his autobiography wrote:

> Father Hildebrand was a truly superior spirit and intellect . . . but became extremely difficult to get along with in our efforts to complete the job and later, in 1964, to change the plan to conform with the new liturgy. Squares of black lines on the east wall behind the altar were superimposed by Father Hildebrand during one of my periodical absences abroad, over my original circles, which I had decided upon in the absence of a contemplated fresco. Squares make no sense and are disturbing.[2]

Because the circles were five, Saint Anselm's became known as the "Olympic Church" during the 1964 Olympics in Tokyo. When the church was renovated after the death of Father Hildebrand, the circles were restored.

2. Antonin Raymond, *An Autobiography* (Tokyo: Charles E. Tuttle, 1973).

Our first letter to benefactors and friends contains an appeal for the new rectory-priory with detailed costs of construction, including each monk's room $1,500 and furnishings $250. A gas stove was also listed because "as everybody else, priests and brothers must eat." News was also included of the summer festival reported by Mrs. Nobuko Utagawa, a member of the parish who is a Thai princess married to a Japanese businessman. She said it was "indescribably magnificent." These festivals not only brought the parish together, but neighboring religious priests, and friends. Much as we try to make our own way, and though our parishioners are doing more as the standard of living has risen in Japan, we still have to ask for help from Saint John's Abbey and friends in America and abroad.

One of the basic experiences of community I remember vividly is the selection of an abbot. Fortunately I was in America making mission appeals and could attend the last election in August 1979. The entire community met, frankly spoke their minds, and then elected Fr. Jerome Theisen as the eighth abbot. He has led Saint John's Abbey with its far-flung activities with patience and imagination.

Gregorian chant was one of the major attractions to Saint John's for me. Before I had a clear idea of wanting to be a monk, I would sit in the old church during prayers and be oblivious even to mosquitoes or mostly so. Frs. Dominic Keller and Gerard Farrell were hard taskmasters, but the results were worth the effort. My novitiate classmate Fr. Jerome Coller encouraged all of us to sing and was a good coach. In Tokyo, for the last two years at the English Mass which we have had since 1981, Gregorian chant is sung at Christmas, Easter, and other special occasions. It is sung so far in Latin, but we are urged to sing it in English by Sr. Cecile Gertken of Saint Benedict's Convent. The chant adds dignity and solemnity. Having been the music of the universal Church for centuries, it is fitting to preserve it.

The "great silence" of the monastery is one of the truly golden moments that monastic life has to offer. Every monastery is busy during the day, especially one like Saint Anselm's which has a parish church. Soon after the evening prayer of compline, it settles into quietness. Difficulties and problems with which one has struggled are suspended in time. Silence is not as absolute as I remember it at Saint John's, but one can find it by ignoring the rumble of trains or earthquakes, both of which are frequent in Tokyo. The night skies of Minnesota are more thrilling than Tokyo for they have stars which can be seen as well as spell-binding displays at times of the *aurora borealis*. The stars in Tokyo are usually few except on some clear night as at New Year's when all usual economic pursuits cease for three days. It was on such a night at Saint John's in the silence of the observatory that Fr. Melchior Freund showed me the constellation of Lyra. From that moment I had an insight into the vastness of the universe which God has created.

Peace shows itself in many places and ways at Saint John's Abbey. The cemetery is a place to work, meditate, and rest, especially the latter near sunset. Many of the monks I knew from the time spent at Saint John's are at peace there, and many I came to know only by name are there too. As novices and clerics, we cut the hedges and grass and came with the community to bury the dead. The long procession of monks and mourners, the inspiring and consoling music at the grave ending with *In paradisum deducant te Angeli . . . Requiescat in pace* remain to this day in my memory.

At Saint Anselm's Church the requiem Mass is heard, but the procession often goes to our Nokotsudo mortuary chapel where the ashes are kept. It is in the basement of the new wing which was designed by Koichi Nagashima who grew up in our parish and became a leading architect. It is quiet and easy of access for families to visit, most Catholic cemeteries being two hours from here. Two of Saint Anselm's founders, Fathers Hildebrand and Joseph, are there. Fr. Emile Butrille is buried in the Old Catholic Cemetery in Chofu.

Many other individuals have made indelible impressions on me, including Fr. Godfrey Diekmann with his emphasis on the Eucharist as a symbol of unity, Br. Kevin Duffy for his grit, Fr. Daniel Durken for his skill in publishing so that even in Japan at the English Mass we have *Celebrating the Eucharist* and a wealth of other material, and Fr. Timothy Kelly who was a confrere in the novitiate and even came to Japan to give us a retreat. After a tour of duty at Saint Anselm's, Br. Isaac Connolly has continued his services on returning home. Fr. Thomas Thole is our most frequent visitor from Saint John's as the enthusiastic advisor to Saint John's University foreign students.

Saint John's and Saint Anselm's have become part of my heart and mind. I cannot imagine being separate from them. They have formed the monks who live and work as Benedictines whether in America, the Bahamas, or Japan. The ease of going back and forth makes the fusion easier, though there are difficulties. All of us have learned to face many frontiers. I have sought to think like the Benedictines were doing when I joined them. At that time, with Marcel Breuer, they were trying to look forward one hundred years. *Ora et labora* has been their motto for over fifteen hundred years and will continue so. I want to be a part in that endeavor of seeking God.

Brs. Douglas Mullin and Charles Kirchner

IN 1937 SAINT JOHN'S ABBEY WAS ASKED BY THE bishop of Saint Cloud to supply a priest as chaplain at the State Reformatory for Men, now known as the Minnesota Correctional Facility—Saint Cloud. At this writing I have completed twenty years as a full-time chaplain. Prison work was something I really did not choose as a first in my vocation. It was more, as one correctional chaplain stated, "going as a reluctant new recruit."

Today we hear that life is a journey and that the places, circumstances, and people shape us for life's tasks. While in college at Saint John's, I participated in the Social Institutes founded and conducted by Fr. Virgil Michel. I had the fortunate experience to learn that liturgy and prayer must become connected with social action. Father Virgil's vivid concern moved me.

After seven years of pastoral work in Minneapolis, I was assigned to Saint Mary's Indian Mission, Redlake, Minnesota. Here as superintendent of the mission I had my first taste of living and dealing with Native Americans. Their culture and way of life was a unique encounter.

My next assignment was to assist in the business office of the abbey and university. There I became acquainted with the Mental Health Institutes, which Saint John's sponsored every summer at that time for priests and ministers. I had years of training in moral theology, canon law, and casuistry in the seminary but no knowledge of psychology and psychiatry. Attending these institutes, I heard from the nation's best such as Drs. Leo Bartemeier, Francis Braceland, Gregory Zilboorg, Paul Meehl, and Frs. James Gill and Noel Mailloux. Their lectures and the discussions opened avenues for more effective pastoral care and counseling. Not all crime was sin, and psychology did not explain away sin, but it helped produce "healthier sinners."

Saint Joseph's Home for Children in the archdiocese of Saint Paul-Minneapolis was my next place of work. The home had changed from a place for the homeless to a facility that cared for emotionally disturbed teenagers—here I was chaplain and served on the treatment team. At the same time I studied clinical pastoral training. With this chaplaincy the archdiocese assigned me to the chaplaincy of the Hennepin County Workhouse, the Women's Detention Center, the County Home School, and the Hennepin County Juvenile Center. At the workhouse I met Blacks and Chicanos as a first venture, as was my experience with disturbed and delinquent people. Ten years at the assignment seemed to have prepared me for a maximum security facility for felons.

During all the years I drove by that foreboding gray, huge granite wall of the Saint Cloud Reformatory—the largest one piece wall in the world outside the great wall of China—I wondered what's "going on behind it?" When I was assigned as chaplain there, I came with a vague awareness. How bad are these people locked up behind these walls? Prisons are artificial environments, but society doesn't make the residents incarcerated there different. Put a face on imprisoned persons, and they are seen as one of us. The degradation of life inside the walls can often add more self-disgust to those who have for the most part always seen themselves as losers. A prison chaplain has the task of helping these people who have known only coldness in life to discover a little of God's love for them. These prisoners are the chaplain's parishioners. It is a pastoral ministry. The difference is they are captive parishioners. In the past prisons were called penitentiaries, run akin somewhat to monasteries. Up to this day the inmate's cubicle or space is still called a "cell," while a monk's room in a monastery is no longer called by that term. One prison chaplain recently referred to a prison as "an imposed cloister" and called the residents "reluctant monks."

Today we are asked not to use the word "prison," but rather "correctional facility." The guards are "correctional counselors." The prisoners are "residents." But whatever we call the incarcerated, they are a mirror of the brokenness of our society, which sees imprisonment as an automatic response to wrongdoing.

Over three-fourths of the imprisoned are from broken homes. In this suffering they become school dropouts. Our present drug culture provides an artificial release from their unhappiness. Crimes are committed under the influence of drugs or to support this expensive habit.

It is easy to point a finger at the imprisoned as representative of criminal elements in our community. Yet on the outside there are people as guilty as those locked up. There are holy people in prison; there are some great sinners outside. From the Christian perspective crime and sin are often not the same. Some of the things that Jesus condemned most strongly don't figure in the calendar of crime. A person can cold-bloodedly break up a marriage by adultery, and he or she is innocent before the law. A person can be quite unjust to his employer, but by keeping within the law he or she is innocent as far as that is concerned. There is no guarantee of such innocence in the sight of God.

People often have a false idea regarding the conversion of felons. Conversion too often means that we look for ways of enabling a prisoner, often a hurt person, never having experienced real love or security and often saddled with anger, to change. To accept them where they are at is a good beginning. The Gospel shows Jesus among the outcasts and sinners, loving and enabling them from where they are. The Church is a field of wheat and weeds. Prayer is always necessary for conversion. I still never have heard a petition for the imprisoned in the Prayers of the Faithful in our churches. Is it still out of sight and so out of mind?

There are, however, people dedicated to the delinquent and criminal from deep inner religious faith and conviction. I mention Charlie Brown, a counselor at the Hennepin County Juvenile Center. Charles Schulz in "Peanuts" made Charlie Brown a household word. Charlie worked with Schulz in the Bureau of Engraving in Minneapolis.

Eventually both quit the bureau; Schulz became a cartoonist, Charlie Brown a counselor for convicted delinquents, often housing them in his own home. Charlie, a devout Catholic, saw his life dedicated to delinquent youth. During all the years I worked with Charlie Brown in the Hennepin County Juvenile Center he never volunteered to say that he was the real Charlie Brown. When the kids came to the Detention Center late at night asking "Is Charlie Brown there?" they had no idea whom they were asking for.

Charlie Brown and Charles Schulz remained close friends to the end. Schulz occasionally offered Charlie a share in the profits from the Charlie Brown commercial spin-offs, such as cards and T-shirts. But Charlie never accepted a dollar. Charlie died of cancer in 1983. It was providential to have met and worked with the real Charlie Brown.

Today Americans harbor a deep-seated fear towards the country's crime problem. There is an ambivalent feeling about what to do with a criminal. Criminologists in the past were debating "rehabilitation" vs. "warehousing" of prisoners. Now the debate deals with what to do with the growing number of offenders. In 1975 the death penalty was reinstated in the United States. This development along with the current disregard for the value and dignity of human life compels a correctional chaplain to speak out against the death penalty. Minors with severe crimes are adjudicated as adults and so should be in line with adult punishment.

In July 1989 a death sentence was carried out on a young adult, somewhat retarded, for a crime committed while a minor. This raises another question: Can a person with an I.Q. below sixty be given a death sentence? The death penalty is a loaded issue. However, whenever we deal with death, we deal with a life issue. The state or the courts ask for the right to kill, calling it capital punishment or "execution." This penalty often evidently discriminates toward the poor and minorities.

A Christian chaplain focuses on a thought that many do not like to think about, namely, relating Jesus with capital punishment. But it is difficult to avoid the connection. Jesus suffered death at the order of the Roman state. Christians everywhere recount his forgiveness of those who carried it out, those who plotted against him, and his solidarity with the men executed beside him. When faced with a woman in clear violation of the Jewish law, surrounded by a crowd ready to carry out the death penalty, Jesus spoke with compassion. His words resound today. Who among us has not sinned? Of what crimes against life are we guilty?

Whether unborn, minor or adult, all human life has dignity and value and asks respect from all. Life comes from God and belongs to him. We only use it. A chaplain defends belief in the inherent worth and sacredness of life, all life, whether or not that particular life has been judged guilty. Were I to begin to judge people's lives as devoid of value, I would be far from the example of Jesus who spent his life among sinners healing and teaching. American polls indicate that a vast majority favor the death penalty for murders and drug crimes. The Supreme Court allowing at present even the execution of minors does not make it right for us to support decisions based on dehumanized values.

To understand what goes on in places in our criminal justice system, consider a letter by Robert West, an inmate on a Texas death row. This letter, published in *The Catholic Worker,* describes how the police had told his best friend Dusty to pack his property and move from the cellblock to an observation cell because his execution was scheduled for the fifteenth of the month. They do this so they can keep watch on the condemned man to be sure he does not kill himself. He states:

> Last year when I had my first execution date, they moved me into the same observation cell. As soon as I got there I tore the sink and toilet off the wall and they proceeded to move me all the way back to the back of the cellblock into a solitary cell with a solid outer door locked behind me. Nobody could see me there.

After they took Dusty away they gave him the option to go down the hall to another dayroom and recreate alone. Imagine the psychological torture that goes along with this. A man is taken out of his accustomed routine and made to live the last days of his life alone, isolated from the only friends he has left, to pace in his cell and to think about being murdered.

The next morning they took Dusty across town to the death house. He stayed there all day preparing to die. That night at 10:20 when Dusty was on the phone saying goodbye to his family, the warden told him he had been given a stay of execution. Dusty will probably next year have to say goodbye again sometime. Why? The Supreme Court has to be heard from. Cases which might reverse the death penalty statute in Texas are in the courts. The game goes on.

Inmate Robert West concludes his letter,

> The next time Iran goes crazy and snatches up a bunch of people, or somebody tries violently to overthrow a government, check the newspaper and listen to the public scream about the other guy being a heathen and what a civilized society we are. They are worked up over these so-called terrorists holding their hostages, teasing them with death, sometimes killing them, sometimes letting them go. They forget the man they left shaking in the local death house, and act like it does not matter. They are ready to do it again. This, my friend, is called justice.

A prison chaplain today finds that his parishioners are young. Most of them come from homes where there was little love, security, or discipline. They are accustomed for the most part to doing whatever they wanted. They have little religious experience and often no commitment to God or to a Church. Many have only a seventh grade or less education. Most are drop-outs. They often lack work experience or work habits. If they worked at all, it was usually for a minimum wage. All this cannot help but make them feel to be losers. They feel the establishment is against them. It includes police, courts, judges, preachers, pastors, and Churches. "Them" represents all the other "losers" who have been arrested and imprisoned.

The criminal justice system relies heavily upon incarceration as punishment for crime. For many, crime is more of an emotional than a rational issue. They are afraid and angry of what they see and hear about what people are doing to other people, to themselves, or their own loved ones. The aim here is to get the offender out of sight and mind. This punitive attitude and practice is not only an emotional reaction. It can also be based on a spiritual attitude. Some believe that their justification for retribution is the mind of God. That's how God is and how he wants it. God is the severe judge. However, they want God to be unchallenging and nonconfrontive with themselves.

The correctional chaplain must look at crime and punishment in the light of faith in a compassionate, merciful God. It is easy for Church people to talk about the legal or psychological aspects or sociological statistics rather than be a community of people who profess the following of Christ.

Christian faith holds and believes that we are created in the image of God. Christ took on humanity, giving it still greater dignity. Those who commit crimes do not lose their dignity as persons nor may those who work with criminals deny it. All members of society, whatever their ethics, heritage, race, sex, or state are redeemed by Christ. To respond with violence against them denies our own dignity. We all are standing before God as sinners. Our misdeeds offend both God and neighbor. God knows weakness and is forgiving. Most people in prison have never known love, and it is very difficult for them to grasp the Christian idea of it.

When hearing of crimes or speaking of those who commit them, feelings of hatred, bitterness, and a flareup of an instinct for revenge may arise in us. We can ask ourselves whether these feelings represent the darker side of our own nature. For the felon who has done the most wicked crime, ought I not still pray for his conversion and ask God's forgiveness? Working in his parish of felons, a chaplain learns that we will be judged more on love than on morality. True love leads to morality. One learns the meaning of compassion and not to be quick in passing judgments on others. One tries to help and discovers that he is helped by them. One retired chaplain said: "You give, and often in turn receive a lot more." Early in my prison work I was a member of the prison labor union, and for a week at the union's request, I wore a union button. The first morning I came out of my office with the button on the lapel of my coat, a black inmate stopped me asking what I was wearing that button for. I said: "It's a union button." He looked me straight in the eye and replied: "There is only one button you ought to wear, and that's God's button."

In my journey that brought me to be with God's people behind bars, I learned not to separate these people as beings different from myself. Once I realized that they are brothers and sisters of Christ as I am, I began to understand better the teaching of Scripture: "Be as mindful of prisoners as if you were sharing their imprisonment" (Heb 13.3).

The role of the chaplain in prison ministry is one of presence, "sacramental presence." As a person of faith, the correctional chaplain ought to profess by his actions a God of unconditional love and forgiveness. The chaplain, as counselor, liturgical leader, prophet, and facilitator of life beyond incarceration, is a powerful symbol of faith in God's presence in an otherwise dehumanizing environment where time is measured by "a clock with no hands."

Br. Robin Pierzina

FROM AGE NINE I ALWAYS WANTED TO BE A PRIEST. It is odd how the idea was planted. There were nine children in my family, five girls and four boys. I was the youngest of the boys. Both parents were Roman Catholic as well as the grandmothers on both sides. All of my brothers had been altar boys. Since I was the youngest of the boys and my next youngest brother was seven years my senior, we were not Mass servers at the same time. They did not continue very long as altar boys. But when I was nine, my mother told me to go over and volunteer for Mass serving. I was reluctant to do so. She told me that either I would go or she would take me. Seldom does a nine-year-old win an argument with his mother. I went to the rectory with angry tears streaming down my face. When the priest answered the door and asked what I wanted, I said that my mother sent me to become an altar boy. He said that it was nothing to cry about and took me into the house. I had my first lesson in the Latin responses and soon became adept at them and at serving Mass as well. I was hooked on the job.

My father often made me get out of bed on cold winter mornings to serve Mass at 6:30. Most days I served the 6:30, the 7:00, and the 7:30 a.m. Masses as the scheduled servers did not show up. And I was obeying my father who said that the priest must not offer Mass without a server. Slowly, over time, the idea came to me that I would like to do what these priests were doing. This was the first inkling that I had a vocation to the priesthood.

Because of the racial segregation that prevailed at that time, I could not attend a Catholic school. One had to be white to attend those schools in Washington, D.C. Even my parish was segregated, for blacks were not welcome to worship in white Catholic churches. However, I did not think, as the idea of a priestly vocation matured in me through continued Mass-serving and attendance at the public high school, that I would meet this racial bias head-on.

At age fourteen I went with a friend, who was also a Mass server, to see our pastor, a crusty old Irishman who frowned at everyone whether they deserved it or not. I was the spokesman and told him of our desire to become priests. He frowned more deeply than usual and said that such was not for us. We would never be able to master the Latin and Greek required. This angered me. I thought that he had no right to assume that blacks could not master the requirements of priestly studies. I never spoke to him again about it, but I continued to serve Mass. Of the three priests in the parish, who surely must have been apprised of what two altar boys had said to the pastor, not one of them in all the years I was a server said to me, "Have you ever thought of the priesthood?" It confirmed for me, though indistinctly, that many whites in the priesthood who were spending their lives working for the salvation of blacks assumed that the Holy Orders they enjoyed were not for blacks.

In addition to serving Mass, I continued to pray, read, and dream of the day when I would also be a priest. As the time drew near for making a decision about where to study, I applied to the archdiocese of Washington. The archbishop was continually going to Ireland for priests. I felt that I could help. What naïveté. For when the archbishop learned that I was not white, he rejected me. "What would I do with you?" he asked. The same occurred when I applied to two religious orders. I was rejected because I was not white. At the time I could not decide whether I should be a priest in a monastery—I had learned about monasteries in my readings—or a priest in the missions, or a priest who teaches. But priest I wanted to be. When my efforts were rebuffed, I was ready to quit the Roman Catholic Church because Jesus taught one thing and the Church was practicing something else: discrimination. But something made me try one more time.

I had heard of Saint John's Abbey in Minnesota. The Saint Andrew's missal that I used had an introduction written by Abbot Alcuin Deutsch. The box the missal came in, published by the Lohmann Company of Saint Paul, had a picture of the Saint Paul cathedral on its front. Besides, Minnesota was where Wheaties came from, those same Wheaties that were advertised on the radio. Finally, the religious calendar that hung in the sacristy had the abbot's name printed on each page, and I had seen this for years as a Mass server. So in my senior year I wrote to Abbot Alcuin to ask whether I could join up. I told him up front that I was not white since that seemed to have been a stumbling block for others. He wrote a very nice letter back in which he indicated that he did not care what color I was, that I should come to Collegeville, and then we would see. Finally, he said in his letter that we could look at each other, and if we liked each other, we would talk about joining. That was how I got to Saint John's from Washington. I was so taken with Minnesota and the abbey that I have never really left either these past forty some years.

While in college at Saint John's, I had the occasion to visit with Abbot Alcuin several times. He was the kind of hands-on chief who liked to talk with each student, especially those considering the priesthood. When five young men, three white and two black, applied for the novitiate at the end of that year, the chapter rejected four of them. To me that was proof that this community at least was color-blind. They considered the merits of the applicants and not the color of their skin. Once inside the community, however, I was to learn something else.

As soon as I graduated from college, I was given a job teaching in the prep school the very Latin which my pastor had said was too difficult for me to master. Of course, he was long dead, and I was unable to let him know how wrong he had been. But, then, I had long known that. His assessment so angered me at the time that I was determined to succeed even if it did me in. At the same time I was taking the regular theology course and following the monastic *horarium* like all the other clerics. In summers I taught special Latin classes in the college for those priesthood aspirants who did not have enough Latin.

After ordination I was posted to the Bahamas for three years to teach Latin at Saint Augustine's College. Then I was recalled to Saint John's because the professor who taught Latin in the university was going to our foundation in Mexico, and I was to replace him. It was then that I began to teach Greek as well as Latin and spent the weekends doing parish work or "livery-horsing," as it was called. Interestingly enough, this work was in white parishes, and it was educational for those parishioners to have the ministrations of the likes of me as a priest. During the thirty-five years I have spent in the priesthood, all my work has been with whites, both in the classroom and in the parish, save for the three years spent in the Bahamas. It has been an education for them as well as for me.

There was one incident among many that I recall which occurred in a suburban parish in Minneapolis. One Sunday morning I had just finished the 8:30 Mass and was returning to the rectory when a white parishioner, a man, accosted me and without preamble said, "I moved out here to get away from you people. The first Sunday I come to Mass, there you are saying Mass. Then I thought about it and realized that it doesn't make any difference!" I had to control my anger, but said, "You've learned something." I then turned and walked away. For the rest of the year I was at that parish on weekends, this man never had occasion to speak to me again. But I am sure that others thought and felt the same way. Indeed efforts were often made to prevent blacks from moving into the area. But there were many other parishioners who became real friends and perdure to this day.

Later on, at the abbey I was tapped for work in the dormitories as a prefect with freshmen. Now that was a challenge and an education for all concerned. Many of these freshmen, Catholics in the main, had never lived that close to a priest before. For many the priest was a distant figure: all head, vestments, and feet. Now here was one living right next door or just down the hall. And he was a black! A new experience.

Saint John's Abbey believes strongly in making the students aware of the monastic setting in which the school is situated. It also tries to place those monks among the students as residents who will impress them with the fact that monastic life is something that can and does enhance their own existence. The effect of having a monk-priest or monk-brother living with these students is a positive thing. My eighteen years with freshmen has been fortunate for me and for them.

Such a prefect or "faculty resident" (as these monks are now called) serves as a spiritual father to all. He is available to those who need direction for their human exigencies. He becomes a facilitator in the workings of the Holy Spirit in the lives of the students. He is there for those who require support when doubts and trials arise. He also has the opportunity to show forth the compassionate Christ. Such a monk living among the students cannot forget that he is a monk-priest or monk-brother and must let those in his charge know that as well by showing himself as that in their midst. The wearing of the monastic habit regularly helps a lot.

Further, such a faculty resident should be concerned for his charges and love them as well. This goes without saying. He must do what he can to keep a vision of Christianity that is current and bright before his charges. A good word when needed, a challenge when called for will do much to stimulate students to greater heights as they strive to learn. The monk-priest or monk-brother faculty resident in all this can be a catalyst. One needs only to try to do this and the rewards, though unexpected, are great. The individual attention given to students in such a residential and rural setting tends to reinforce the emphasis we place on Benedictine values.

The young men with whom I have lived are seventeen to nineteen-year-olds. They are in the main away from home for the first time and are eager to try out their newly acquired freedom. Many are seeking an identity as well as social, psychological, and educational development. Over time it has been my experience that there is much mutual learning taking place. One is kept abreast of the latest music of the young as well as the terminology that is current among them. Many have admitted years later that they chafed under the restrictions they endured in the dorms, but that they now realize that it was beneficial, and they are grateful that it occurred. At least it impressed them that someone in the Church cared. For the faculty resident must above all be father to all, confidant to some, and a friend to most while at the same time showing by his manner of life that the monastic setting of the school makes a difference in the type of education one obtains in this place.

In 1968 the dean of students position was bestowed upon me, and I found myself in a delicate situation. Student unrest was rampant on college campuses in the '60s. Saint John's was not an exception. My predecessor had been hanged in effigy. The students served notice that I was their next victim: not for hanging in effigy, but for shooting. Needless to say, this was the time when a serious effort was being made in the university to diversify the composition of the student body by recruiting minorities. We then had a number of black students enrolled.

One of the first things I did as dean was to establish a Black Students Association as a rallying point for the blacks in the student body. There was much alienation at the time. The biases of the Catholic Church and the attempt on the part of the African-Americans for self-determination were patently clear. The faculty as well as the student body and the monastic community had much to learn about having these minority students in their midst. The curriculum was inadequate, the social life was non-existent, the needs of these minorities were not being addressed as they should have been. The students themselves, mainly from Washington, Chicago, Saint Louis, the Bahamas, and Africa, felt alienated and wished to do something about it all. The association was one means I thought would give them the vehicle to do just that. However, the African students wanted no part of it, and the Bahamian students were unable to identify completely with the plight of the African-American students. It was a difficult task, but the association did get off the ground and helped the community through some very difficult times.

The black students pointed up some glaring problems that not only were evident in our society but also in our Church and in our community. Yet many of these same students were successful in the milieu that is Saint John's and are today a credit to their communities as doctors, lawyers, and administrators in schools and banks. One has even begun his own manufacturing company in conjunction with an African alumnus; others have entered the business field as junior executives. Still, there is a lot to be done regarding prejudice in our society, Church, community, and religious house.

Just the other day I was reminded of the covert bias which may be unknown to some. A monk, whom I respect and who was a member of this community long before I joined it, asked whether I was a Bahamian or a Jamaican. He had assumed all these years, more than forty, that I was not a United States citizen and that a black must have come from the "islands." That kind of covert bias is a bit hard to take after all these years. Why would anyone assume that a black face in Saint John's must be a foreigner?

When I look back over the forty-one years that I have been a member of Saint John's Abbey, I see that the community *qua* community is color-blind, but that individuals in that community are as prejudiced as any white in American society. Yet I must admit that when all other doors were closed to me in the late '40s, Saint John's Abbey gave me a chance. For that I am and will ever be grateful. The community has changed in character over the years, and its composition is more representative of the country as a whole. With that change comes a tolerance that was not evident heretofore. It must be said, however, that there were many in the community when I joined who were broad-minded enough to give this fellow an opportunity. They have been supportive ever since. People like Frs. Cosmas Dahlheimer, my novice master, and Godfrey Diekmann, whose classes gave me a new way of thinking and a new approach to matters theological, have made a big difference in my life as a monk. I cannot overlook Fr. Eric Buermann, who gave me my first chance at teaching Latin. Nor must I omit recalling Fr. Michael Blecker, who as president of the university encouraged me at every turn and insisted that I prepare to get African and other minority literatures into the curriculum. I must not forget to cite Abbot Alcuin who was so encouraging and supportive. All these have had a profound effect on me and have made me realize that persons like myself can make a contribution as can every monk who enters this community and perseveres.

The monastic priesthood is something that has made my life complete and meaningful. Before I said that I could not decide whether I should be a monk-priest, a missionary-priest, or a teaching-priest. I have had all of that at one time or another, thanks to Saint John's Abbey. It has been a rewarding experience as well to be in a position as a faculty resident since it has afforded the opportunity to witness to my beliefs as a Catholic, a priest, and a Benedictine monk among those who would benefit much. The jobs that have come my way in this monastic setting have been rewarding indeed. Yet somehow, I have to agree with Bishop Emerson Moore, who was present at the last bishops' meeting held at Collegeville. He noticed that I was to give a retreat that summer. I mentioned to him that I had never had the opportunity of doing that before. He said quietly, "What a waste!" My hope is that as time goes on, more chances will be given me to serve the community better, a community that has given me so much.

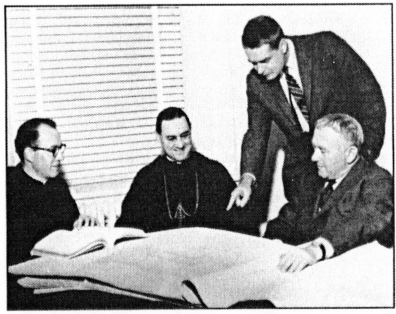

Subprior John Eidenschink, Abbot Baldwin Dworschak, Hamilton Smith, and Marcel Breuer

KILIAN W. MCDONNELL

I T SMELLED DIFFERENT. ODOR WAS THE FIRST sense to distinguish Saint John's from other places. The abbey church smelled, a soft pungent aroma of old incense, of decades of holy smoke which clung to the walls, the pews, the curtains. When the new church was built and the old church was converted into the Great Hall, what disturbed me most was not the removal of the Twin Towers, which had been the signature of Saint John's. What I missed was the smell. It was gone.

For me there was a link between that smell and the angels painted by Brother Clement in the apse of the church. The adoring angels were veiling their eyes before the glory of God, singing Holy, Holy, Holy. The old church was not particularly distinguished architecturally, but the sanctuary with the golden baldachin, the adoring angels, the hanging lamps, the Christus in the apse, was for me a thing of great beauty. The smell of the abbey church carried the whole visual experience: *Terribilis est iste locus:* "Full of awe is this place."

The church which Marcel Breuer built doesn't smell, not yet. Though acoustically a disaster, visually the church has its moments of greatness. Stand at the back of the church at night, when only the lights under the baldachin fall on the blonded crucifix. Silence and awe. *Terribilis est iste locus.* This view can hold its own with anything in Christendom. Sanctuaries we do well.

There was a view of monasticism expressed in the words *propter chorum fundatum:* "a monastery is founded for the sake of the monastic choir." While this overstates the case, nonetheless the choir stands at the center of my experience of Saint John's. Without it we monks are not ourselves. The greatness of having a vocation to the monastic life at Saint John's is the insertion of a novice into a daily framework of prayer and work in the context of a real family of men all seeking God according to the monastic way of life, not invariably "running the way of God's commandments with unspeakable sweetness of love" (Prologue to the *Rule*), but at least stumbling together in the right direction.

When I entered in 1945, the monks rose at 4:10 a.m. Though I loved the life, it nearly killed me. There was nothing much wrong with me. However, from birth I was not strong constitutionally. The rigor of the monastic schedule meant that I was hanging on by my fingernails. When the end of the novitiate came, I was in poor health and had lost weight. In order to get me through the monastic chapter, Fr. Basil Stegmann drew up a letter stating that if my health had not improved by the time for final vows came, then I would not press to be accepted. The law was that a monk in simple vows could not be dismissed for poor health. On that condition I was accepted by the chapter.

When it came time for final vows, my health had deteriorated, my weight had slipped to 115 lbs., and I needed a lot of rest. The cleric master, Fr. Vitus Bucher, tested me during these years. Sometimes when I really needed to sleep over for a few days, he kindly refused permission. On other occasions when I did not think I needed extra rest, he told me to stay in bed that morning. Mostly he kept me on even keel, protected me, and saw to it that I made it to the monastic chapter which would consider my application for final vows. But I had signed that letter and the chapter was free to send me packing. At the chapter meeting on the candidates for solemn vows, the letter drawn up by Father Basil was presented only to have it sabotaged by Fr. Adelard Thuente, who denounced it as immoral, unconstitutional, anti-monastic, a scandal, and legally not binding. He requested that I be given solemn vows. I was accepted and made vows. Fr. Wilfred Theisen, who has a deadly eye for the incongruous, suggested that I was the only monk in the history of the abbey who made his solemn vows in a bathrobe. Where can one find such a community of support, one monk drawing up an accommodating document, a second monk torpedoing it, and a third monk keeping you from taking yourself too seriously? This is typical of the great support I have received from the community over the years.

During these years when I was struggling and needing special rest, one of the monks asked me if I did not feel a little guilty receiving special consideration. I told him, yes, but added: "I handle guilt extremely well."

Sometime within the last few years a group of religious women in the East were asked whether they would chose the convent if they had to do it all over again. More than 50 percent said no, they would not enter religious life. This is tragedy of monumental proportions. Nothing is so depressing as a trapped life, a life spent in a school of God's service which is a matter of regret. Religious women find themselves in a special situation, which I think I understand. For myself I am eternally grateful for my vocation and wonder why I have been so fortunate as to receive this great grace.

In many ways monastic life is one of the best kept secrets. Were it widely known that this life of modest discipline, a chance to seek God with a round of prayer and work, a community of support which will be both one's greatest burden and one's largest joy, the opportunity for a wide variety of work within the monastic framework, were all this known would we be able to accommodate the applicants? The big impediment is celibacy. If society places such a high premium on sexual expression, monastic life will have problems recruiting. But why not turn that disadvantage into an asset? From my novitiate days here at Saint John's, I remember the teaching on the monastic vows which Father Basil gave. The sexual urge, and the possibility of having one's own family, was described as one of the highest human goods. The monastic vocation is a call to lay that greatest gift on the altar. We do not offer up some diseased sheep which was going to die within the week anyway. No, we offer that which is noblest, purest, which, in a daily struggle, must be laid on the altar each day. That was the challenge with which my novice master presented me here at Saint John's.

When millions of people go to work each day, hating their jobs, marking time until 4:30, waiting only for Friday, dreading Monday, when I think of all these millions and then think of the eagerness in the morning with which I look forward to the interesting, challenging work of my day, I again wonder why I have been so fortunate to be called to such a life. Were the deep, quiet satisfaction of monastic life, the chance for prayer scheduled into the day, the deep commitment to God and each other of a community stumbling toward God, were all of this really known, candidates would be breaking down the doors to get in. How can we get out the great good news in a way which will be credible?

A few months ago Fr. Emeric Lawrence and I were talking about our monastic vocation at Saint John's and what that vocation had meant beyond the specifically religious quality of life. We concluded that Saint John's presented us with educational opportunities neither of us, as North Dakota boys, could have expected: Emeric to Harvard and I to German universities. Heady stuff for lads from Fargo and Velva. None of this would have been possible had Saint John's not been a specific monastery, located in a specific place, which really provides for a whole range of supports. I think of the support I received from the monks for my writing, for my work in the ecumenical bilateral national and international dialogues. This all necessitated a great deal of travel and spawned a sizable array of Kilian jokes, such as the abbot has to keep two monks in the air at all times, one of which is Kilian, so that if there is nuclear war, the two can carry on and be the link to the pre-war Saint John's. Or the time Fuller Seminary, Pasadena, California, arranged for a helicopter to pick me up in front of the church to take me to the airport to catch a flight to Los Angeles. My seat strap in the helicopter came undone shortly after take off, and then a door opened. The noise of the helicopter taking off, landing, and taking off again was so loud it stopped the monastic choir. This flurry of winter snow and helicopter blades came to be known as "the grand exit." All of this was grist for travel jokes, in response to which I could only answer "if one has the burden of the universal Church on one's shoulders, one has to travel."

Most significant was the support the monastic community gave in the founding of the Institute for Ecumenical and Cultural Research. Because the institute has played such a large role in my life at Saint John's, I have been asked to write of its beginnings, about which up to now there is no public record.

When it had been decided that I was to go on for further studies and that it would be to study Protestant theology in Protestant faculties in Germany, I told Abbot Baldwin Dworschak that I thought I could get funds for such a venture, which in the late '50s was still unusual. I wrote a two-page application and in one mailing sent it to ten foundations. Eight said no, two were affirmative. I accepted the offer of $5,000 of the Aimee Mott Butler Charitable Trust and was off to Ottawa for a year; if I had no major health problems I would go on to Europe and then to Trier, Germany.

One of the reasons for going to Trier was the presence of a Reformation scholar, Professor Irwin Iserloh. Because our national traditions are historically more pronouncedly Calvinist than Lutheran, I had decided to do a thesis on John Calvin, which eventually came out as a book: *John Calvin, the Church and the Eucharist,* a title suggested by Fr. Colman Barry.

Most German students have attended more than one university, the educational system being more oriented to the professor than to the university structure. So after a year in Trier I spent from a semester to a year in Tübingen, Münster, Paderborn, and Heidelberg. You move around to sample the best professors working in your field.

Each year I would write a long newsletter to Mr. Patrick Butler in Saint Paul telling about the people I was meeting, the new issues which were surfacing in university life, what it meant for an American to be studying in Germany during Vatican II, how I was managing cooking my own meals and living in various student dormitories.

Being in Germany but reflecting back on the situation of the Churches in the United States, it struck me that the Churches, especially the Catholic Church, had long been out of the missionary stage. We were no longer wholly dependent on European Christianity for a whole range of religious needs. Though no longer a missionary country, we were in many ways still living in a missionary mentality. As regards scholarship, that meant that we still lived off the translations of European research. That could not go on. Certainly we would always be reading the books of European scholars, but we have our own national history; we need to write out of the American experience. Mostly we need to stop living in adolescent dependence on the research of others. All of this was included in the letters I had written to Mr. Butler. No response was given, and I did not think it was appropriate to expect one.

When I received my degree and returned to Saint John's, one of the first things I wanted to do was to meet and thank Mr. Butler. In a luncheon conversation with Mr. and Mrs. Butler at their Summit Avenue home in Saint Paul, I learned that Patrick had multilithed my yearly letter from Germany and sent it to his friends. It helped to show that their money had been well spent when I told them that the thesis was being published as a book in England by the Oxford University Press and in the United States by Princeton University Press.

In the course of our conversation about my experience in Germany, Patrick asked "Where do we go from here?" I took up the lead and said that I would go back to Saint John's and consult with my confreres. Back in Collegeville I am sure I spoke with Fr. Colman Barry and Abbot Baldwin Dworschak. Most distinctly I remember speaking to Fr. Michael Blecker. What emerged was the possibility of erecting a combination retreat and research institution. Quite early, I am not sure of the exact point in time, it was seen that the combination would not work out; it had to be one or the other, and the post-doctoral research institute was chosen. The post-doctoral level would define its essential character, but it would not necessarily exclude other persons with serious research projects. Patrick Butler said he would think about it and would let me know.

A year later, and still no word. I decided to take the risk, and I approached Mr. Butler, pointing out that we were riding the crest of a popular ecumenical wave, which might be helpful were the project to go forward. Being a clumsy young man in a hurry, I am not sure I phrased it that well. Mr. Butler invited me to come down. I returned, I think with Frs. Florian Muggli and Gervase Soukup, and again talked about a post-doctoral residential ecumenical research institute. We were presented with a grant of $250,000, at that time one of the larger physical plant grants Saint John's had received.

For the remote planning for the institute, I traveled to Princeton to see the Institute for Advanced Studies, whose housing units were designed by Marcel Breuer. From the work he had done at Saint John's already and from what I saw at Princeton, I knew that he should be the person to design the institute. I traveled on to Union Theological Seminary in New York City to speak with members of the faculty and get ideas. When I returned I wrote to Dr. Raymond Morris, librarian in the divinity school of Yale, asking him if he would inspect our library holdings to ascertain whether it could support post-doctoral research, which would predictably be mostly theological. I also checked the local grade and high schools. Scholars are very choosy about the schools to which they send their children. The schools of central Minnesota were well above the national average.

I proposed to call the center the Institute for Ecumenical and Cultural Research. There was both a theological and a non-religious reason why I wanted to give prominence to the cultural dimension. Theology has its own source and method, which distinguishes it from the other disciplines. Though distinct, theological discourse which does not relate itself to secular disciplines will be remote from the great issues of humanity, and will, ultimately, languish. The humanities would best serve theology when they assume their own proper autonomy. They do not acquire worth only as handmaids to theology. This integrated view of the institute's task would enable it hopefully to make a significant contribution to the life of the Church, to ecumenism, as well as to non-theological disciplines.

An institute which is ecumenical must itself be ecumenical both in intent and in structure. Therefore the institute could not be a Catholic institution, but needed to be ecumenically constituted, as an independent legal corporation, having its own board of directors. In this it differs from Saint John's University which, in my view is rightly a Catholic university, and should remain so. When the institute was being planned and built, Father Colman gave ideas and inspiration. He was among the ecumenical pioneers of the community.

To insure that ecumenism not be conceived of as a complex series of mergers much like the merging of the Great Northern and Soo Line Railroads, I asked Marcel Breuer to express the centrality of prayer architecturally. The chapel in the administration building is a reminder that the ecumenical task can only be approached in repentance and petition, that is, on our knees.

When the bids came in, it became evident that the cost of the ten units and an administration building furnished would come to $350,000. I returned to Patrick Butler and proposed that we go ahead and build half of the institute, see how it prospered, and then we could later decide on the second half. But Patrick said: "If we are going to do it, then we have to do it right by building the whole institute at the beginning." He gave us another $100,000.

About this time I asked Abbot Baldwin for another monk to aid me in the work of the institute. In response to this request, he appointed Fr. Philip Kaufman, who had an important role in the formation of the institute in its first years.

If I were to exaggerate the extent of my administrative skills, I would say that they were minimal. The man who professionalized the institute was Dr. Robert Bilheimer as executive director. He brought with him years of experience at the World Council of Churches and an informed vision. Sr. Dolores Schuh, C.H.M., now executive associate, is the living memory of the institute. What is not down on paper, she remembers. During the first years Father Philip and I were the Benedictine presence at the institute. Fr. Jerome Theisen also did so, and now Fr. Wilfred Theisen fulfills that function, dispensing welcome and wisdom. At one time Fr. Godfrey Diekmann was on the board of directors. Bob Bilheimer is a hard act to follow, but Dr. Patrick Henry has built on the strengths already in place and moved on in creative ways. Few can match him as a moderator of a discussion.

In 1989 we celebrated the institute's coming of age, twenty-one years, with a concert in November at Orchestra Hall in Minneapolis. Philip Brunelle conducted a sixty-piece orchestra and a 250-voice chorus from Saint Olaf College, the College of Saint Benedict, and Saint John's University in a specially commissioned "Christ Metaphors," an oratorio-type of composition by the American composer Merrill Bradshaw of Brigham Young University.

The institute has had 234 scholars in residence from North America, Europe, Africa, and Asia; has sponsored fifty-six consultations; has published studies gaining national attention such as *Faith and Ferment,* edited by Robert Bilheimer, a multidisciplinary study of religion in Minnesota authored by Joan Chittister and Martin Marty, co-published in 1983 by Augsburg and The Liturgical Press. Another of Robert Bilheimer's achievements is the introduction of the first-person approach, where people speak of what it means to believe in God today, which resulted in *God on Our Minds* (P. Henry and T. Stransky, C.S.P., co-published by Fortress and The Liturgical Press in 1982).

The success of these twenty-one years is due to a number of factors, including a very supportive board of directors, talented executive directors and associates, the continuing support of the Butler family and others. But if I write not of its success, but of its special character which enabled it to achieve some eminence, I would point to its relation to the monastery. Being situated in a Benedictine community of prayer makes it unlike any other similar institution. Some scholars have joined the monastic community regularly at Divine Office. Whether actively participating or not, Benedictine life and the monastic tradition are topics which, over the years, have surfaced the most frequently in our coffee hours. Some scholars have been influenced by the monastery at some depth. The presence of the Hill Monastic Manuscript Library, the building of the Episcopalian Center, the construction on the grounds of the abbey and university of nine significant buildings by an architect of international reputation, the founding studios of Minnesota Public Radio, The Liturgical Press, the Jay Phillips Chair of Jewish Studies, a preparatory high school and a liberal arts university, the residence of two nationally known novelists and a colony of artists make Saint John's and the institute an interesting, sometimes an exhausting place. My expectations for the future are wide. Mostly I wait for the Breuer church to acquire its own smell.

THE ANCIENT ROMANS USED TO BUILD SHRINES
to their gods. Sometimes they would mark out a sacred area in
the middle of a field and dedicate it to an agricultural god. The
sacred area was called a *fanum*. The rest of the field surrounding
the shrine was *pro fanis,* profane.

The inside of the monastery is called the enclosure, the cloister.
We no longer make as much of the idea of enclosure as we used
to, and we don't consider everything outside the cloister as profane either. But we do have a sense of the sacred associated with
what is inside the cloister.

It seems to me that this is the place to start when we are reflecting on what a monk at Saint John's understands by a sense of place.
We can start with the very concrete boundary that separates out
the place where we live, eat, sleep, recreate, and worship from those
areas where we work and connect with our friends and colleagues
who do not live inside the cloister.

What one finds inside the cloister is important because it speaks
of who we are. Just as when you walk into a home, you can find
out a lot about what kind of family lives there, so also if you could
explore the rooms inside the monastery, you would find out what
kind of people we are and what is important to us.

Here's what we would like you to notice. The church first of
all. The most important thing for us is worship. Unlike most
churches, what is distinctive about ours is the choir where the monks
gather to pray as a community at regular times during the day.

The choir stalls speak of our priority enshrined in the motto that nothing is to be preferred to the work of God. The work of God is communal prayer.

The next place that is important to us is the refectory, where we eat together. The refectory is the extension of the church. We are nourished in the church, and also in the refectory. Eating together is a priority exceeded only by praying together.

Also distinctive are those common areas where we find our mail boxes, newspapers, space to play cards or watch TV, in general, those areas where we can associate with each other in a casual and relaxing way.

The emphasis up to this point has been on the community dimension of our lives. This in itself is very distinctive. We define ourselves as monks. We are members of a community. We vow ourselves to this particular group of people, and the stability that is part of our commitment ties us to each other in a network of common purposes and responsibilities that are reflected in the common areas of our home. Each day we do rotating tasks that remind us of the contribution that we are expected to make to the community, tasks like leading prayers and waiting on tables.

We have not lost any of our individuality, not to mention our eccentricity, by entering the monastery. Each of us has his own private room as well, and there, as is true of anyone, can be found those items of furniture, books, plants, pictures, and memorabilia which tell us so much about the person who lives there. As a matter of fact the common life of monasticism tends to foster individuality, in my opinion, rather than suppress it. The variety of life styles expressed in the living quarters of the individual monks defies general description.

Nevertheless, there is a constant and pervasive communal pressure that tends to mold us into the kind of community we are. Not only is there a recognizable corporate personality that constitutes Saint John's community, but one of the better ways to find out what that personality is like is to look at our home and the way we live in it.

Most people know about us because of our work in education, in publishing, and in parishes and missions away from the confines of the land that is our home. Through our work the personality of the community extends into the prep school and university, where we worry a lot about a Benedictine presence, especially in these times when that presence is diminishing. The buildings on campus express that work dimension of our lives, and we find our work significant not only because of the inherent value of a liberal education but also because of the values of monasticism that influence the rationale of what we are trying to do in the business of education.

One cannot understand Saint John's just by looking at what is going on in the monastery today. Like any individual person, we as a community are known when you know something about our history. One has to be able to detect the spirit of Abbot Alexius Edelbrock, Fr. Virgil Michel, and Abbot Alcuin Deutsch in the corridors of the quadrangle to be able to appreciate what we are and how we got this way.

My personal history is connected with this history of the community. I remember where I talked with Abbot Alcuin when I wanted to come to the prep school. I remember the place where I graduated from prep school and college, where I pronounced my religious vows, and where I first taught. None of these places serves the same function today that they did for me in my early days here. Knowing about the history of Saint John's includes knowing how different buildings have been transformed to serve new purposes. If you know where the print shop was in the quad, you have some idea about a lot of other changes that in themselves tell us about the history of the place.

Especially do I remember locations that are for me packed with emotion. I remember where I was when President Kennedy was shot. I remember the hallway in a dormitory where a student threatened me with a knife when I was his prefect. I remember where the motorcycle accident occurred on campus which I came upon and which took the life of a student. I remember the room in the monastery where a couple of other monks and I found one of our confreres dead.

As I walk through the buildings and go down the rows of grave markers in the cemetery, a wealth of associations come to mind, all of which contribute to what we mean by Saint John's. The same is true of all of the monks. And as I get older I do what older people do. I recall the good old days. But I like to tell younger people that contrary to what is implied in their ridicule of the good old days, I am not just trying to recover the past. I am trying to make sense out of my own and my community's current identity, and I do that by recovering the history of Saint John's.

But our identity does not have to do only with the past. It has to do with the future as well. As a community that is very much alive, we have a stake in what kind of place Saint John's will be like in the future. At this moment in our history, we are being pushed to think imaginatively about our future.

This strikes me as being the most salient feature of the character of Saint John's today. We look at the dwindling numbers of our community. We look at the historical crossroads that the Church throughout the world is approaching. We wonder about the changing role that we will have to play in the work of the Church. We are at the point where we need not only to remember our history but also to make judgments about whether and how we want to alter the course of our development in the future.

We know that we enjoy a good reputation. Sometimes we are a little embarrassed by the praise we receive from people. We think that we may be resting too much on our laurels, that we need to scramble a little bit to measure up in the future to what has been achieved by those who have gone before us.

What is healthy about the situation is that we are aware of the need to look into the future with hope, imagination, courage, and our ideals intact. We know that the past is important because we stand on the shoulders of those who made Saint John's what it is today, and so we have a strong foundation for the construction that will be Saint John's in the generations to come.

But I want to emphasize that I think Saint John's, like the Church, is indeed at a crossroads. The community will never be the same internally as it was a few decades ago, when being a priest was important, superiors ruled with forceful authority, and the individual monk lived a life which manifested the details of an earlier spirituality. Nor will our external work be the same, as we search for the appropriate contribution that we can make to the apostolic work of a changing Church.

We stand poised in that juncture between a clearly defined past and a somewhat uncertain future. In order to make the adjustment that will bring us to the next level of development in our corporate personality, one of the things we hold onto is a sense of place.

RYAN T. PERKINS

WHEN STUDENTS, FACULTY, STAFF, GRADU-
ates, lounge lizards, and other members and hangers-on at the Newman Center of the University of Minnesota, Minneapolis, discover
that one of their campus ministers is a monk, that discovery almost always becomes the topic of an interesting conversation. Those
who have a connection with Saint John's seem delighted to have
a representative from "behind the pine curtain" in their midst,
even as they wonder how this came to be. As becomes quickly apparent to every monk who travels, almost everywhere there are
people who have heard of Saint John's—and they all have an opinion. "That place!" they will say with every accent from rapture
to disgust.

Yet despite the incredible reach of Saint John's Abbey, people
frequently seem surprised to meet me at the University of Minnesota. Perhaps it is the seeming incongruity of it all. "The U"
is everything Saint John's is not—big, urban, and secular. And
for those few unfamiliar with Saint John's, it is a curiosity to meet
a monk so far outside his monastery, a representative of the sixth
century at a supposed cultural crossroads of the twentieth. What
all of this gives me is the repeated opportunity to reflect on and
discuss whence I've come, what I represent, and what I contribute to this university, in brief, what I'm doing here at this Newman Center, a city of God in a megalopolis.

I have no trouble remembering how I came to Saint John's. I was living in my home state of California, working for hotels and enjoying it. Still, at age twenty-seven I felt something was missing, and I decided to pursue an old interest in religious life and ordained ministry. A priest friend suggested the Benedictines. I had never met one or been in a Benedictine monastery. "Try Saint John's in Minnesota, that's the outstanding house in the country," he said. My pastor groaned in response: "Anyplace but there. They started it all!" Nevertheless, I wrote and, in turn, was invited to visit. To tell the truth it was not love at first sight. Saint John's was completely different from what I expected, indeed, from anything I had ever experienced. After a few days I began to feel the rhythm of life at the place, but I was hesitant about joining such a way-of-life that seemed odd and eccentric.

After consideration I decided to give it a try and returned for candidacy in January 1977. Immediately, I was struck with an impression much different from my first one: I felt very much at home, as if I somehow belonged at Saint John's, and began monastic life with great enthusiasm, most of which still remains. I think the difference in my reaction is due partly to the difference in the campus between January and July, but more so in that I was no longer an observer from the outside but a participant. I was actually invited to enter into the mystery that is monastic life and discover for myself what makes Saint John's tick. Moreover, I could do this with a group of fellow-travellers, a class and a community.

The first thing I discovered about monastic life is that it is a system in a specific context. It is a method of living ordinary Christian values in a systematic fashion according to a particular tradition. To my surprise I found that however methodical the system, there are some extraordinary individuals living it and shaping it. This gave that ordinary Christian life a particularly focused and somewhat more intense character than the Christian life I had heretofore known. To get to know Collegeville, the place, then, meant getting to know the rich combination of people who lived there—past monks as well as present—and the setting in which they come together and the monastic culture and spirituality which comes out of their interaction. In this search I was doubly fortunate. First, the then Fr. Jerome Theisen was a wonderful novice master. Novitiate was for us a long introduction to a series of widely diverse monastic personalities, practices, and events, along with the invitation to begin a life-long critical reflection on these as well as to begin the formation of a monastic worldview. Along the way the novice master was good enough to provide some tools and skills as well as a historico-theological context and framework for us to live the life and do the reflection which forms the basis of the conversation with God in community which is monastic life at its essence.

The second fortuitous event was the opportunity to work in the archives, following the death of Fr. Christopher Bayer. When Fr. Vincent Tegeder was appointed abbey archivist, he asked me to help him, and thus began my most important monastic relationship. In exchange for a little organizational work, I had the opportunity, through Father Vincent, to meet, converse with, and get to know the monastic giants and characters of 130-plus years in Collegeville. Through Father Vincent, and also Fr. Colman Barry and Dr. Bill Franklin, I came to see and understand how the genius of Saint John's grew and developed. This contribution of our forebears is the momentum or historical imperative that impels us; it is the accumulated wisdom of the monastic generations. It is their vision that continues to form and inform the rhythm of our lives, and it is synchrony with that rhythm that is the engine for Saint John's greatest success, its ability to affect profoundly all those whose lives it touches, drawing people in, sustaining, transforming. This consonance with a dynamic tradition ensures a unique and distinctive character for Saint John's, one that is easier to experience than describe. But it is a character rising naturally in response to the vows each Benedictine takes.

Monastic life is not supposed to be a mainstream movement. Monastic life is different from the world, an alternate life-style, and the difference gives monks the opportunity to converse with God in ways the majority cannot. This on-going conversation is, of course, a wonderful way to run the path of God's commandments. It is a full and rich way-of-life. But the perspective of difference allows monasticism to practice an intense form of Christian living as a counterpoint to the profane values of the world. I say counterpoint because monasticism, while seeking a life apart, does not disdain or disparage the world. Rather it seeks a continual discovery and rediscovery of the presence of God in all of creation. Monasticism points to the divine presence wherever there is beauty, whether in a forest and lake, a poem or philosophy, a scientific discovery, a hymn or inspired song, or, especially, in the unction of love and fellowship. In this sense monasticism and the world are complementary.

Monastic life points outward. People are drawn to this great experience, this conversation with God. Because it changes forever the way they look at themselves, their world, creation, God and religion, monasticism is forever teaching—it affects people's lives. Monks through their vows publicly commit themselves to this goal and process we call *conversatio,* day in and day out. This is done in *obedience* to a common vision of Christian life and worship as set down in a rule and articulated by an abbot.

There is a third distinctly Benedictine vow. Monks commit themselves to a specific group of people and to a particular tradition. They promise *stability,* that they will throw in their lot with this common enterprise, invest themselves in this center and culture, join in the unfolding of this tradition. It is this third vow that ensures Saint John's will be a "place." The natural beauty of the setting aside, it is the combination of people that is unique, that over the years has given Saint John's its striking personality. I walk in the footsteps of generations of monks, such as the late Frs. Alexius Hoffmann, Roger Schoenbechler, Othmar Wirtz, Othmar Hohman, Cornelius Wittmann, and Basil Stegmann, not to mention what I share with the 250 living monks.

Campus ministry is interesting and exciting. Newman Center at the University of Minnesota is one of the oldest and largest such centers in the country. It has six ministers, including two priests, and a support staff of about ten. My title is director of education. I program ten to fifteen classes and presentations each quarter, teach some of them, and hire teachers for the others. I also direct all sacramental preparation. Another one-third of my job is to be available for spiritual direction and pastoral counseling. Finally, the other priest-minister, a Dominican, and I split sacerdotal responsibilities. We offer five Masses each weekend and all the usual sacramental services, including about one hundred weddings each year.

My appointment to Newman was a happy coincidence. For some years the center has been a Dominican stronghold. When the Order of Preachers was unable to fill a vacancy, the center asked our abbot if he had anyone available. Abbot Jerome thought this was a good opportunity to have Saint John's represented (as we had been previously at the University of Illinois) at such an influential institution as the University of Minnesota, and he asked me to apply. I had never considered campus ministry and went into the position with not a little trepidation. But I was quickly able to see what the abbot had in mind—it is an excellent match. There are many with Saint John's connections in the Twin Cities, alumni, parents, oblates, and friends, and many more who have heard about Collegeville. That connection gives me a certain entry-point and a lot of credibility to begin with. I represent Saint John's and people are interested in the monastic point of view. They ask lots of questions and listen to the answers.

This monastic-state university connection is much more appropriate than it might first appear—the two have quite a lot to say to one another. First, Newman people are often fringe people. For many, Newman is their last stop on the way out of the Church or their first stop on the way back in. Frequently, Catholic students find themselves adrift in a secular ocean. They are learning to question, and there is considerable internal debate about many of the sacred tenets of their childhood. Many are dealing with experiences of hurt or trauma, and several have had bad experiences with the Church. All of this is common in working with college students. What is different about this university is that its size and diversity are so daunting. Many young people haven't the grounding or context in which to make a critical reflection. They certainly don't have the skills. On a campus so huge some students see more people in a single lecture hall than live in their hometown. They have trouble making friends and finding mentors they can trust. They are liminal people, existing on the edges of a complex society they don't understand and one which seems cold and threatening.

Students are by nature immersed in a period of transition, on the fringes, so the liminal aspect of monasticism is especially attractive to them at this time. Marginal people seem to recognize one another and reach out to make contact. When they find in us an attitude of openness, acceptance, and hospitality, if they see in us a certain ease or comfort in dealing with our own identity as people in transition, our own liminality, they respond eagerly. Students see that they do play an important role in a society which then seems much less threatening than before. The way is open for them to begin to truly appreciate themselves as lovable members of God's family.

Also, monastic stability is appealing. It suggests that it is possible to find a supportive context and ground for a life's journey, that such is within their reach, and that this can provide the basis for growth. Here the idea is to invite those to whom we minister to get to know themselves, to examine their own living tradition. In helping them to do this, I draw on the experience of my own novitiate. I invite a critical reflection and teach some basic skills and techniques for making one. I also introduce major figures and ideas in their Christian tradition, help students to construct a hierarchy of values and to examine how these values relate to their everyday lives. I provide some background information and explanation and translate Church teaching out of "church-speak" and into a language they can more easily understand. This is the major activity of my ministry, linking people in continuity with their own, larger tradition. It is what the Newman educational program is about, it is the major part of my one-on-one work, and it certainly is what sacramental ministry accomplishes. All of this for me is simply passing along what I've learned in monastic life, from novitiate onward, informed as well by a good education from our Saint John's School of Theology. Giving people a context in which to make a critical reflection helps ensure the success of that reflection. The Benedictine world-view is an excellent context for such an exercise.

Another aspect of Saint John's is one with obvious appeal. The size and intellectual breadth of the University of Minnesota make isolation and alienation inevitable and endemic. We offer community as the antidote, and this simple exchange sums up what we are all about as Catholic Christians—community is the natural consequence of belief in Jesus Christ. The corporate experience of God is primary for us. It is not the only experience, to be sure, but the most important one.

This leads to a natural opportunity to invite Newmanites to study and appreciate what is distinctive about Catholicism. Richard McBrien points out many distinctive features about our faith in his *Catholicism*. Many of them are also descriptors of the Benedictine ideal: the experience and expression of faith is inclusive, comprehensive, detailed, and articulate. God's presence is mediated through our community, the world and culture. Our view of humankind is optimistic. The sacramentality of Christ, the Church, and the people of God are expressed in key moments we call sacramental. The central role of the Word is still vital. Tradition, history, and the world form a powerful context, and also the way the faith is lived out affects and informs what we believe. Authority, teaching, ministry, structure, organization, and law are important parts of the way we do religion. As a Benedictine I feel very much in touch with these facets. It is easy for me to make others aware of them and also to help create a milieu where these values are cherished and practiced.

American Church history is my field. I once wrote an essay suggesting that Saint John's was a logical place for Virgil Michel to have begun the American Liturgical Movement. Saint John's was a leader in promoting and protecting German *Kultur* from loss of identity resulting from the assimilation into the broader melting-pot of American culture which was so relentlessly pushed by the Irish. Community was the organizing principle, both at Saint John's and in the communities served by its monks. When *Kultur* became politically untenable during World War I and could no longer be used as the focal point for community, the door was open (so I proposed) for the Liturgical Movement to take the place of *Kultur* and champion community as the antidote to the social alienation engendered by the Enlightenment and Industrial Revolution.

The alienation and isolation of today are just as strong and keenly felt as that of the nineteenth-century immigrants and the poor and oppressed of the '20s and '30s. We deal with its effects daily at the Newman Center. Again, I think Saint John's through its version of living the Benedictine ideal is in a unique position to respond to the problem. It is a sense of place, of the City of God in megalopolis that can offer so much to so many, a community with continuity and a living tradition. We offer an opportunity to learn to live life in harmony with life's deepest rhythms and to know that God is present in all life, even on the far side of the pine curtain.

Br. Alan Reed

JAMES PHILLIPS

"**I**N THE MIDST OF LIFE, WE ARE IN DEATH,"
declares a somber Dominican antiphon for the *Nunc dimittis* (Canticle of Simeon) at Compline during Lent. "Do not reject us now that we are old," it pleads, "when our strength fails, do not forsake us, Lord" [cf. Ps (70)71:9]. We feel our mortality more perceptibly the further we progress on life's journey. Yet while aging is part of the natural cycle of life by God's design, the changes it brings can catch us unawares, life a thief.

> There was a man going down from Jerusalem to Jericho who fell prey to robbers. They stripped him, beat him, and then went off leaving him half-dead. . . . A Samaritan who was journeying along came on him and was moved to pity at the sight (Luke 10:30, 33).

Saint Benedict did not have to look far to discover the unfortunate man who fell prey to robbers. That victim of the human condition bore the face of every sick and elderly monk in the community infirmary. Those who travel the monastic path to God are not spared illness and advanced age that deprive them of vitality and strength. But Benedict, like Jesus, the true Good Samaritan, was filled with compassion for the sick and provided amply for their care.

In his *Rule*, the "gentle teacher of monks" prescribes that

> Care of the sick must rank above and before all else, so that they may truly be served as Christ, for he said: "I was sick and you

visited me'' (Matt 25:36), and, ''What you did for one of these
least brothers you did for me'' (Matt 25:40). Let the sick on their
part bear in mind that they are served out of honor for God, and
let them not by their excessive demands distress their brothers who
serve them. Still, sick brothers must be patiently borne with, because serving them leads to a greater reward. Consequently, the
abbot should be extremely careful that they suffer no neglect (36:16).

Benedict revered the sick because they participate even now in
the suffering of Christ; the sick incarnate the suffering Christ in
the midst of a monastic community. To serve them is to serve Christ
in a most tangible way. Thus it is not surprising that the ''man
of God'' considered care of the sick to rank before and above all else.

He approached him and dressed his wounds, pouring in oil and
wine. He then hoisted him on his own beast and brought him to
an inn, where he cared for him (Luke 10:34).

Benedict's inn for the sick took the form of what he called ''a
separate room.'' Such was the provision for the sick at Collegeville
until Saint Gregory's Hall, a separate three-story infirmary building for monks and students, was constructed in 1907. According
to Fr. Alexius Hoffmann, up to that time Saint John's had no distinct infirmary, but only ''sickrooms'' reserved for students. ''The
last 'sickrooms' in the main building,'' he noted in 1926, ''were
the two large rooms at the west end of the third floor in the middle
building—each room was about twenty-five feet square and sixteen feet high. Food was carried up by a small elevator connected
with the kitchen.'' Ailing monks were cared for in their rooms or
in ''a common sickroom, at least for clerics and brothers.''
    In reporting the renovation of Saint Gregory's Hall in 1933, the
Saint John's *Record* of September 28 that year observed that

Those inclined to be superstitious may not get a great deal of comfort from hearing what is going on in the hospital. Without regard
to whether increased accommodations may bring more patronage,
the home for sick students, or those who feel the need for a respite
from scholastic labors, is getting an extensive remodeling. . . . The
contagious cases which were formerly kept in the rear section will
now be taken care of on third floor. A stairway and porch are being built on the west side so that the third floor may be reached without making any contact with the rest of the building. The porch
will be used for students needing plenty of fresh air and sun-

light. . . . On the north side of the building a chapel room is nearing completion. This addition is a necessity as the old chapel located on third floor will be used by the contagious patients.

The new chapel was adorned with oil paintings and murals by Saint John's monk Br. Clement Frischauf, who had studied at the Abbey of Beuron in Germany under Fr. Desiderius Lenz, founder of the Beuronese school of religious art. God alone knows how many fervent prayers for healing and restored health were offered up before these sacred images.

Members of the monastic community who served as infirmarians during this century include Frs. Fridolin Trembreull, Edgar Kees, Boniface Hain (who entered the monastery as a registered pharmacist), Christopher Bayer, Severin Lauer, Egbert Goeb, Maurice Hurrle, Ignatius Candrian, and Br. Gerard Wojchowski. Since 1958 Br. Andre Bennett has served as the Saint John's University infirmarian.

After Fr. Boniface Hain died of a heart attack in 1928, Etienne Dupuch noted that this priest's labors as infirmarian and guest master had brought him into contact with more students, parents, and friends than many another monk. What Dupuch said of him was true of those who preceded and followed him: "In his path he scattered seeds of kindness, affection, love, and his daily life was a splendid round of self-sacrifice" (*The Record,* February 3, 1928).

Brother Gerard began to follow that path of self-sacrifice soon after he completed his years of monastic formation, when, as he relates, he was "asked to 'take a try' at learning the art of nursing." This he did at the Alexian Brothers' Hospital in Chicago from 1946–48. During that time, he also studied allied health sciences at De Paul University.

Upon his return to Saint John's, Brother Gerard began assisting students and confreres with his newly gained knowledge of the healing arts. He later observed that

> nursing now for the past thirty-four years, I am daily amazed at what the Lord has brought into my learning experience. I have come to see what a truly magnificent creation the human physiology of a person is. How rightfully each person has the duty to return the ability to know, love and serve God for the gift he has received. In the process of helping to heal my fellow men, I have gotten to know myself better, understand better what makes other people

what they are, and above all, learned to know Christ better—and how he alone is the life-sustaining factor in our lives.

During the past several years, illness has weakened Brother Gerard physically but not spiritually: "For health reasons I have also been taught to slow down and perhaps to reflect a bit more how love is made perfect in infirmity. This too can be very pleasing to God, as it unfolds new mysteries in the divine plan."

In 1973 a monastic housing committee began planning for a new infirmary. Its members included Frs. Roger Botz (chair), Walbert Kalinowski, Hugh Witzmann, and Finian McDonald, and Brs. David Erceg, Kelly Ryan, Kurt Kaiser, Walter Kieffer, and Luke Dowal (consultant). Their good work resulted in Saint Raphael's Hall, where monks who are retired, chronically ill, infirm, or recuperating from major surgery now reside. This complete nursing-care facility occupies the second floor of the health center, a building erected in 1976, as well as part of the second floor of the quadrangle, renovated in three separate stages for this purpose. There are private rooms, visiting and recreation rooms, a chapel, nursing station, kitchen, and dining room. A physical therapy room was added, which has proved to be an invaluable asset not only to residents of the hall but to other members of the community as well.

Presently, twenty-one of the thirty-six retired monks reside in Saint Raphael's Hall. Their wisdom that comes with age, love of prayer, and faithfulness to living the monastic life are gifts that the community needs and cherishes.

Except for those who are physically too weak, the majority of residents are engaged in some kind of work. Among their pursuits are writing, translating, photography, gardening, distributing mail, visiting the ill, driving others to doctor appointments, hobbies, and even supplying the community with fish from our lakes. Most are able to work at their own pace, giving them extra time for spiritual and recreational activities. Some find it difficult to undertake work that differs from what they did in the past or to remain content with a reduced level of productivity. Yet Saint Raphael's Hall ideally provides time and space for what the residents always wanted but never had time to do.

This community within a community is located at the crossroads of the monastery's traffic routes, at its very heart. It was intentionally placed there, so that the sick and elderly would not be isolated from the rest of the community. It is also uncloistered, so that women as well as men may serve as nurses and visit the residents. Its location facilitates conversation between monks residing there and monks passing through.

There, in past years, one might encounter Fr. Sylvester Harter, who suffered from convenient deafness. If he did not want to speak to you, he could not hear you. But if he did want to have a conversation, he could hear every word you said. One might overhear Fr. Denis Parnell teaching French to the nursing staff. Or, every morning after breakfast, one could observe Fr. Linus Schieffer lighting his pipe while warmly greeting the nursing staff. Invariably he would stand under the smoke detector and set off the fire alarm. The dining room has been a premier place for memorable conversation. Bishop Paul Leonard Hagarty would sometimes stand up during lunch and give a speech to the retired monks gathered for the meal. "I want to thank you all for coming to this special dinner. . . ." Fittingly enough, he would usually close with a prayer.

On the other hand, the sick and elderly sometimes make their presence felt in other ways, in other places. One Halloween night Fr. Damian Baker climbed up the back stairwell with his walker, all the way to the fourth floor, which then was the attic. He kept wandering back and forth with his walker, groaning with each arthritic step. The novices below heard the groaning and the "clunking" of the walker. Thinking that the abbey was haunted, they sat in the novitiate frozen with fear. In fact, one brave soul reportedly hid under his bed.

Clearly Benedict knew what he was doing when he prescribed that the sick be served by "an attendant who is God-fearing, attentive and concerned" (the *Rule* 36:7). Accordingly, Saint Raphael's Hall is staffed by a dedicated and competent nursing staff of monks and lay persons. In consultation with physicians, they try to understand the residents' particular illnesses and meet their demands, as long as these are reasonable. Like the Good Samaritan, they pour the oil and wine of compassion lavishly into the physical and spiritual wounds of those under their care.

> The next day he took out two silver pieces and gave them to the innkeeper with the request: "Look after him, and if there is any further expense I will repay you on my way back" (Luke 10:35).

The coin of physical care that the Saint Raphael's Hall staff expends so generously is matched by the coin of spiritual care.

"You must . . . visit the sick," Benedict exhorts his monks (the *Rule* 4:14, 16). Yet it must be admitted that multiple and conflicting demands on monks' time and energy can make this inconvenient. Now that the members of the community no longer take assigned turns in bringing breakfast trays to the residents of Saint Raphael's Hall, it is important that other contact between the residents and their confreres be maintained.

Each resident of Saint Raphael's Hall is "adopted" by one of the other living groups within the monastery known as deaneries. The intention is perhaps not so much that they attend deanery meetings and discussions, but that the members of the deanery take an interest in a particular resident, spending time with him in reading or prayer, perhaps assisting with correspondence, accompanying him on an occasional walk, if possible, or a drive in the summer.

At present, Fr. Baldwin Dworschak, retired abbot of Saint John's, serves as chaplain and celebrates the Eucharist daily with the residents in their chapel, whose altar is the one formerly used in the first infirmary chapel of Saint Gregory's Hall. Also from the former chapel is Br. Clement Frischauf's painting of the crucifixion, whose saintly figures of John the Baptist, the Virgin Mary, John the Evangelist, and Mary Magdalene gaze upon the worshippers. On Wednesdays, Abbot Jerome Theisen visits the sick in their rooms before presiding at the 5:00 p.m. Mass. The prior of the monastery also takes responsibility to minister to the sick and elderly in the hall.

The entire community's spiritual care for the sick is most visibly manifested during the annual retreat, when residents of Saint Raphael's Hall join their confreres for a communal anointing of the sick in the abbey church. Those to be anointed are seated in the sanctuary for the service. After the greeting, introduction, opening hymn and a prayer by the abbot, all listen to the Scripture reading and the abbot's homily. Then the abbot invites the entire assembly to follow him in imposing hands on the heads of those to be anointed. This ancient gesture of blessing and strengthening, happily received when gently given, has come to be a much appreciated part of this celebration. A litany of petition for the sick, set to music by Fr. Henry Bryan Hays, accompanies this sacred action.

After the oil is blessed by the abbot, he anoints the forehead and hands of each of the sick. Meanwhile a litany of praise, again in a setting by Father Bryan, celebrates the healings recounted in the Christian Scriptures. The Lord's Prayer and a blessing by the abbot conclude the service.

The smiles on the faces of the anointed remind all present that the Lord's healing is to be our gift to each other. Such a liturgy may not result in dramatic cures, but surely it brings smaller though no less real miracles of spiritual strengthening to those weakened by sickness and age. Following the anointing in church, those who were unable to participate are anointed in their rooms.

> "Which of these three, in your opinion, was neighbor to the man who fell in with the robbers?" The answer came, "The one who treated him with compassion." Jesus said to him, "Then go and do the same" (Luke 10:36-37).

Our love for our neighbor is the power of God's love at work in us. God's unlimited love for us, made manifest in Christ, becomes the model for our love of neighbor and the power of our service. While some Saint John's monks are charged more directly with the care of their sick and elderly confreres, all are expected to serve as ministers of compassion to them. In addressing the community on the care of the sick and retired, former Prior Julian Schmiesing said: "We need to be compassionate with those who are suffering and at times we need to remind ourselves and them just how close they are to Christ in their suffering." Because the sick share in Christ's passion, they can confidently hope to be one with him in his glory. As fellow travellers along the "road that leads to salvation" (*Prologue* to the *Rule* 48), monks are to be zealous in "supporting with the greatest patience one another's weaknesses of body or behavior" (the *Rule* 72:5).

No matter how many or how great the wounds of body, soul, and spirit, Jesus always lavished the healing oil and wine of his compassion on those in need. He now bids us do the same.

Brs. Isaac Connolly and Linus Ascheman

THE DAMP OCTOBER WEATHER OF 1987 CHILLED
Sr. Jacqueline Sailer, D.H.M., and me to the bones. The slow
drizzle dampened our flesh but not our hearts. We were determined
to do something positive and practical in the way of founding a
house of hospitality and prayer. Sister Jacqueline and her friend
Phillis Needham had located a home in Saint Paul at 763 Butternut. We had to decide before November 1 to rent for $425 a month,
continue the search, or give up entirely.

Despite limited funds, we took the risk. Phillis volunteered to
live in the house and pay $200 per month. Some money was bor-
rowed from Sister Jacqueline's Motherhouse, and we began operations. Nazareth House soon became our household name.

We moved in on November 1, and after the furniture was arranged, my friend Fr. Robert Hamel and I spent our first night
in Nazareth House. We were the only ones there that cold November night, and we will never forget it. The wind whistling and
strange noises upstairs forced my friend to seek refuge downstairs
on the couch.

We survived that night and arranged for the owners to rid the
house of rats or squirrels. On weekends we visited the house and
helped Phillis install plastic over the windows. Later we hung curtains, shades, and decorations that gave the home a touch of warmth
and coziness. Soon we would invite roomers to stay and guests to

come for visits and use the prayer den for reading and meditation. While praying there I recalled in flashbacks the previous two years of our search for "creating a new community."

In 1978, at age fifty-seven, I began studies for the priesthood after thirty-three years of undergraduate work as a brother monk. I noticed almost every exam touched on "community" in one way or another. Society had become sour, but "community" still held up an ideal that was both sweet and bittersweet. In my assigned essays I tried to put my theories on community to the test. My teachers did not always agree with me, but they did not discourage me. I was convinced society needed a remedy for its ailments: alcoholics, drug addicts, alienated divorcees, etc.—all hurting and being rescued one at a time.

It all seemed such a waste of time, though downstream, helping and pulling in drunkards and others one at a time. I was trying to perceive an upstream solution to the problem, such as "the family that prays together, stays together," a cliche that could work if applied to community.

How could I create a community of alienated, hurting people reviewing themselves spiritually and emotionally? My concept of common life included both lay and religious persons, married and single, stable and unstable. It seemed to me that three or four families living in a house or fourplex, sharing their possessions, and praying regularly as a semi-monastic dedicated group could help to rescue someone who is weak or faltering and thus function as a healthy extended family unit for the good of society.

I noticed as a clinical pastoral education student in 1982 that a drug addicted person who was cured "in" community did not find "community" once he or she returned home. They were already labeled "rejects," and soon they fell off the wagon and returned to the hospital.

At Nazareth House a dual operation gradually took place. Sister Jacqueline and Phillis invited former friends of the original Nazareth House, as well as friends from their respective parishes, to spend a few days of relaxation and prayer at the house. Also in those early days, Sr. Helen Connors lived in one of our upstairs rooms, held a part-time job, and paid us a minimal $50 per month. Bill Mann also lived with us and paid $100 a month until he found a better job as a cook. When the first tenants left, we decided to make a new resident policy that invited them to be part of a community family.

About this time in the spring of 1988, Matt Harrington rented a room at the house. He belonged to a charismatic prayer group called "People of Praise." He was open to our intentions to have meals and prayers together but was not always able to attend. Because he was employed regularly, he paid $225 a month for board and room.

Some of our other residents were street people recommended by Catholic Charities. We were able to house Bob and Mike for some six months without cost to them; when they had jobs they would contribute something. At this time we had a full house, and when Doug wanted to join our household we experienced our first major conflict. It was one thing to tackle material problems like no heat or lights or leaking faucets, but it became very trying for Phillis to handle personality conflicts.

Our guests Bob and Mike were very upset because we invited Doug into our household without first consulting them. Maybe they had a legitimate complaint. We weren't prepared for the verbal conflict that ensued. In the end Doug felt obliged to leave, although we believe he needed the spiritual and physical comfort Nazareth House could provide.

One weakness in our overall operation was that we had no full-time core member to direct the household. Sister Jacqueline worked at Saint Mary's Parish in downtown Saint Paul. Phillis worked at Saint Peter's Rectory in Mendota, and I worked as a full-time chaplain at Saint Therese Home in New Hope. I spent Sunday afternoons until Monday night at Nazareth House.

Although Phillis lived at Nazareth House, it was difficult to have full control of phone calls, visitors who would drop in unannounced, and there were the problems of residents. Somehow we managed to please most of our guests and visitors by pre-arranged appointments. It was a great learning experience.

Because I requested a sabbatical from Abbot Jerome Theisen to make a study of various life styles of communities in Europe, Israel, and the United States, and because Phillis entered a second marriage in June 1989, we at Nazareth House determined it would be best to rest awhile and evaluate our next step. With the permission of the board of directors, we suspended all activity at

763 Butternut, stored the furniture, and set our hearts on renting or buying a bigger house with some property and service buildings that would meet all our needs.

My major mentor in helping me form ideas about community and fellowship is Jean Vanier, who uses his home to care for disabled and retarded children. In his *Community and Growth,* he explains how he mastered the technique of love and care. In a June 1, 1989 article in the Washington, D.C., *Catholic Standard,* Vanier wrote:

> The parable of the wedding feast is the story of our twentieth century; no one is coming to the feast because all are too busy. God is hidden in those people who are most rejected by today's society. Our world is truly a world of war. In the richer countries, people's hearts are soiled with materialism. This is its own form of persecution. The poor and the weak and the broken are crying to be included to have their humanity recognized. In order to find their place, they must first find a place in someone's heart.
>
> But to live with the poor is not easy, for it means accepting their anger and pain. The heart of those excluded is a broken heart . . . love is not doing things for people, but is rather the ability to reveal to them their own beauty. But community will reveal the enemy inside, the enemy that must be illuminated by Jesus. The secret of the heart of God is forgiveness.
>
> Many people come to L'Arche communities because they want to help the poor, but the ones who stay are those who become poor, those who allow their defenses to come down and be willing to act out the littleness and dailyness of ordinary life, those seemingly irrelevant things that can only be done with love. The Good News is that all that is broken within us can become a source of life.

These quotations remind me of Mike, the Nazareth House guest mentioned earlier. He came from an undisciplined family, was heavy on drugs, and wanted a chance to start over after separating from his wife. At age twenty-two Mike shared this insight with us:

> For the first time in my life I felt the real presence of family life and a home here at Nazareth House. I experienced peace of mind, solitude, personal attention, challenge to improve, and a sense of personal worth. I will always be grateful for that.

Sometimes I become discouraged at the enormity of the task at hand when I perceive a society that will not admit its sins. If only

I could gather together six to ten people of like mind, determined to live in community for the love of Christ. Hopefully this core-group membership would meet regularly every week or two. Through study and firm purpose of application, perhaps we could perfect what was lacking in the original Nazareth House. Prayer no doubt is the foundation of any work or edifice. For two years at Nazareth House we met at 7:00 a.m. and 7:00 p.m. for morning and evening prayers. Phillis and I were faithful in observing these prayer periods, and sometimes as many as ten or more guests would join us in this prayer of the Church. After our Monday evening prayer service, I would offer the liturgy of the Eucharist. Guests too would join us. Our prayers and liturgies were offered for the special intentions of our friends and benefactors, especially the living and dead listed in our book of memorials placed in our prayer room.

Every empty begging hand is an invitation to see Jesus in our hungry neighbor and to do something about it. At present I observe six movements in the world that make us conscious of our Christian tradition of fellowship, oneness in Christ and our duty to reach out to others: The Ecumenical Movement that is bringing our Christian traditions into one Body of Christ; the spirit of fellowship that draws Christians into small groups of people sharing and caring for one another; the programs that have regenerated local parishes spiritually by small groups studying the Bible and sharing personal life experiences touching on faith; the Basic Ecclesial Community movement in South America whose lay leadership has kept the faith alive in a land short of priests and religious; the Marian phenomena at Lourdes, Fatima, Garabandal, and Medjugorje where Christians have renewed their spiritual lives and love for Christ; the charismatic impact of the Holy Spirit in all areas of the world: "Where the Spirit is, there is the truth; where the truth is, there is the Holy Spirit."

All of us who are aware of these worldwide movements ought to rise above the mundane and create a community of fellowship that reveals Jesus Christ in action in our midst. Nothing does that better than the sign and sacrament of breaking bread together in fellowship on the parish level where we associate with our neighbors. That is our Nazareth House dream.

Fr. Dunstan Tucker

THE PRACTICE OF CARPENTRY WITHIN THE SAINT
John's community is as old as the community itself. When the
founding monks arrived in Saint Cloud in 1856, they immediately
began to work with wood so that they might create the life they
hoped to live together. Initially they found shelter in two small log
cabins along the Mississippi River, but they had no place they could
worship in. So under the hand of Br. Benno Muckenthaler
(1817–59), the space between the two cabins was made into a very
simple chapel. It was enclosed with wooden rafters and covered
with hay and straw. When the other monks were not doing mission work or tending to the daily affairs of the household, they
helped Brother Benno build this chapel and the small kitchen and
frame building that together comprised the first monastery.

In the winter of that same year the monks staked out claims in
the "Indianbush," the northernmost part of Saint John's present
property. To validate the claims, they had to build cabins on each
of them. These cabins of tamarack logs, covered with brush and
sod were a far cry from the later evidences of Saint John's carpentry, but they partook of the same spirit—a determined effort to
create an environment in which a group of men could seek God
together. The monks struggled to clear part of the land, planted
crops in the rocky soil, and built sheds, a log cabin, and a primitive frame house. All these tasks were part of a common effort and

thus the specific contributions of individual monks have faded from memory.

A little more information has survived from the time when the community moved south from the Indianbush and settled permanently on the northern shore of Lake Sagatagan. The Old Stone House was constructed in 1865–66, in what is now the monastic garden. Br. Placid Brixius (1831–71) worked on the structure, along with a number of men from nearby farms. Peter Eich (1834–1920), long a craftsman in the carpenter shop, was among them, earning a hefty $.025 for each foot of lumber he fastened up.

The old frame house from the Indianbush was moved to the new location in 1867. The chapel and housing for the monks occupied most of this modest structure, but significantly one room was set aside for the use of the carpenters. It was a "dingy apartment," as Fr. Alexius Hoffmann recalled, but for the next eleven years it at least served as a base of operations.

In 1868 a saw mill was built along the Watab. The monks were thus able to use their own oak and maple trees for the extensive and more sophisticated construction of the first parts of what later became the quadrangle: the south wing (1868), the middle building (1870) and the northern addition (1873–74). Brother Placid worked on the first two structures with a crew of monks and lay workers.

While putting up buildings was a massive part of the carpenters' work, it did not exhaust their craft. The new buildings were constructed one after another, as the community and its school grew. However, the interiors of the older structures changed each time, as the chapel and student dormitories leap-frogged north from one structure to the next. New users were found for the vacated spaces. Inevitably the carpenters were called in to redefine the space by constructing a new wall or ripping an old one down. This has become characteristic of Saint John's life, one of the enduring coordinates that defines its universe.

The early carpenters also produced furniture, but barely a trace of it remains. Equally as sparse are written testimonies to individual pieces. Fr. Alexius Hoffmann recorded that the first chapel had a few pews, all of which were "home-made and simple," and that the second chapel had a "home-made" altar. Beyond his off-hand references nothing else was recorded about the quality or design of Saint John's furniture. Presumably cost alone demanded that most of it be produced by the abbey carpenters. No doubt, the furniture was as austere as Saint John's first buildings and as functional as the pioneer monks required. Perhaps the very simplicity and extensive use of Saint John's-crafted furniture by the community made writing about it a bit unnecessary.

In 1878 the carpenters moved out of their dingy quarters in the old frame house to a new building, north of where Engel Hall now stands. This new carpenter shop was in a two-story brick building that also housed the blacksmith shop. A lumber shed was constructed near it. Wood could now be stored indoors once the sawyers had cut up the logs down by the Watab and the wood had been allowed to age outside. This solidification of the carpenters' enterprise was accompanied by the arrival of two carpenters who wished to join the community—Brs. Leo Martin (1849–80) and Andrew Unterburger (1848–1916). They and the new facilities were immediately mobilized in the community's greatest undertaking up to that time: the erection of the first abbey church. Brother Andrew assisted Fr. Gregory Steil in drawing up the plans for the building. He and Brother Leo had to design special low-bottom wagons that could carry the huge foundation stones to the building site. They built all the scaffolding needed by the masons and carpenters brought in for the job, and supervised all the carpentry work. On October 9, 1880 Brother Leo lost his life when a plank slipped high up on the scaffolding and sent him plummeting fifty feet to the ground.

After this tragedy Brother Andrew was left in charge. With his crew of young monks, he concentrated on smaller aspects of the over-all building and worked diligently at ironing out the structural problems that developed as the plans were executed. Fr. Philip Bahner recalled that Brother Andrew was a good worker who held a pretty lively temper in reserve. Presumably both qualities helped him to direct the project. Once the abbey church was finished, Brother Andrew was placed in charge of the carpenters who added the whole western half of the quadrangle to the existing buildings in 1883–86. As always, many of these carpenters were young monks and lay workers from the area. Brother Andrew evidently trained the raw energies of the former so expertly that the building still stands today, and got along so well with the latter that he was made foreman of all the abbey's workmen after the quad was completed. Abbot Alexius also sent Brother Andrew to construct a number of buildings outside Saint John's during those years: the station house in Collegeville, the church and rectory at the community's Indian mission at White Earth, the priory at West Union, and Saint Clement's Church in Duluth. His skills at cabinetry have been passed down by oral tradition, even though we cannot identify which pieces of his survive.

Brother Andrew headed the carpenter shop until his death in 1916. Under his leadership it flourished. Peter Eich worked along with him, doing some marvelously detailed carving along with the regular day-to-day work. As Peter Eich grew older, he was joined by Theodore Dillenburg (1868–1943), who worked for Saint John's for many long years and was a master craftsman. Furniture-making was his specialty. He was very meticulous, refusing to ever put so much as one nail in the furniture he made. Year after year trees in the woods matured and were chopped down, sawed, and left to age in the open air. Year after year the carpenters erected new buildings for the abbey's shops and farm and assisted in building new buildings for the college. Year after year they adapted older buildings to new needs of the community. They still built wagons and sleds for the farm and the ever-busy abbey teamsters. And year after year they worked the wood from the forest into furniture. Young monks worked alongside the masters and then moved on to other jobs in the community. During part of each school day from 1885 to 1896, the abbey carpenters took youths from Saint John's Indian Industrial School and trained them in carpentry. Thus their craft flourished at Saint John's and at the same time passed out of the community to those in need.

Sometime toward the end of the nineteenth century the saw mill was moved from the Watab to an eighty-acre tract in the northeast part of the woods. Fire had twice destroyed the old saw mill and the new location perhaps afforded the opportunity to build the whole operation from scratch. In 1903 the carpenter shop moved to a three-story brick building where it is now located. However, the carpenters could not immediately use all their new space. In the summer of 1904 they turned the second floor of their new building over as a temporary residence for Saint John's new cooks, eleven French Sisters of the Presentation. Needless to say, as part of a typically busy summer, the carpenters worked long hours helping build a proper convent that the sisters could move into with dispatch.

The work of the carpenter shop continued after Brother Andrew died. Theodore Dillenburg provided the continuity needed. He was soon joined by John Pflipsen (1892–1971) after World War I. John worked primarily on maintenance carpentry, mastering the difficult art of making doors and windows. He also built some furniture in his long years of working in the shop. Karl Schmoll, a native-born Austrian who never spoke a word of English, did a good deal of carving during those years, though his main vocation was painting. In 1925 the lumber shed was constructed behind the shop. The saw mill and lumber yard were moved to the north of this shed, thus centralizing the shop's activities more than ever had been before. Maximilian Schmoeller (1869–1959) was the man in charge of the shed. He was very particular about how the lumber was to be stacked. As a local resident recounted, ''He was the only one who did it right.''

This group of craftsmen was joined in 1929 by Br. Hubert Schneider, who had been asked to choose between training in shoe-making or carpentry when he entered the community. He chose carpentry because he thought there was a longer future in it. Brother Hubert worked in every aspect of carpentry in his early years and in the late '30s became head of the shop. On January 29, 1939 he and the other carpenters were faced with a major crisis. A fire broke out in the shop in the middle of the night. It destroyed the roof and upper story and severely damaged the interior. The next day the carpenters were up building a new roof so that the building would escape further damage by the elements and also retain heat. Brother Hubert recalls with a chuckle that it was the coldest winter of his life.

The traditions of Saint John's carpentry continue to the present day with basically the same dynamics that developed in Brother Andrew's day. Farm implements are no longer made. The abbey's timber has been sent to neighboring saw mills since 1958 for sawing and then brought back to Saint John's for aging. But beyond these minor changes, construction, renovation, and furniture production still vie for the attention of the shop. Significant changes in Saint John's life since the late '40s have merely accentuated these long-existing elements of the shop's life.

The great growth of the university made it necessary to call in outside carpenters for the massive building programs. Saint John's carpenters worked on support and detail work for these programs, much as they had worked on the first abbey church. The exception to this was the new monastery (1956), where all the interior carpentry, including the wooden floors, was done by the carpenter shop. It was thought important that monks work on their own house with greater intensity than they were able to invest in other new buildings. But the shop has not ceased constructing buildings, even though its role in the larger building program is an auxiliary one. Br. Philip Heitkemper built Edelbrock House and the Gagliardi residence in the '40s. John Eich supervised the building of twenty-three buildings since 1939.

The traditional job of renovation has continued to be a constant shop activity. This is a telling sign of the community's respect for the buildings left it by its forefathers. It speaks of a strong desire to adapt inherited buildings to present community needs and abhorrence at the mere thought of tearing them down.

Furniture production has continued and even grown. The expansion of buildings and activities has increased the demand for abbey-constructed furniture and a reputation gained over the years has added to the number of outside requests. Brother Hubert has concentrated his energies on this aspect of the shop's activities. Br. David Manahan worked in furniture production as well. Besides these two craftsmen, a whole host of young monks and older monks cultivating hobbies have given many hours to furniture work. Brothers Hubert and David, along with fellow carpenters Brs. Gregory Eibensteiner and Kurt Kaiser, designed much of the furniture. Other members of the Saint John's community have designed pieces later executed at the shop. Among them are Fr. Cloud Meinberg, Br. Placid Stuckenschneider, Fr. Roman Paur, Br. Alan Reed, and Br. Frank Kacmarcik. Marcel Breuer, Ray Hermanson, and Michael Keegan—all people with strong ties to Saint John's—have designed a good deal of the furniture recently produced by the carpenter shop.

The paucity of the references to Saint John's furniture in the early days and the careful documentation of the more recent past tempt the historian to judge that the carpenter shop is succumbing to the mania for categorization and specialization. There is something compelling about a piece of furniture whose designer or builder is unknown. It forces one to let the piece speak for itself and drives him back into that collective world of craftsmanship known only as the "Saint John's carpenter shop"—a group of men intent on using the resources of their land and involved in creating their living environment with their own hands. The furniture we live with speaks more eloquently of their concerns than any label or written account. It is exciting to hear talk of possible accentuation of furniture production and once again opening the shop to people anxious to learn from experience. But such prospects are also fraught with peril. If the carpenter shop becomes a low-keyed assembly line or a school, there will be fine furniture. But if its roots in this land and its place in the life of this community are lost, we will all be the poorer because of it.

This essay was written for the exhibition catalog Saint John's Furniture 1874–1974, *edited by Marcia Lavine and Thomas Williams. The entire exhibit was dedicated to Br. Hubert Schneider, then and still the venerable figure connecting the craftsmen of Saint John's founding era to the craftsmen of the current woodworking shop. A future exhibit would certainly give significant space to furniture crafted since 1974 by the shop's present director, Br. Gregory Eibensteiner, and cabinetmakers Larry Notch and Michael Roske. But it is enough, perhaps, to let this essay stand as it is. It was written by a twenty-five-year old, skittish in the presence of a band-saw, unable to drive hammer onto nail without somehow getting thumb in the way, someone who—fifteen years later—is more convinced than ever that turning timber into furniture, the chance work of nature into the crafted context for human community, is a parable of things far greater than we often realize.*

MARTIN E. SCHIRBER

MY ASSOCIATIONS WITH SAINT JOHN'S BEGAN
in the academic year 1901–02, five years before I was born. That
was the year my father Frank and his older brother Martin, the
two oldest sons of a large Millerville farm family, attended the commercial course at Saint John's Preparatory. This course was
designed to equip eighth-grade graduates with basic business skills
much in demand on the frontier.

The commercial course was offered in the prep school for farm
boys who did not feel qualified to pursue the so-called classical course
for priesthood students. It was an ingenious adaptation to the special conditions of Central Minnesota and to the frontier and made
the name of Saint John's familiar to me from my earliest years.
It was indirectly responsible for my coming to Collegeville as a student in the '20s because six of my uncles had followed that route
to prepare themselves for employment in business careers on the
frontier. They held Saint John's in high esteem.

In response to lurid descriptions of the healthfulness of the climate and fertility of the soil by the early missionary priest Fr. Francis Xavier Pierz and other pioneers, German immigrants were
pouring into Minnesota seeking homes on the land. They brought
with them their age-old Catholic culture, a love of the land, an
intense family life, and a devotion to the Catholic parish. They
adapted readily to the type of farming developing in Central

Minnesota—namely dairying. In the days before the invention of the milking machine, but after the invention of the cream separator, each pampered cow had to be milked by hand. Dairying was a labor-intensive type of farming and an extra child was looked upon not so much as an extra mouth to feed as an extra pair of hands to help with the milking and the care and feeding of the cows. This need for labor exerted an upward pressure on the size of family in Central Minnesota. Msgr. Luigi Ligutti, dynamic rural-life leader who collaborated with Saint John's in the rural-life movement in the middle decades of the twentieth century, used to maintain it is the large family which can typically spare a son for the priesthood and a daughter or son for the religious life. In any case, in due time Saint John's became the largest Benedictine monastery and Saint Benedict's the largest Benedictine convent in the world.

A confluence of these social and economic factors gave rise to the unique social enclave known as Central Minnesota, more especially Stearns County. The one element needed to complete a transplantation of an organic Catholic culture was priests to celebrate Mass, administer the sacraments, and take leadership in developing this new homeland in America. This need was perceived by Bishop Joseph Cretin of Saint Paul, who in 1856 invited Abbot Boniface Wimmer of Saint Vincent Abbey in Pennsylvania to send Benedictine monks to Minnesota—a mere ten years after the Benedictines had established their first monastery in the United States at Saint Vincent.

The little band of five Benedictines—one priest, two clerics not yet ordained, and two brothers—who answered the call, arrived in Saint Paul in May 1856. They soon moved to Saint Cloud, acquired land along the Mississippi River, established a monastery, and in 1857 received a charter from the territorial legislature to establish a seminary, later changed to "university." After the title to the land was called into question, the community picked up and moved west first to Saint Joseph, then to a site near the present Collegeville station, and eventually to the shores of Lake Sagatagan and the Watab.

What is remarkable about this westward movement of the Benedictines was that despite several changes of location, they continued without interruption the school of higher learning for the education of priests which they founded in 1857. This makes Saint John's University the oldest institution of higher learning in continuous existence in Minnesota. For the purposes of this essay, just as remarkable in the adaptation to the needs and conditions of Central Minnesota was the commercial course as a special department of the prep school in the early 1870s.

The significance of this development derives from the unique social and economic conditions of Central Minnesota. Since dairying was labor-intensive, the farms tended to be small. That was also promoted by the size of the claims (160 acres)—through which early settlers could acquire or "prove up" land at very low prices.

Another result of the type of farming was that the villages were small and close together. Fred Schilplin, a past editor of the Saint Cloud *Daily Times,* used to say that there was a hill not far from Saint Cloud from which he could count six or seven Catholic church steeples. Such proximity made it easy and natural for inter-parochial activities such as baseball games, parish festivals, barn dances, and other forms of interchange to develop.

Education was not overlooked in this transplanted village economy. As soon as the plaster was dry on the walls of the parish church, the pastor and his lay supporters would plan a parochial school. The next problem was staffing the schools. This need was met by the generous and heroic response of the sisters of Saint Benedict's Convent, Saint Joseph, and later also by the sisters of Saint Francis of Little Falls.

However, the villages of the area were too small to support a parish parochial high school. A few attempts to do so outside of a population center like Saint Cloud ended in failure; farm families had to look elsewhere if they wanted their children to progress beyond the three Rs. One way to get a higher education was to study for the priesthood or become a nun at Saint Benedict's. This is the time-honored route followed by the sons and daughters of the Kapsner family of Buckman—Fathers Celestine, Roland, and Oliver, and two of their uncles, and Sister Benedict of the Convent of Saint Benedict. But for eighth-grade graduates of the parochial schools of Central Minnesota who did not feel that they had a vocation to the priesthood or religious life, there was no readily available route to a high school education. This need was answered for boys by the commercial course at the prep school. There sons of the large farm families who saw no future in farming or didn't like what they saw could take from one to three years in bookkeeping, typing, stenography, commercial law, business correspondence, etc., along with English, geography, history, and religion. The commercial course was in effect a boarding school offering elementary business training, but it was eminently suited to the need of the time. The remarkable thing about it was how thoroughly it prepared its eager young graduates for on-the-job training.

Although my father and Uncle Martin were only seventeen and eighteen respectively when they graduated in 1902, there was no thought of returning to the farm. The remaining six brothers and four sisters were able to meet the demands of milking and providing care and feeding of the dairy herd, along with tending a big garden and orchard and a flock of hens. After graduation, therefore, my father and uncle took a breather from farm work and took advantage of the opportunity to attend a summer course in a business school in Minneapolis. Uncle Martin then found a bookkeeping job in Minneapolis. My father took Horace Greeley's advice and bought a ticket on the Milwaukee Railroad, which took him as far as his last pay-out from the Millerville farm would take him. That whistle-stop on the Milwaukee was Selby, South Dakota, the county seat of Walworth County. After fortifying himself with a sandwich and a cup of coffee since he couldn't afford a meal on the diner of the train, he walked up to the courthouse and asked if there were any job openings. The official who met him asked if he could type and take dictation. When my father answered yes, the official almost shook his arm off and told him to report for work the next morning. This warm reception was due to the fact that it was harvest time and most of the county officials were either out harvesting on their own farms or those of their daughters or sons. In later years, during the busy farm seasons, county officers would turn their keys over to my father, deputing him to answer complaints and inquiries of the local citizenry, while they pitched bundles or stacked hay.

It was not long before my father found a more promising opportunity in the bank at Mound City, the seat of Campbell County, twenty miles north of Selby. He also became county abstracter, a service he provided for many years and which gave him a broad education in real estate sales and transfers. He had not been in the bank at Mound City very long before he was invited to participate in the organization of the State Bank of Herreid, seven miles north of Mound City. The group of businessmen promoting this venture were looking for a young live wire to head up the new banking operation, and my father suggested Uncle Martin, who was still holding down the bookkeeping job in Minneapolis. He was given an opportunity to buy stock in the bank and was elected cashier and manager of the Herreid State Bank, a post he held until the bank fell victim to the twin disasters of drought and depression in the '30s.

But before those calamities there was a parade of Schirbers to the frontier. In the prosperous times preceding and during World War I, conditions seemed favorable for founding another bank in an unbanked town. This was Artas, sixteen miles east of Herreid. It was then Uncle Nick's turn to come west and head up a bank organized by his two older brothers and local businessmen. Uncle Nick graduated from the Saint John's commercial course in 1910 and was hoping for something to break. While waiting he came out to South Dakota and took on-the-job training in the Mound City Bank. He paid for his board and room with our family by providing professional care to the family cow Julia, who had sole access to the forty-acre pasture back of the family home in Mound City.

Julia was mercifully freed from the rigorous discipline of Uncle Nick, who had grown up on the Millerville farm making cows toe the mark, when his older brothers recommended him for the position of cashier and manager of the bank at Artas. He held this position until the Artas bank also fell victim to drought and depression.

Next in line was Peter who finished the same commercial course in 1915. The older brothers and their associates organized a bank for him on the real frontier—at Glencross across the Missouri River from Mobridge. Meantime the brothers and their associates had bought out the First National Bank of Mobridge and elected my father president in the early '20s. This is why my last mailing address as a layman was Mobridge, South Dakota.

The next three brothers reached high school age in the '20s. By that time the commercial course had been absorbed into the prep school curriculum, so they enjoyed the luxury of a standard high school education strongly laced with subjects like bookkeeping, business law, typing, etc. The increase in the family income as a result of keeping records of production, weeding out "boarder" cows, and raising more corn and alfalfa as feed made it possible to hire additional workers at peak times, thereby releasing the last crop of Schirbers for four years at Saint John's Prep.

The first uncle to finish the expanded course was Leo, who graduated in 1922. The brothers had run out of banks by that time but had other enterprises which needed staffing. One of these was the Ford dealership and garage in Herreid, and Leo was soon installed as manager of that operation. By careful cost control, Leo survived the depression, and in the late '30s bought out a larger dealership and garage in Mobridge. I no longer used the term of address "Uncle" when speaking to or referring to this younger crop of uncles. None of them is much older than I.

Two younger brothers, Richard and Al, completed the prep school program in 1927 and in due time took on-the-job training at the Artas State Bank under Uncle Nick. But drought and preliminary rumblings of the Great Depression made the opening of a new bank in the Dakotas a risky undertaking. Richard and Al therefore looked elsewhere for greener pastures. Richard ended up as the chief officer of the Warren State Bank, Warren, Minnesota, and Al opened a public accounting office in Jamestown, North Dakota.

By 1929 the Great Depression struck with unprecedented fury, and along with it came drought and grasshoppers. Several thousand small unit state banks succumbed under these twin disasters with repercussions similar to the wave of failures of the savings and loan associations in the 1980s, except that the federal government had not at that time guaranteed bank deposits, and the depositors took it on the chin. The banks at Herreid, Mound City, and Artas all were obliged to close their doors. The First National Bank of Mobridge was saved by selling it to the Northwest Bancorporation, now called Norwest Banks, after the stockholders had removed the questionable paper. Because of his reputation as a careful banker, the new stockholders elected Uncle Pete to take my father's place as president and eventually promoted him to the presidency of the larger James River National Bank of Jamestown, a position he held until near the end of his life.

One other Schirber bank survived the disasters of the '30s. That was the Glencross State Bank managed by Pete until he became president of the First National Bank of Mobridge. After the depression the Glencross bank was moved to Timber Lake and re-named the Dewey County Bank, and Uncle Martin and Uncle Nick became its chief officers until after World War II. For a time since then it was owned by a group of investors who were not Schirbers or graduates of the commercial course. More recently it came again into the hands of Uncle Nick's son Walter '39 and his son, Walter, Jr. '64, who is now vice president and chief executive officer.

Only one of the seven Schirber brothers did not attend Saint John's. In the mid '20s my grandfather sold the Millerville farm and moved to Saint Cloud. John, the youngest brother, and Rose, the youngest daughter, attended Saint Cloud Tech, and John went on to earn a B.A. in math at Saint Cloud State. He taught math in the Saint Cloud school system until his retirement in the early '80s. He followed his seven brothers into eternity in 1987.

With this set of precedents, it is not surprising that it was taken for granted that I, as the first of the second generation, would attend Saint John's, presumably to take a pre-legal course and then go to law school to become legal counsel to my banker father and uncles. Uncle Martin promoted this idea by starting a savings account for me on my first birthday and adding to it each year after that, and I added to it whenever my cash flow would permit. One particularly hefty addition occurred as a result of the gift from my father of Julia's bull calf about 1916. My father allowed me to sell the animal along with a shipment of steers from a Schirber brothers' farm when it reached maturity. That bumped up my savings account by 25 or 30 percent.

In 1926 I entered Saint John's along with my stepbrother Mahlon Gann, who became a football star under Coach Joe Benda and helped Saint John's win its first championship in the Minnesota Intercollegiate Conference. I didn't tell anyone that I was thinking of the priesthood, but I registered for Latin along with the standard pre-legal course. That probably tipped off Fr. Mark Braun, dean of the college, because at the end of our mid-year retreat he called me down for an interview. Despite my somewhat unpriestly style of life, in a masterpiece of counseling, he got me to admit that I wanted to study for the priesthood. He said he wasn't surprised and would arrange for me to take additional Latin with Fr. Clarus Graves, dedicated language teacher, as my tutor.

I absorbed the additional Latin and signed up for an advanced course in my sophomore year. After the retreat Father Mark again called me down for an interview. This time by delicate questioning he got me to admit that I would like to engage in teaching and study, and I asked him if he thought the bishop of Sioux Falls would like to have a priest teach in one of the diocesan high schools. Father Mark said he was sure that the bishop would welcome such a prospect and offered to write to his friend the chancellor of the diocese about it.

Then he asked me if I had ever thought of joining an order like the Holy Cross Fathers who run the University of Notre Dame. No such thought had ever crossed my mind, but every red-blooded American boy knew about Notre Dame, Knute Rockne, George Gipp, the Four Horsemen, etc. My interest was aroused and I asked Father Mark more questions. He told me that after their fourth year of college, the young members of the Holy Cross Congregation study theology and are then ordained. After that they are sent to study in a special field to prepare themselves to do research and teach in the university. They live a community life under a superior and enjoy the intellectual stimulation of communal life while presumably making progress toward eternity. He never mentioned that I could find much the same sort of regime at Saint John's—perish the thought. He just let me come to that conclusion on my own. Our interview ended up something like this:

>"You priests live together and engage in study and teaching, don't you?"
>
>"Yes."
>
>"You can do priestly work along with teaching, can't you?"
>
>"Yes."
>
>"Well, why shouldn't I become a Benedictine?"

He said he could see no reason why not and offered to arrange an interview with Abbot Alcuin. His masterly counseling consisted mostly in asking me carefully framed questions that helped me to think about my future and come to a realization of what I wanted to do.

Since I had had a rather pieced-together training in Latin, Abbot Alcuin judged that I ought to have a test in that language. He picked up his breviary, opened it at random, and asked me to translate the psalm (thank heavens it was not an abstract discourse by

Saints Augustine or Leo) on the righthand page. I passed that test satisfactorily, and on July 10, 1928 had my hair clipped down to one-sixteenth of an inch, was invested with the Benedictine habit, and entered upon the happiest year of my life.

I said that Father Mark made me see the obvious parallels between Saint John's and Notre Dame. That is true, but there are differences. After living the monastic life for one year, and even more so after sixty years under the gentle yoke of the *Rule,* I have become more and more impressed with the uniqueness of the Benedictine way of life—its simplicity, moderation, humaneness. I could illustrate my appreciation for this community life by a couple of incidents of my experience. In the fall of '29, just after I had emerged from the novitiate, my Uncle Al '27, came up from Minneapolis for a football game. As a fledgling monk I was eager to share my enthusiasm for the religious life with anyone who would listen. Al made this easy to do by commiserating me for sealing myself off from all that was worth living for. This was before the stock market crash of '29, and Al was a typical product of the "roaring twenties." He really felt sorry for me for passing up all the fun and excitement of that gilded age. My reaction to his misplaced sympathy was simply the one-liner: "Al, I've got more brothers than the ordinary man has friends." Al never forgot my *apologia* for the way of life I had chosen.

Many years later, in August 1979 to be exact, as an accompaniment to the election of Abbot Jerome Theisen as eighth abbot of Saint John's, the community held a discussion as to the direction in which Saint John's was going and where change of direction was needed if we were veering off course. I wanted to give emphasis to my conviction that Saint John's—any Benedictine monastery in fact— is primarily a community in which all members have much in common, look upon each other as brothers, and support one another in our quest for spiritual and other kinds of fulfillment. I therefore sprung the one-liner I had used on Uncle Al fifty years before: "I have more brothers than the ordinary man has friends." The assembled brethren seemed impressed by this aphorism coming from such an unexpected source and wove it into the ensuing discussion.

I could illustrate this brotherliness of the members of a community living under the *Rule* of Benedict. One of our confreres is not a born Catholic, but after observing Benedictines at one of our larger parishes, he decided to become a Catholic so that he could become a Benedictine, which he did.

Additional evidence as to the brotherliness of the Benedictine way of life is the result of observation. This brotherliness of members to one another and to our students, friends, alumni, and hangers-on in general was enhanced at Saint John's by the prefect system beginning in the prep school and continuing through college. The prefects, in this more refined age called "faculty residents," live among the students, play on their intramural teams, and get just as mad at members of opposing teams as the students do themselves. One of the present community members still limps and carries a cane as the result of a block thrown by Ray Fesenmaier '51 of New Ulm in a touchball game. And if any of the prefects had to coach a prep football team and fielded a team which ran up against another intramural team coached by Fr. Pirmin Wendt, he learned the meaning of humility.

There were many other associations between students and prefects and members of the community in such activities as dramatics, band and orchestra, as well as water sports on the lake and winter sports on the ski hills. The prefect was the key element in this student-faculty relationship, a bond that persisted for years after the students had become alumni.

The warmth and attractiveness of the Benedictine way of life has been noted and dwelt upon by many writers of recent times. One of the most eloquent of these is Esther de Waal, wife of the dean of Canterbury in England and mother of four sons. After living for years in the shadow of the cathedral of Canterbury—"in the context of that greatness" of the past—she finally felt impelled to read the *Rule* of Benedict in order to derive a deeper understanding of the thinking that went into the development of such greatness. This changed her whole outlook and served as the inspiration for a perceptive look at Benedictinism. In her book *Seeking God* she summarizes the distinctive qualities of the way of Saint Benedict by quoting from Thomas Merton, "who wrote of 'that concern with doing ordinary things quietly and perfectly for the glory of God which is the beauty of the pure Benedictine life.' "[1]

1. Esther de Waal, *Seeking God: the Way of Saint Benedict* (Collegeville: The Liturgical Press, 1983) 30.

ONE EVENING A COUPLE OF YEARS AGO A freshman dropped in at my dorm room to fulfill an assignment he had, to interview one of the Benedictines. One of his first questions was: "How long have you been here at Saint John's?" Since he was sitting down I thought it safe to tell him: "About forty years." This eighteen-year-old's response, loaded with amazement, was, "Holy smoke!" After he had recovered a bit he asked: "Are there others who have been here longer?" There are, and after I had told him that he was practically speechless.

In my own way I'm impressed by the fact too. To have found a place and life which, despite unsatisfactory and even exasperating moments, has been so congenial seems to fulfill the desires and hopes of many a person. A happy marriage seems to do the same; a position or occupation too which is satisfying and enduring is similar.

Getting there (or here) was, as I presume most happily married couples can also attest, not always easy or smooth. The unforgettable Fr. Walter Reger arranged for me to come to Saint John's when there were some considerable difficulties to overcome. Once here as a freshman, attending a Catholic school for the first time in my life and going more than three blocks to school also for the first time in my life, I was very homesick and sorely tempted to quit. The situation taught me a lot about prayer of petition, as well as about endurance and perseverance. My first possible visit home was at Thanksgiving. After returning to Saint John's I began experiencing a growing attachment. I had come here with an interest in religious life. During my first three years I investigated different types of religious life but finally applied for entrance into the Saint John's monastic community. And forty some years later . . . .

As the free spirits or footloose among us (or, probably more correctly, within all of us) would remind us, all this stability and contentment with a life and place means you have closed off other options and at least risk smugness. Does stability equal self-satisfaction?

Many of us at Saint John's, myself included, have had and do have opportunities to distance ourselves from the place and experience other possibilities. My early life as an ordained member of the Saint John's community brought two years of teaching and parish work in the Bahamas, plus two years in a parish in the Bronx, New York. After returning to Collegeville to be college chaplain and to teach, I spent five summers at The Catholic University in Washington, D.C. After ten years at Saint John's, I went to graduate school in the Berkeley of the late '60s. While there I was awarded a trip to the Orient to visit and study at Hindu and Buddhist sites, in fact, had a trip around the world. After another ten years at Saint John's, most of it again spent as chaplain, I had a sabbatical year in Paris and repeated that after another seven years of teaching.

I detail all these movements to suggest that my attachment to Saint John's, its people and the place, is not simply the result of ignorance of other possibilities, places, and persons. Despite the fact that I cannot imagine a more delightful climate and exhilarating atmosphere than the Bay Area or a more endlessly fascinating city than Paris, I have returned—a number of times now— to Saint John's with the conviction that it is the place where I can grow and work best.

Like any life that involves commitment and a concomitant routine, monastic and academic life also have the danger of not only becoming smug but also dead and lacking in innovation, closed to change. Despite my own failures in these areas—it is always a battle—I am very proud of the steps Saint John's has taken especially since Vatican II to carry out the hopes of the great Pope John XXIII that the Church and its life be updated, made more open and more responsive to genuine, human values in the world around us, especially among Protestant Christians and Jews and even in the other world religions.

The American poet Wendell Berry has a wonderful line to the effect that it is only the impeded stream that sings. The boundaries and promises of a commitment, despite the way they seem to cut off other choices, are what channel and direct our powers and abilities and give us some joy in their exercise. The impediments of a committed life, whether in marriage or religious life, drive us to practice the qualities or virtues of perseverance, forbearance, patience, mutual respect, etc., which otherwise remain simply dreams and imaginings.

Whether we succeed in all these is not as important, it seems to me, as the fact that we stay committed to trying to practice them with *these* people, in this situation, rather than continually running off to supposedly greener pastures (back to that poet—Benedictines do sing a lot).

I can't conclude this without saying that even more than the beautiful setting, the easily accessible woods, it has been the people I've met and come to know at Saint John's who are absolutely priceless and irreplaceable, from fellow members of the community, living and dead, (among the latter, Frs. Walter Reger, Conrad Diekmann, Michael Blecker, Ivan Havener) to the students who fortunately so often are able to see their relation to us as much more than that of client or consumer to producer or vendor.

For one who has lived in student dorms for many years, as a prefect or faculty resident, it's always a delight when the student-Benedictine relationship is not that of inmate and warden. Probably the most satisfying aspect of my academic life at Collegeville has been being able to retain as friends at least some of the extraordinary students who have spent their college years here. Like the many other loving people in our lives, they are signs of God's love for us, these people who light up our life when present and whose memory does the same when they're gone. Conversely, the greatest sadness of academic life at Saint John's is seeing so many students leave year after year and knowing that some of them will never or very rarely be heard from again. Because Saint John's is such a place for us Benedictines, we always hope it's something similar to and for our students and alumni.

Fr. Walter Reger

VINCENT G. TEGEDER

ON MAY 20, 1856 WHEN THE FIRST BENEDICTINES arrived at Sauk Rapids, in the Minnesota Territory, they entered a unique geographic region. The impact of the glaciers was evident on all sides. As one Minnesota historian has colorfully observed: "The real Blue Ox that left footprints on the land was not the fabled animal of a mythical Paul Bunyan, but snow and ice, forming, moving, melting" over a myriad of centuries.[1] As a result majestic rivers appeared, such as the Mississippi, on whose west bank two miles south of the present Saint Germain Mall in Saint Cloud, Minnesota, the early Saint John's community was located. Central Minnesota eventually was transformed into an area of lakes, forests, and rich prairie farming land. Granite beds, too, varying from steel gray to red in color, and very accessible for quarrying were found close to the surface. Clay deposits abounded. The manufacture of bricks would become commonplace.

After ten years of wandering back and forth from the original Saint Cloud site which was in litigation, the pioneer monks of Saint John's located permanently in an area which exhibited additional glacial features.[2] It was inland, about fourteen miles northwest of

1. Theodore C. Blegen, *Minnesota: A History of the State* (Minneapolis: University of Minnesota Press, 1963) 9.
2. Colman J. Barry, *Worship and Work: Saint John's Abbey and University, 1856–1980* (Collegeville: The Liturgical Press, 1980) 51–52. This is a basic study of the history of the Benedictines in the upper Midwest. Cf. also Vincent G. Tegeder, "Benedictines in Frontier Minnesota," *Minnesota History* 32 (Spring 1951) 34–43.

the 1856 river foundation. Large isolated granite boulders sometimes measuring five to ten feet in length dotted the terrain. There
were also heavily wooded sections on the claims. One of the major
features of the community's new location was a picturesque lake
that covered about 360 acres. It was first known as Saint Louis
Lake in honor of ex-King Louis I of Bavaria, an early patron of
the German Benedictines in America. It was likewise referred to
as Saint John's Lake, especially by the pioneer students. In 1896
the name Sagatagan, an Ojibway word, was popularized by Fr.
Alexius Hoffmann, a noted archivist and interpreter of the early
history of Saint John's. He was of the opinion that the term means
"spunk" or "punk," a shelf-like hard fungus used for tinder and
obtained by the Indians from trees near the lake before the appearance of the early settlers.[3]

Another story comes from the diary of Abbot Peter Engel. We
read under July 16, 1920:

> Today "John Smith" the oldest Chippewa Indian living (they say
> he is 130 years and his wrinkled face indicates it) was here on a
> short visit. He used to be around here before Saint John's was
> thought of. He said that our lake was called "Sagatagan" not be-
> cause there was a greater amount of punk-Sagatagan found around
> it but because an Indian by the name of Sagatagan was buried in
> its south shore.[4]

Fr. Bruno Riss, one of the original band of monks entering Minnesota in 1856, always considered the Sagatagan the prize of the
claims that he filed for the benefit of the community. The lake has
been outstanding in the development of Saint John's. The great
complex of buildings beginning with the Old Stone House and the
quadrangle and culminating with the completion of the spacious
Saint John's Abbey and University Church in 1961 was placed
near the north shore of the lake. From the adjacent hills came the
red clay which would be kilned into bricks for future buildings.
Countless numbers of students would experience joy and relaxation on its placid waters, and on its western slope the monks would
find their final resting place on earth. Saint John's truly grew up
"High Above the Sagatagan," as the university song proclaims.

3. Saint John's Abbey Archives [hereafter cited as SJAA]. Alexius Hoffmann,
"Natural History of Collegeville, Minnesota, ms. (1934) 22.
4. SJAA, Peter Engel "Diary: 1916–1920."

The claims which Father Bruno and his associates legally established during the pioneer period eventually provided the community with approximately twenty-nine hundred acres of land and water located now in four townships of Stearns County: Collegeville, Avon, Saint Wendel, and Saint Joseph. Fr. Alexius Hoffmann described how these holdings were acquired:

> Our community, or better, members of it, acquired this property by claiming it under the Federal Pre-Emption laws, partly by means of Land Warrants issued to soldiers after the Mexican War (1846–47). Soldiers (ex-soldiers) holding such warrants did not care to have land and consequently sold their warrants. These were in the market in the '50s and '60s of the last century and Abbot B. Wimmer purchased a number of them, giving them to various members of our early community, who filed for lands and paid for them with these warrants.[5]

These land transactions by Abbot Boniface in part involved the use of 3,000 *gulden* ($1,280) contributed by King Ludwig I of Bavaria for the benefit of the sisters of Saint Benedict who had just arrived in Saint Cloud and were not firmly established. Abbot Boniface as their protector decided at this point to use the funds to purchase some of the military warrants which were on the market at a favorable price but had to be purchased immediately. He explained his action in a series of letters to King Ludwig and received royal approval for the way he had disposed of these funds.

The early superiors of Saint John's, particularly Prior Othmar Wirtz and later Abbot Alexius Edelbrock, were very conscious of this action by Abbot Boniface in 1858 and began early to aid the sisters once they had obtained official ecclesiastical approval for the establishment of a Benedictine women's foundation in central Minnesota. Prior Othmar built the first frame convent in Saint Joseph in 1863 with funds from Saint John's. In 1881 Abbot Alexius provided the bricks kilned on the abbey grounds for the first unit of the present convent.[6]

5. SJAA, Alexius Hoffmann, "Natural History of Collegeville, Minnesota," 1934.

6. Cf. Letters in Sr. M. Incarnata Girgen, O.S.B., *Behind the Beginnings: Benedictine Women in America* (Saint Joseph, Minnesota: Saint Benedict's Convent, 1981) concerning the use of funds designated by King Ludwig I of Bavaria for the sisters of Saint Benedict in Saint Cloud and their appropriation by Abbot Boniface

Although this property now in the Lake Sagatagan area may appear in size to resemble a baronial estate, it is well to note, as Father Alexius did, that "it is for the greater part poor soil, covered with small lakes or ponds, marshes and timber that is used for fuel."[7] The better farming land in the vicinity was left for acquisition by the German immigrants.

The hills, stones, forests, and lakes on this property proved especially suitable for a college environment. Many unique opportunities for sharing the benefits of a scenic campus were developed. Walks, paths in the woods, and lawns featuring outstanding floral designs have always been a Saint John's tradition.

Brs. Placid Tlusty and Maurus Held for many years proved to be outstanding designers of flower beds on the front lawns. Their floral creations were eagerly awaited each spring and became a colorful summer feature of the campus.[8]

In the woods nearby a series of paths were early laid out. They became a favorite walking area for generations of students. The course was referred to as going "Round the Beat." The distances involved could be covered in about twenty minutes. A local poet proclaimed joyfully:

> And their arches overhead
> Tame grim winter's chilling breath
> And summer's heat.
> There's no walk that will compare
> With that humble path we wear

Wimmer for the purchases of some of the holdings of the monks in the Lake Sagatagan area in 1859. Cf. Wimmer to King Ludwig, (December 12, 1858) 133–34; Mueller to Wimmer (May 15, 1859) 140–41; Wimmer to Ludwig (April 5, 1859) 141–42; Wimmer to Ludwig (April 9, 1859) 142–50; Ludwig to Wimmer (May 29, 1859) 150; Mueller to Wimmer (June 1, 1859) 151. See statement in a ms. written by Fr. Alexius Hoffmann in 1934; cited by Girgen, 181–82. See also Barry, *Worship and Work*, 53–54, 62–65.

7. *Ibid.* Br. Innocent Kratz checked the precise location of the various claims in the '40s. He left a massive set of notes and charts, which are now in the Saint John's Abbey archives. The 2,900-acre figure has been reduced over the years. As of November 6, 1979, the property held by Saint John's now is 2,541.01 acres. Statement of Fr. James Tingerthal, director of corporate enterprises, to Fr. Vincent Tegeder, November 6, 1979.

8. Br. Placid Tlusty died on June 26, 1947 and Br. Maurus Held on January 19, 1950.

As we make our daily circuit
"Round the Beat."

The woodlands on the Saint John's property are still extensive
and diverse. They first featured tamarack, cedars, birch, oak,
maple, poplar and some pines. However, many of the pioneer members of the community came from Bavaria where conifers abounded.
They proved to be very forestry-minded and encouraged the planting of pines. Frs. John Katzner and Adrian Schmitt, and later Br.
Ansgar Niess, fostered the development of a nursery and the regular
planting of a great variety of pine trees, such as white, Scotch, jack,
Austrian, red and ponderosa pine, Norway and white spruce, Douglas and balsam fir, and northern white cedar. More than 117 acres
of trees were planted as the years advanced. More than 1,500 acres
of the total property are still in forest. This aspect of the campus
is so striking that students still refer to Saint John's as the "school
behind the pine curtain." Today a very visible evergreen border
lines the eastern approach along I-94 as the motorist approaches
the Saint John's exit. In the development of these tree plantations,
Saint John's had the benefit of much advice and forest planting
stock from the Division of Forestry of the State of Minnesota.[9]

Cuttings of these trees have frequently been at the rate of 55,000
board feet per year. Sawmill operations have also been a regular
feature of the Collegeville scene until recently. After a hiatus, Fr.
Paul Schwietz, land manager, started cuttings again in 1985–86.

According to one description:

> Workmen combed the woods during the winter season and culled
> out the mature trees and hauled them to a spot about where Ber-
> nard Hall now stands. Here for a few weeks in spring, before the
> farm was quite ready for the ploughs, Br. Julius Terfehr and work-
> men cut the logs for the presumed needs of the carpenter shop. The
> steam engine burned up the sidings from the logs and made more
> steam to rip more logs into usable sizes. For students and monks
> the scene became the place of daily pilgrimage in a period when
> the puffing of the steamer was the most excitement on the campus.[10]

9. Henry L. Hansen and Lawrence B. Ritter, "St. John's Forest Plantations,"
The Conservation Volunteer 14 (May–June 1951) 28–30. See also Saint John's *Record* 54 (October 16, 1941).

10. SJUA, Alfred Deutsch, *St. John's Furniture, 1874–1974* (A Centennial Booklet). Other articles therein dealing with the history and products of the carpenter
shop are by Br. Dietrich Reinhart and the former Br. Austin Gray.

With the availability of this regular supply of lumber, the basic material for new buildings and shops was at hand and the wood from the forests could be worked into quality furniture such as study tables, chairs, bookshelves, and wardrobes. In the production of these articles, Br. Hubert Schneider has been a guiding force for over forty years. Possibly the most extensive contract which he and his dedicated staff of workmen and monks undertook was the preparation of flooring, wardrobes, and bookshelves for the new monastery wing built in 1955. At that time "30,000 feet of flooring screamed through the machine, and the sound delighted the ears of monks who lived in memory of self-subsistence and remembered that Benedict wrote "for then they are truly monks when they live by the labor of their hands, as did our Fathers and the Apostles."[11]

The Saint John's woods also have produced a regular supply of high quality maple syrup. Periodically in the spring, usually during April when the temperature is freezing at night but is warm during the day, maple trees are tapped. The warm daytime air and the nightly freezing causes the sap to run up and down the trees. The spout inserted in a hole drilled into the tree catches the sap, which is deposited in the attached bags. This sap is boiled down into syrup. As recently as 1985, 1,900 catchbags were set out, producing 22,000 gallons of sap, 549 gallons of syrup. According to Brs. Michael Laux, Arnold Jirik, Walter Kieffer, and Frs. Sebastian Schramel, Fintan Bromenshenkel, and Julian Schmiesing, veteran directors of the operations, it takes about forty gallons of sap to make one gallon of pure syrup. The finished product is used in the monastery or given away as a choice gift from the community.[12]

The Saint John's forests and campus have long resounded with the cries and songs of birds. Local watchers have recorded their observations. Some of the common species are chickadees, orioles, woodpeckers, swallows, bobolinks, shrikes, larks, martins, loons, hawks, blue herons, Canada geese, scarlet tanagers, bluejays, and owls, along with robins, sparrows, and crows. Fowl, such as ducks, quail, grouse, pheasants, and snipe also inhabit the woods.[13]

11. *Ibid.* 7.
12. Cf. "Maple Syrup Is Sweet Ending to Springtime Tradition in St. John's Woods," *The Saint Cloud Visitor* (April 13, 1978) 5.
13. SJAA, Lambert Thelen, "Ornithological Notes, 1894-98."

The presence of so many birds in the Collegeville area has encouraged the monks to provide for their care by constructing bird houses of all types and styles. Possibly the prize creation is a three-story house constructed by Fr. Maurice Hurrle in the '30s, which is still located on a platform overlooking the west shore of Lake Sagatagan. It contains dozens of openings for martins. Students have named it "The Saint John's Bird Hotel."

The environment has also encouraged the care and taming of animals. Gray squirrels, raccoons, ducks, and deer have often been adopted and fed by animal-loving monks. Fr. Sylvester Harter had his tame squirrel "Patsy"; Fr. Corbinian Hermanutz, a pen of raccoons; Br. Edward Zwak, a flock of ducks; and Br. Michael Hurth, Fr. Joachim Watrin, and Abbot John Eidenschink several fawns which they nursed between 1950 and the '70s. The deer were given such names as Mike, Echo, Abigail, Jubilee (who was found during the monastery's centennial year of 1956), and Heidi.

The campus has likewise featured colorful shrines, grottoes, and a striking lakeside chapel. The latter construction has had a long history at Saint John's. In 1872 the younger members of the community under the direction of Fr. Vincent Schiffrer resolved to build a chapel on the south shore of Lake Sagatagan. They worked energetically and by the end of the summer the project was finished. It had Gothic lines and measured 16 by 12 feet. It had some ornamental brick work on the exterior and a wooden spire which was painted white. It was commonly known as the *Stella Maris* Chapel.[14] Humble as its appearance may have been, it caught the interest of Dr. Hermann Zschokke, chaplain to the Austrian Imperial Court and rector of the University of Vienna, when he visited the campus in 1880. In a book which he published under the title of *Nach Amerika und Canada*, he wrote glowingly in the Victorian prose of the period:

> On the shore of the lake there stands a small chapel surrounded by trees, *Stella Maris*—built by the students in honor of the Mother of God. It was a sunset picture so exquisite that one could not imagine anything more perfect. The sun, which had just disappeared below the horizon, poured a flood of orange hued light over the western sky; the placid lake caught and mirrored the glorious light

14. Erwin M. Kuehne, "Chapel Island," Saint John's *Record* (April 29, 1916) 215.

which transfigured the thick foliage of the forest; from its height the little chapel looked calmly upon the scene; and when, finally, the bell sounded the *Ave Maria*, and its voice was wafted over the woods, I found myself transported in spirit back into the early centuries, when the sons of Saint Benedict penetrated with holy zeal into the wilderness, cut down forests, founded monasteries, enkindled everywhere the light of faith and civilized Europe.[15]

As time advanced, ready access was provided for visiting this woodland shrine. In 1892 a path leading "Round the Beat" and along the shore to Chapel Island was developed. This picturesque edifice stood on this site until 1903 when a fire broke out in the vicinity and the flames destroyed it. In 1915 it was rebuilt. This time the chapel was constructed of red cement blocks in the old Romanesque style with a very visible steeple. A series of white steps with balustrades led from the landing place on the lakeshore to the hill on which the shrine is located. This structure, although renovated a number of times— the latest 1988—still stands and remains a notable feature of the skyline of the south shore of Lake Sagatagan.[16]

Another aspect of the development of the Collegeville site was farming.[17] For many years barns, silos, stables, and machine sheds were familiar sights on the grounds. Gardens, orchards, apiaries, vineyards, and grain fields received much attention and care. The maintenance of a large herd of milk cows, beef cattle, hogs, and chickens definitely affected the diet of the monks and students. Farming and food processing made Saint John's economically quite self-sufficient during its first fifty years. Wholesome home-grown food was regularly available at mealtime.

In the peak period of farming about two hundred and fifty acres were under cultivation and approximately one hundred and thirty additional acres were used for pasture. Rye, barley, and oats were the major crops until the '30s when corn and alfalfa were also important. Potatoes, too, were planted, producing about six thousand bushels in a favorable year. A large "truck" garden of nearly

15. *Ibid.* 215–16.
16. *Ibid.* 216–17.
17. The township of Collegeville was organized in 1880. It was so named in view of the existence of Saint John's College in section 1. Cf. William B. Mitchell, *History of Stearns County, Minnesota* (Chicago: Cooper, 1915) 2:1265-66.

ten acres yielded a variety of vegetables, such as celery, lettuce onions, carrots, cabbage, and melons. This produce was stored in a huge root cellar and could be drawn upon daily to satiate the appetites of the monks and students.[18]

Until the advent of the ubiquitous tractor, much of the farm work was done with draft horses. George Klein, a long-time farm employee at Saint John's and supervisor of field operations from 1937 to 1943, loved to recall how an early procurator (the abbey business manager), Fr. Herman Bergmann, proved to be an excellent judge of animals. He always made certain that the stock was of superior quality.[19]

A dairy herd under the supervision of Br. William Borgerding was also an important element in the Saint John's farm experience. It was carefully developed and was composed of Holsteins with superior blood lines. It was one of the finest herds in the state. Buyers would come from all sections of central Minnesota whenever young bull calves from this herd were offered for sale. At one time this herd numbered about one hundred and fifty with approximately eighty milkers. A pasteurization plant was installed in the '30s. Quality and approved milk was thus regularly available for local consumption.[20]

A beef herd was also maintained, at times numbering 150. The cows and steers, know as "canners," were fattened and then processed in the abbey butcher shop under the expert management of Br. Ansgar Niess. Before the advent of a complete refrigeration plant, ice was the usual preservative. As a result, an annual feature of the winter at Saint John's was the ice harvest on Lake Sagatagan. For three days most of the work force cut ice and stored it in a large ice house for use during the rest of the year.[21]

Due to the changing economy during and after World War II, farm costs tended to mount excessively. A monastic group studied the picture carefully:

> It is becoming increasingly more difficult to keep losses at a minimum because of rising labor costs. When these enterprises were

18. SJUA, Jeffrey S. Meyer, "A Short History of Farming at St. John's," ms. (1975) 9.

19. *Ibid.* 8.

20. *Ibid.* 9.

21. *Ibid.*

introduced and expanded, labor was a relatively minor item in the total cost of the product; today labor costs are becoming an increasingly major factor of product cost. In addition, two other factors have changed the picture, making our semi-self sufficiency too costly: (a) mass production, (b) advancements in transportation. As related to our enterprises, this means that many of our operations have become uneconomical, as compared to competing mass produced commodities and unnecessary, because truck transportation has brought things right to our door. We do not say that farming has become generally uneconomical, but it has become such for us. The wages of farm labor have risen to the level of other labor; we are unable to produce a sufficient quantity of feeds, which demands that we purchase raw materials and feeds in a controlled market; and we are dissipating our managerial and investment potential. . . .[22]

Some of the conclusions of this investigation were (1) the Saint John's pasteurization operation was non-economical. The cost per quart of milk was more than twice that of the dairies in the Saint Cloud area. (2) The feed requirements for the care of the present herd far surpassed that furnished by the farm. (3) Currently 38 percent of the fresh milk needed was being purchased from a Saint Cloud dairy. (4) Sell the dairy herd and go into beef raising. (5) The hog farm should be sold; this enterprise has consistently lost money.[23]

As a result of this study, farming operations were drastically reduced. At present only a few acres are devoted to a small garden. Instead of horses and tractors, large produce trucks are daily appearances in Collegeville.[24]

Thus, over the years since 1866 when the monks established the abbey and school "high above the Sagatagan," the features of the Collegeville environment have been utilized for monastic, educational, and agricultural purposes. The woods and lakes have offered opportunities for meditation and reflection; the scenic features have enhanced campus life and activities; and the soil has yielded daily

22. SJAA, Report on the Farm and Shops Commission to the Building Committee (May 25, 1953) 1-2.
23. *Ibid.* 3-4.
24. Although farming may no longer hold the importance that it did at Saint John's during the first half of the present century, definite achievements can be recorded, particularly in the areas of horticulture and crop yields.

sustenance during the formative years. So outstanding has the site been that monks and students early gloried in the cry: "The school in the heart of a landscape paradise."

Fr. Alfred Deutsch

Lee Hanley

.

BY FOCUSING ON WHAT SAINT JOHN'S HAS
meant and means to me, I hope to clarify to some extent what this
monastery means for the Church and society. I did not come to
Saint John's in 1949 because I was cognizant of the monastic life
or because I wanted to enter the monastery in Collegeville. I came
because Saint John's University was recommended to me as a place
where I could receive an accelerated course in Latin. In those days
the equivalent of six years of Latin was required for entry into the
major seminary. I came to study Latin and I discovered a special
place. I was particularly attracted to the sense of community which
I found on campus; the monks, the students, the support staff, all
seemed to form one large family. I experienced no difficulty in mesh-
ing my life with the routine of the place: worship, sacred reading,
meditation, study, work, sports, music, recreation. I found monks
leading the way in all of these areas. The place fit and its routine
made sense. I became a novice in 1951.

Upon entering the monastery I came to realize only gradually
that what looked like a well-ordered and coherent monastic life had
many flaws and drawbacks. Some rules and practices seemed to
foster immaturity: no newspapers or radio, little privacy, rushed
psalmody, etc. I also found that the men in uniform, the monks,
were not uniform. Some were zealous, most were steady, some were
lax, at least in the standards of those days. Monks were people of

diverse talents, moods, friendliness, and capacities to work. No two monks were alike in spite of the same monastic profession. Behold, I discovered the monastery was like a family or a group in society with diverse members, most functional but some dysfunctional.

The life was regular and athletic; it required a sound body and a willingness to live with others in close quarters. We lived next to each other, we prayed next to each other, we studied next to each other, we worked next to each other; but we did not engage each other very deeply in exchanges about the meaning of prayer or the monastic life. The life tended to be more objective than subjective. It formed us by its routine. I learned that monastic life is a way of living; I learned by living with others.

My monastic world was expanded considerably when I was sent to Rome to pursue theological studies at the Collegio di Sant' Anselmo, the international school for Benedictines. I was exposed to Benedictine observances of various types, some like our own at Saint John's, some very enclosed, some outward looking in missionary activity, etc. I heard some European monks state that the members of Saint John's were not true monks because they were too active, too engaged in education, parochial life, and missionary activity. I had to assimilate these statements. At first I was defensive, then I no longer cared about the negative judgments of Saint John's. I came to realize that our type of Benedictine monasticism was indeed found elsewhere and had its own strengths. I was not tempted to live my life in a French or Beuronese monastery, though I felt quite comfortable when I visited these monasteries and stayed for extended periods of time; I found the monks hospitable and prayerful.

In 1960 I completed my graduate studies and returned to Saint John's to teach theology in the seminary program and in the undergraduate college. I returned with a greater appreciation of what Saint John's stood for in the panorama of Benedictine monasteries and observances. I appreciated its openness to the arts. When I first came to the monastery, two to three dozen monks played musical instruments, many in the university orchestra. I enjoyed the monks' acceptance and engagement in athletics; some were coaches in varsity sports. I saw in better perspective the liturgical movement which Fr. Virgil Michel became acquainted with in Europe and promoted in this country. I was in tune with the sense of history which I found on campus, a sense that was expressed in the in-house publication *The Scriptorium* and Fr. Colman Barry's *Worship and Work;* it was a sense that accorded well with the history of theology and of the Church that I learned at Sant' Anselmo. I liked the forwarding looking architecture which was being developed on campus (in 1960 the abbey church was two-thirds completed). I appreciated the endeavor to bring together psychiatry and pastoral life. The Mental Health Institutes for clergy of different traditions were six years old by the summer of 1960.

In 1960 I also noticed an interest in ecumenism at Saint John's, a movement that I had only casually heard about at Sant' Anselmo. Our seminarians were holding quasi-secret dialogues with their counterparts at Luther Seminary in Saint Paul. About this time too an official though non-public dialogue was held on campus between Roman Catholic and Protestant theologians.

In 1960 I also found a much improved Liturgical Press that was publishing books on liturgy and the Bible. *Orate Fratres* had already become *Worship* magazine (the change took place in the early '50s), and it was regarded as the leading publication of the liturgical movement in the United States. The magazine and The Press generally became more involved in the publication of Bible materials because the Bible was seen as the foundation of the liturgy.

In 1960 I found an endeavor to provide more theological education for Benedictine sisters. A few years previously the Benedictine Institute of Sacred Theology was initiated at the Convent of Saint Benedict, Saint Joseph, Minnesota, with the participation of some monks of Saint John's. This institute developed greatly in the early '60s and eventually became the graduate school of theology of Saint John's University. At first it served Benedictines only, but later it opened its doors to other religious, to lay persons, and to students of other Christian traditions. The school testified to Saint John's commitment to liturgical and theological education for others besides seminarians.

In 1960 Saint John's Abbey staffed dozens of parishes and chaplaincies; it ministered to American Indians on a number of reservations; and it was in the process of founding new monasteries in several places such as the Bahamas, Mexico, Puerto Rico, Kentucky, and Japan. Saint John's itself was a busy place, and many of its monks lived and worked away from the monastery.

It was a vital place, a center of much activity that impinged on the Church in Minnesota as well as the Church in the United States.

The year 1960 was pivotal for me since it was the year of my re-entry into the monastic life of Saint John's. I could look back on my experience of Saint John's since 1949, and I could look at the monastery of 1960 in the light of my Roman experience and of my visits to many monasteries in Europe. I was happy with the educational, pastoral, liturgical, ecumenical, artistic, and missionary directions of Saint John's.

All of these dimensions and movements continued after 1960. In fact, all of them continue today, but they have been modified and shaped in different ways through the years, especially in the light of Vatican Council II (1962–65). This is not the place to narrate how each of these areas developed before and after the council; it is sufficient to say that all of them were profoundly affected by the ferment of the council and by movements within society.

One area is necessarily central to Saint John's; it is the sense of monastic life. I was taken up with this sense when I entered the monastery in 1951; I was forced to reflect on it when I encountered other forms of monastic life in Europe; I was confronted with it upon my return to campus in 1960. The type of monastic life I found suited me well when I returned from graduate school. Our practices nourished me as I plunged into the work of teaching theology.

Vatican Council II, however, forced me and all of us to look at our monastic worship services, our monastic practices, and our relation to the world of Church and society. Saint John's changed much as a result of the forces of Vatican II. Monastic life continued, but in a different mode: English in the liturgy, a reduced burden of public worship, more independence and privacy, fewer candidates entering the monastery, many monks departing from the monastery, less stress on the clerical and priestly, a greater focus on the common and basic vocation of monastic life, etc. In short, the monastic place of Saint John's changed much between 1965 and 1975.

My understanding of Saint John's as a monastic place was challenged in 1975 as a result of my appointment to the office of novice master. To some extent I left the world of theology and ecumenism to enter once again the realm of monastic studies. I was obliged to teach the *Rule* of Benedict to novices and to provide these newly arrived candidates with an understanding of the practices and spirit of the monastic movement, specifically those of Saint John's Abbey.

In the next three years I grew to appreciate the wealth of wisdom in the *Rule* as well as in the monastic tradition that we inherited from the Abbey of Metten in Bavaria by way of Saint Vincent Archabbey in Pennsylvania. We had no reason to feel inferior to other monastic traditions. At the same time I realized that the way in which monastic life was lived in the early days of our monastery was not fixed forever, that in some ways it was determined by the nature of the immigrant Church among which it was born and grew. The Church of Minnesota is no longer immigrant, and the monastery is no longer in a fledgling stage. It is time to reemphasize the basic features of cenobitic or community monasticism: public liturgy, private reading and prayer, mutual service, self-support, silence, humility, hospitality, etc.

Saint John's as a place, as a monastic space, must continue to attend to the basic features of monasticism in order to retain a vital community. Saint John's as a place cannot be simply a staging area for apostolic works that take the monks away from Collegeville. The monastery as a center and as a place must remain strong and vital in its sense of prayer, silence, service, and mission. This does not mean that all monks must live within the walls of the cloister; some will carry on the work of the community by serving elsewhere as teachers, pastors, and chaplains. But their presence elsewhere cannot jeopardize the vital character of the monastic place of Saint John's. Careful discernment is needed to achieve a balance in this matter.

One aspect of Saint John's that needs to be continued and even enhanced is hospitality. The *Rule* legislates for the reception of guests; it advocates a stance of welcome to guests but not to the point of disrupting the regular life of the community. Guests may share the goods and prayer life of the monastery, but they are not to make it impossible for the monks to carry on with their regular practices.

Hospitality is the kind of service that monks can provide people without losing their commitment to a community life of prayer and silence. In fact, guests come to the monastery expecting to share the liturgy of the hours and solitude. Monks can provide an atmosphere of prayer and a good word without greatly altering their mode of life. Saint John's as a place must continue with its apostolate of hospitality and even increase it in the form of a guest house where relatives, friends, and persons of all faiths or no faith can come for days of quiet, retreat, and conversation.

If Saint John's is to remain vital, it must recapture its monastic tradition. This is being accomplished by the introduction of monastic studies in the school of theology of Saint John's University. It is possible now to pursue graduate courses in the history of monasticism, monastic spirituality, and monastic practices. These studies, together with a better sense of our monastic heritage, are designed to strengthen the notion of Saint John's as a place that stands in direct line with the early monastics of the Church. Formal studies are not sufficient in themselves, but they provide a framework within which Saint John's can evaluate its present monastic observance.

A recapturing of monastic values leads to a renewed interest in monastic space. The monastic community is identifiably located in a place and in a space. The monastic community, large or small, takes up space. It is defined by a worship space, a living space, a working space, a reflecting space, an eating space.

Talk of space does not imply that all monasteries must be in the desert. Historically monasteries have taken shape in cities and towns, in woods and mountains, in deserts and islands. Physical surroundings vary considerably but still the monastic community stands out against or within the environment. Monasteries are shaped by their surroundings, and at the same time they must be identifiable. They must have a space which is defined and conducive to the practices of community life, worship, silence, etc. Monastic communities do not exist in a vacuum. They thrive in mutual relationship to the characteristics of a place.

Saint John's has been important to me as a theological place, that is, a place where monks, at least some monks, engage in the professional study of theology. The education of seminarians for the priesthood forced Saint John's to espouse a program of theological studies and a library to match. Professional theological studies are not necessarily a part of the monastic movement, but they have accompanied Saint John's tradition from nearly the beginning.

For me personally and for many others in the monastic community, the study of theology has provided the framework within which one could understand the place of monasticism in the Church and the world. The study of God, the interpretation of the Scriptures, the reading of history, etc. support the goal of Benedictine monasticism, that is, a seeking of God. Theology, of course, does not offer absolute clarity in matters of faith, but it can assist a person in a life which demands faith for its very raison d'être. Professional study of faith underpins the professional search for God. Saint John's as a place stresses the importance of theology both in its work of pastoral ministry and in its pursuit of the monastic vocation.

Saint John's is a place of struggle and mystery. It is a struggle for the monks to come to some realization of who they are as human beings, Christian believers, and monastic persons. Saint John's is a place of trial, discernment, and decision. Some react to the discovery of themselves and to the mystery of the divine by leaving the space. Confronted by the mystery they realize that they do not belong here or in any monastic space. They may come to realize that they should seek and serve God elsewhere. The monastic space of Saint John's provides many with room for enlightenment about God and themselves.

Saint John's is not utopia (no place). It is some place. It is not the kingdom to come; it is not a perfect community. It is not a place without problems, nor a people without problems. But it is a place to seek God. It is a place where one is constrained to seek God. It is a monastic space.

M Y INTRODUCTION TO THE PSALMS OC-
curred at Vespers on July 1, 1947, two and a half hours after I
had crossed the threshold of the cloister at Saint John's along with
seven other candidates for the novitiate.

It was a bright summer afternoon. There was a short rite of reception at Abbot Alcuin Deutsch's office. Then Fr. Cosmas Dahlheimer, the new novice master, opened the iron gates into the enclosure
and led us by the shortest route along a silent corridor and up three
flights of stairs to the novitiate, an enclosure within the enclosure.
There the novices who were just finishing their year greeted us,
showed us to our assigned beds and desks, gave us pious but in
our gullible state plausible new names—such as Simplicius, Ethel-
wold, Suitbert which we later learned were unofficial—helped us
to don winter-weight wool cassocks and scapulars which we were
to wear during most of our waking hours for the next twelve months.
A change of habit would be provided if and when we made first
vows a year later. They then sat us down to introduce us to the
books we would need for Vespers at 5:30 and from then on for
the Divine Office, the daily round of the canonical hours in choir.

The *Rule* says that monks should be contented with the poorest
and worst of everything, and on the general principle that one learns
by doing, the novices were issued the oldest and most cumbersome
breviaries in the abbey's possession. The breviary was the basic

Office book, a compendium of antiphons, psalms, prayers, and readings in Latin arranged according to Benedict's *Rule* and the liturgical year. The breviaries the novices used came in four-volume sets, dictionary-sized, one for each season, and as I recall were published in Ratisbon in 1871. As they came off the press they were undoubtedly handsome examples of the printer's art with rubrics, initials, and the names of greater feasts in red; but seventy years on they were worn and, what is worse, out of date. Jerome's Vulgate version of the psalms had not changed since A.D. 400 nor had Benedict's distribution of the psalms from a century later, but in seventy years new feasts had been added to the calendar with their own texts. For these we needed the Supplement, and to know when to use it we needed the Ordo, the day-by-day liturgical calendar crammed with Latin abbreviations for everything from ferial days with no commemorations to doubles of the first class with privileged octaves.

This may sound elementary, and indeed mastering the complexities of the Office was of necessity one of our first accomplishments as novices, but to start with we simply had to be told on what pages we would find the texts for our first experience in choir. This our mentors proceeded to tell us, setting the colored grosgrain ribbons at the psalms, the *Magnificat* antiphon, the text of the *Magnificat* (printed at only one place in the book since monks soon learned it by heart), and the oration plus any commemorations for the day.

We would come back again after supper to set the ribbons for Matins and Lauds at 7:30, but for now we lined up in order in the novitiate corridor, then filed down the stairs and along the corridor to the enclosure doors where *statio* formed for the monks' procession into church. We led the way, conscious of not stumbling on the hem of our new habits, conscious that we were newcomers, conscious that we were not to talk to monks in vows without permission, conscious that any slip in what seemed a complicated protocol would display our awkward self-consciousness.

This long preamble about my first hours in the monastery is meant to set the context in which I began to recite the psalms, morning and evening, day by day, year in, year out, in a rhythm occasionally interrupted but essentially unbroken till now. Early on I learned that the *Rule* provided that monks sent on a journey should not neglect the Office but pray the Hours as well as they could by themselves. Later this was reinforced by the canonical rule that those in Holy Orders must pray the Office daily under the pain of sin, a good example of a wholesome principle turned into a nagging legalism.

The psalms made up the larger and constant part of the Office. Readings, prayers, hymns, antiphons varied with days and seasons, but the *Rule* stipulates that all 150 psalms are to be said each week, observing in passing that our stronger monastic forebears accomplished this task in a single day. In fact some psalms were repeated every day—psalms 3 and 94 at the beginning of Matins, psalms 66 and 50 and psalms 148, 149, and 150 at Lauds, psalms 4, 90, and 133 at Compline. The last three Abbot Alcuin expected us to memorize, observing that our stronger forebears had known all the psalms by heart. We assumed that these were the same people who said the whole psalter every day.

The manner of recitation in choir never varied. One side of choir said one verse, the other the next. For the longer Hours the choir sat during the psalms, rising and bowing profoundly—from the waist, forehead to the bookrest—at the *Gloria Patri* at the end of each psalm. When I entered the monastery Vespers was sung on Sundays and solemnities. Otherwise the psalms were recited on a singing monotone set by a gong sounded by the prior at the start of the psalmody and repeated from time to time when the pitch sagged egregiously as it tended to do. On rare occasions—perhaps once or twice a year—the whole choir got into the spirit of the thing at the same time and tossed verses back and forth across the sanctuary with verve. This mysterious phenomenon was entirely unpredictable, and nobody counted on it to dispel the sense that Benedict knew what he was talking about when he described the Office as the *Opus Dei,* the Work of God.

This account would be incomplete if I failed to note that some years into Abbot Baldwin Dworschak's reign as the numbers in choir overflowed into pews behind the altar the gong became completely ineffective and we began reciting the psalms to the accompaniment of the organ. This pretty well guaranteed that the choir would keep the pitch, but if anything it heightened the lulling effect of psalmody on a single note.

If all of this suggests that my early experience in reciting the psalms was more or less mechanical, that is uncomfortably close to the mark. Latin was an obstacle for me. No doubt I would have found it difficult to focus my mind on texts in English amidst the welter of new impressions during my first days in the monastery. No doubt either that routine always risks being dulling. Nevertheless I soon began to appreciate many of the variable texts of the Office: the antiphons and verses for feasts and seasons, the orations, sometimes even the hymns despite their difficult vocabulary and syntax. Their annual recurrence gradually made the Office a world of thought and color and affectivity for me. I cannot say as much for the Latin psalms. They were the warp and the woof of the Office, but reciting them lulled me into reverie more often than it roused me to thought or feeling.

The trouble was that Latin wasn't my native tongue. The psalms are after all poems—exultant, martial, plaintive, didactic, mystical. The appeal of poetry lies in its form, its rhythm, its power to evoke our assent: Yes, this is what a rattling thunderstorm is like: this is how grief feels; this is how I yearn for peace. Poetry in our native tongue works automatically. "There is a tide in the affairs of men;" "I wandered lonely as a cloud;" "Here in the wind's terrain." Our response to such lines is instantaneous, rooted in the names we have learned for things since infancy, their associations, the way we have formulated our own experience.

To achieve such instant resonance to poetry in a second language is rare and fortunately was not a requirement for joining the monastery. Luckily, I made some headway. There were eventually Latin verses and some whole psalms that came to be spontaneously expressive for me. By and large they had easily recognizable cognates in English and a word order natural to English: *Benedicam Dominum in omni tempore* (I will bless the Lord at all times); *Dominus illuminatio mea et salus mea* (The Lord is my light and my salvation); *In lumine tuo videbimus lumen* (In your light we shall see light).

Other words and phrases passed me by completely. For some reason I think of a verse from psalm 130 in the Vulgate: *Sicut ablactatus est super matre sua, ita retributio in anima mea.* There is a textual problem in the Hebrew and translators work around it. Nonetheless in English the verse presents a lovely and tender simile expressing trust in God. The Grail version says, "A weaned child on its mother's breast, even so is my soul." Somehow *ablactatus* never suggested the image of a child to me and *retributio* (an abstract noun from *retribuo,* to give back or pay back) did not, to my mind, connote any kind of affection.

Besides the disadvantage of not having spoken Latin at my mother's knee, I think the unvarying practice of reciting the psalms antiphonally—one verse this side of the choir, the next verse the other side of the choir—often worked against appreciating what we were saying. Some of the psalms are composed in distichs, but most of them develop a thought over several lines and reward recitation as verse paragraphs. Moreover the steady antiphonal back-and-forth rhythm was inherently monotonous, an effect heightened by the deliberate monotone decreed by monastic custom.

All in all I greeted it as a passage from dawn into full day when twenty years into my monastic life at Saint John's the liturgical reforms stemming from Vatican Council II in the early '60s cleared the way to recite the psalms in English. As time passed I regretted leaving behind much of the rich content of seasons and feasts, some of which we have gradually recaptured in English, some of which was intrinsic to the Latin culture of the Middle Ages and doesn't translate to a different time and a different tongue. A few verses from the Latin psalter remain a part of my consciousness and spring to mind naturally in prayer, but only a few.

Along with English came changes in choir etiquette. Gone was the *Gloria* at the end of each psalm, the singing monotone, the strict antiphonal recitation of the text. Psalms were now said in a speaking voice, divided into verse paragraphs, traded between solo readers and the choir, followed by intervals of silence.

These changes aided my understanding of the psalms and appreciation of their range of themes and moods. They did not guarantee that I would be attentive; one can be absentminded in any language. They did not altogether dispel the risk of monotony; any pattern, even a pattern of variations, can become monotonous. They did not assure a very expressive recitation; contemporary translations are accurate and serviceable but rarely sonorous; readers—at least in Minnesota—seldom trust themselves to dig into words and phrases and sentences for all they are worth. Perhaps that is just as well when the words will be heard over and over again for a lifetime.

On a first reading most of the psalms have an easy and evident meaning, but on the whole they gain in depth with the reader's experience of the Scriptures and of life. For readers like myself who have led sheltered, comfortable lives, vicarious experience has to lend urgency to the cries for justice from depths of oppression and destitution we have never known. And—let's face it—the psalms include some bloodthirsty prayers for revenge that echo a primitive moral code incompatible with the Gospels although all too evidently—see the daily news—still ingrained in human nature. Someone learned in the Scriptures and steeped in the love of God can perhaps pray them as metaphors for rejecting whatever is evil, but I think it wise to pass them over in common prayer. They too easily lend themselves to animosity and hatred toward real people when our prayers should be for forgiveness and blessings.

But even aside from the cursing psalms, which are not numerous, the psalms are not all sweetness and light. The fullness of life is reflected in them, from naive wonder at the powers of nature to sober recognition of the joys and sorrows of life to exultant praise of God's truth and holiness. Anyone who turns to them only for pious sentiments will be disappointed. Their fiber lies in their rock-solid assurance that God is, that justice and peace and love are possible, that people everywhere and at all times share the same needs, that prayer is valid.

I hardly knew how the psalms would shape my interpretation of life when I clutched my cumbersome breviary with the ribbons set for Vespers forty years ago. Now I cannot imagine doing without them.

THREE TIMES A YEAR SAINT BENEDICT'S *RULE* IS read out, day after day, a few paragraphs at a time, at supper in the Saint John's monastic refectory. And three times a year we hear Benedict begin addressing us again in the prologue of that *Rule:* "Listen, my son! Listen!"

It was forty years ago in the fall of 1949 that I arrived at Saint John's as a prep freshman. It was a whole new world to me, a little kid raised in the flat lands of the Red River Valley. Actually, my first impressions came the year before, when I had journeyed by bus to visit my older brother, then a prep senior, during homecoming festivities to see for myself and decide whether I wished to come to Saint John's for high school. The smoking, wheezing Greyhound dumped me at the old brick gateway at the Highway 52 entrance to the campus. It was a blue and bright October day, and alone I had to find my way into the campus as best I could, walking through all those trees, those magnificent red and orange and yellow and green trees. Past too the landscaped roadbanks with their plots of patterned plantings, and shrine to Saint John Berchmans, the well-kept walkways, the bronze plaque with the names of the veterans of World War I, the old water tower, and finally the twin towers of the abbey church. I had never seen any of this before, nothing like it ever in my life. This was a whole new world. All those buildings in the middle of nowhere!

A new experience of religion also immediately began. A long file of monks was processing in front of the old buildings, entering the church for the funeral of a confrere. I had never seen so many "priests" at one time. There must have been hundreds of them. With suitcase in hand I skulked as unobtrusively as possible into the church behind the elaborately-robed abbot celebrant. There in the apse were those angels, their faces covered, bright beads of red light burning at their feet, and the great Christ hovering over the black-robed choirs. Out rushed the full-voiced sound of the chant. "Religion is a masculine thing," it all seemed to say. This indeed was a revelation! Where I came from, women did the praying.

The rest of the weekend was a masculine experience too, you may be sure—the football games, the variety show, the band, the student liturgies, the open dormitories, the noisy and jammed refectory. What boy who wanted to be a guy wouldn't decide to stay in a place like this?

So I did, and so I have. Of course, it wasn't always like that. First impressions are usually overwhelming. But you get the idea: Saint John's was new, which is a strange thing to say because the place was ninety years old by that time. But that's just the point: Old as it is, for this part of the continent, at least, Saint John's somehow comes across as new.

That, at least, is the way it has always been for me. Yes, routine set in during those adolescent years. So did homework. Boredom too, especially in the long winters. Loneliness also, I suppose, though you never had a moment to yourself. But "trapped" there as students always are, something began to happen. Friendships developed. You found more than a few comfortable people a teenager could deal with. You began to develop a common sensitivity and outlook. Community was forming.

I didn't know it then, but I was listening. I was being made into a Benedictine. Through eyes and ears, nose and mouth, through touch and every sensation, through emotion and intuition and intellect, it was pouring in. You listened or you didn't fit for very long. You listened or you didn't last. You listened with your whole self or you packed up and left.

Somehow I managed to stay, and in 1955 I entered the novitiate with my younger brother. The monastery was another wholly different world. I was twenty by this time, but it seemed that I didn't know a thing. The monastery was another culture: We got up before the sun and went to bed as it set; contacts with the wider world were minimal; there was silence, prayer, public and private reading, elaborate and lengthy liturgy, physical labor, and study—always more study. We studied the Church Fathers and the Desert Mothers, monastic history, Thomistic philosophy, and Roman theology. We were steeped in "The Tradition," and as we were dunked into it year after year, more of it seeped in, more of it clung. We listened. All of it was new. It was all right.

By the time all that was over, I was twenty-seven and an ordained priest. By now I had seen everything, except the '60s, of course. Except Vatican II, of course. Except *aggiornamento,* which was the ecclesiastical equivalent and forerunner of *glasnost* and *perestroika,* and we know how much disruption and disorientation that has led to in the Communist East these last few years. If all this has been aggravating for the lay Church these last decades, it has been nothing short of maddening for monastic communities. We who studied, preserved, and practiced "The Tradition" to a greater degree and intensity than others were wrenched even more severely than they by all the change. When we lost the Latin, we lost our music too. We lost our ceremonial. The social structure gave way, and the non-ordained no longer accepted secondary status in the house and all that entailed in terms of rights, rank, responsibilities, housing, education, and even spirituality. While the wider Church heard statistics about religious leaving their commitments, we experienced confreres departing: classmates, friends, admired mentors. The young, restless, left altogether; older men, alienated, moved to the fringes of community involvement and were rarely seen again. It was hard to watch all this, hard to endure, hard to listen.

What perhaps cushioned all this for us to some extent, though we probably didn't realize it at the time, was the new Breuer Saint John's Abbey and University Church. It had been long in building, and even longer in planning. Theologians and liturgists, as well as architects, studied and dialogued about what the Church, the People of God, itself is, and how that is best expressed in a church building. Their deliberations were shared with the community in the late '50s and early '60s, and we found ourselves praying within a structure that expressed in concrete, wood, brick and glass the best of the Church's ecclesiology and spirituality. The experience of the new church helped to ease our transition into the New Church. The new structure opened our ears and our hearts as well as our eyes. We were hearing a little of Vatican II a few years early.

The experience of those years simply highlighted, it seems to me, what life at Saint John's has always required. You can't settle in. You can't say, "I've got it. I know Saint John's." Whether it was the missionary explosion under Abbot Alexius Edelbrock in the 1880s; the development from the seminary, junior college, and preparatory school into a liberal arts college in the '20s; the growing liturgical movement of the '30s; the war years of the '40s; the loss of the farm in the '50s; the building of the new campus in the '60s; the increasing presence on campus of women in the '70s due to the cooperation between Saint John's University and the College of Saint Benedict and the development of the graduate program in theology, or in the '80s the strengthening of the relationship with our sister monastery Saint Benedict's Convent itself, Saint John's would no longer be an exclusive bastion of monastic maleness. Whatever it was, there was always a new Saint John's in the making. You had to have your ears cocked. You had to keep tuned in. And that is never easy.

I have been on the "outside" the last ten years, living with and serving as chaplain for the sisters at Mount Saint Benedict in Crookston, Minnesota. At a distance I become more aware, perhaps, of the changes taking place at Abbey Central. On my infrequent trips home, there always seems to be a new dormitory to inspect, a renovation to check out, a venerated old building recycled, gutted of all the accumulated memories and meaning from my earlier years. A familiar face or two is now gone, and I didn't even get to say good-bye. And there are several new faces too, along with new names that are so hard to remember for sure. There are new hymnbooks in the choir stalls and new table practices in the dining room. It gets annoying, all this change. It even gets overwhelming after a while. You want to stop it by tuning it out.

Trips home to the abbey have taught me that I am a conservative, which surprises me because when I am circulating in the larger Church community, I feel quite liberal. In fact, clergy and others who know Saint John's presume you to be liberal. They almost expect it. Some even greet you with suspicion. But at home, someone is teaching a new approach to Scripture, or somebody else is off studying electronic music. And you find rising within you conservative mutterings like "What was wrong with the *old* New Testament?" or, "If we have ten organists, why are we singing a cappella?"

It is interesting, this experiencing of the liberal and the conservative within the same heart. For I suspect that that is the reality of Saint John's itself. The abbey is sometimes castigated by elements of its public as being too liberal, of fostering aspects of theology and liturgy that are corrosive of the Church. Yet there are others who look at Saint John's and weep at what they consider its rigidity, its conservatism, its provincialism, its comfort with the way things are. Strangely enough, both interpretations are probably true. Much as others would wish to categorize and thus dismiss Saint John's as irrelevant to their lives, I find Saint John's to be an expression of what we used to call Catholic humanism. There is undoubtedly present at Saint John's "The Tradition," and there are not many of us who would apologize for that. But present too is the realization born of that tradition that it must be played with, reexamined, and reevaluated in each generation, or "The Tradition" will cease.

It is, in the last analysis, this deep respect for "The Tradition" and the desire to keep it alive that continues to make Saint John's an interesting place to me. I feel at home there, and yet never at home, because it is ever evolving, always speaking to its members with another voice, in another tone. The careful listening required to live there can be exhausting, but it is always an enriching experience.

Viewed from almost any angle, the abbey church has the features of a huge megaphone. The voice box of that horn is the monastery behind it. I like to think that because of the prayer and liturgy that takes place in the church, that because of the student graduates who go out from its folded concrete walls, that because of the thousands of visitors who come to marvel at its expanses—that because of all of this Saint John's continues to speak and to teach the Christian and Catholic humanist tradition to the Church and somehow to the world. I would like to believe that by its continuing hospitality to students, scholars, politicians, and business leaders, as well as the merely curious, Saint John's will be able to give them an experience of the richness and excitement it has given to me. I would like to think that because Saint John's itself listens, it will continue to have something to say for some time to come.

Br. Robin Pierzina

WHILE READERS MAY CONSTRUE SOME LIT-
erary mischief on my part when they read what I call in this essay
"a place of sense," this is not my intention. What I wish to achieve
by this simple inversion of word order, however, is a means to emphasize what lies at the essence of my reflections on being both
a Benedictine monk and a scientist. "A Place of Sense," as a title, is
admittedly in no manner as engaging as "A Sense of Place," but
hopefully it will provide a reader with something of the same meaning as it has held for me in my twenty-four years as a member of
the monastic community at Saint John's. In using the word "sense"
here, I employ its meaning from the Latin *sensus,* the faculty of
perceiving, and from the past participle of *sentire,* to perceive through
knowledge of the known, the masonry of the scientific method.

From my earliest years I had always been taught to be and to
learn as an observer of reality, of the perceptible. I have often at-
tributed this to my Scottish-English Protestant origins which held
rigor, order, reason, and practicality as virtuous, exemplary, and
above all, essential, as a point of departure for any task at hand.
While I still strive to temper these qualities with those that invoke
equity for creativity and freedom of the spirit, the basis of my life
and philosophy has remained steeped in empiricism. One might
have well predicted that monastic life would have been somewhat
at odds with this willful and perhaps, in part, hereditary pragmat-

ic raison d'être. Yet, as I was to discover in the earliest years of monastic formation, the pulse of the orderly *horarium* of Benedictine life had a profound appeal to my sense of order and provided what I saw as a most reasonable approach to learning more about God and my relationship to others.

After I professed vows to our community, I pursued graduate studies in science and have worked in diabetes-related research for the past twelve years. During that time I established a research laboratory for the particular purpose of investigating the unfortunate disease that afflicts many in the human family. In many ways to undertake a serious and professional research program at a small, private liberal arts university seems unrealistic and impractical. Admittedly, there often arise those moments that are haunted by the memory of Gulliver's travels to the Grand Academy at the capital city of Lagado in the land of Balnibarbi, where people insisted on doing everything in an impractical manner. There, Gulliver met the researcher who had for eight years worked "upon a project for extracting sunbeams out of cucumbers . . . to supply the governor's gardens with sunshine at a reasonable rate."

Reasonable or not, what I have come to discover is that my scientific instinct, my search of sense, has considerable historical precedence. While much of what we are as a Benedictine community at Saint John's is understandably recognized in the significant merits of those distinguished monks who contributed their talents in the pre-eminent areas of theology, Scripture, liturgy, literature, and the humanities, there has been a long, enduring tradition of scientific Benedictine *sentire* at work as well. From time to time I find my thoughts reflecting on particularly notable characters of the past who lend a thread of continuity to both my commitment to monastic life and my scientific interests. In playing the unauthorized role of a historical detective, I have often attempted to ferret out the minds of my early predecessors in the hope of discovering therein how the empirical mind can find harmony and meaning in a monastic vision absorbed in faith. These archival expeditions have provided considerable insight into the timelessness of human nature.

Consider for a moment, Fr. James Hansen (1874–1934), our noted biologist in the early years of the university. As he left Vespers on July 18, 1934, he collapsed and was taken to the infirmary, put to bed, and instructed by the nurse to rest. Shortly thereafter she returned to find him moving his limbs about, and in response to her orders to keep quiet, he replied: "I've got to know how it feels so I can write up the experiment." He died the following day of a cerebral hemorrhage. A scientist to the end some might say, knowing that his final *vade mecum* was not with beaded consolation, but an objective reflection on his own mortality—certainly a supremely sacred moment in the mind of the created and in the eyes of a creator.

No doubt the details of that reflection, had Father James survived, would have been carefully noted in his diary of over thirty-five years. This diary, represented by a series of small notebooks penned in ink, contains the frank and candid chronicled annotations of an astute observer. Having read the diaries, I have little doubt that Father James was not keenly aware of his clinical state during those last moments and would have wanted to die as he had lived: concluding by Baconian methods the premises of a final syllogism, or resolving through Aristotelian processes, a consummate hypothesis.

Amid the infinite details of his earlier activities as a professor of zoology, botany, entomology, physiology, and experimental psychology, recording his tireless efforts at keying species, mounting slides of various molds and cellular mitosis, prosecting specimens for his laboratory sessions, testing well water, cleaning and dusting his lab, and the list goes on, are references to his community commitments and, as might be expected, observations of his physical health. From October 28, 1933 to his death in July 1934, Father James recorded ten entries related to his health which included three key observations: transient mental confusion and forgetfulness, a persistent headache localized at the base of the skull, and a periodic bloody discharge from his left ear. The entries are not voiced out of complaint or self-pity; they are often in the form of salient observations frequently assessed through lines of inquiry as in the case of his entry four months prior to his death:

> *March 18/34.* That headache at the base of the skull was rather intense, particularly on the right, from the mastoid bone over the top of the right eye. This appears anomalous: it is my left ear which continually discharges—why is not the ache on that side also? It is quite strange.

Perhaps, what very few knew, including those in our community, was that Father James, aside from his detached visage born of scientific objectivity was very privately a deeply spiritual man. Following many entries in his diary regardless of the day's events are brief excerpts, written in Latin and taken from Scripture, antiphons, or readings from the Divine Office, the lives of the saints, or from the coffer of classical philosophy. It was not uncommon to find such entries as on June 16, 1934: "Worked most of the day in lab. making mounts of Scotch Pine pollen tubes and preparing frog skeletons. *Si Deus pro nobis, quis contra nos!*;[1] or for April 16, 1934: "Began the *'Dogfish'* today in zoology. *Existima enim quod non sunt condignae passiones huis temporis ad futuram gloriam, quae revelabitur in nobis.* Ep. ad Rom. VIII 18-19."[2]

Not all references, however, embraced such passive reflections on Scripture but revealed on occasions the natural and polemical dilemma that arises between the heart and mind or within the mind itself as it strives to resolve conflicting images of quiddity. This is evidenced in his question of contradiction arising from the text of Psalms: January 14, 1934: "The usual program for Sunday. *Servite Domino in laetitia.* Ps 99.1. *Servite Domino in timore.* Ps. 2.11. How can we do both at once?"[3] Father James will be vividly remembered for his outspoken defense of organic evolution and his episodic and vigorous flirtation with sophistry. But, he will also be long remembered for his personal quest to solve the complexities arising from the natural order of things and his prophetic vision of the value of science in the intellectual formation of young minds.

In those early and subsequent years, many of our monks, like Father James, strived to place Saint John's solidly on a path that led into an increasingly complex world of science and technology, often with little or no resources except for their own talents. Among those who left their footprints as early life scientists are Fr. Urban Fisher who began a systematic study of plant life on the Saint John's property and founded our first greenhouse; Frs. Bruno Doerfler (1866-1919), Bernard Kevenhoerster (1869-1949), Albert Erkens

1. "If the Lord is for us, who can be against us?"
2. "For I reckon that the sufferings of the present time are not worthy to be compared with the glory to come that will be revealed."
3. "Serve the Lord in rejoicing." "Serve the Lord in fear."

(1874–1956), and James Hansen who amassed an extensive entomology collection still in use today. Fr. John Katzner (1850–1930), whose specialty was horticulture, spent years in experimental grafting of fruits which could better survive the frigid Minnesota winters. Among his most successful efforts was the "Alpha" grape, a cross between the wild variety and the Concord which could survive a -40° F. without protection. Fr. Hilary Doerfler (1876–1950) erected the first experimental fish hatchery to stock the Sagatagan. Fr. Wendelin Luetmer (1889–1977) assisted Father James in introducing bacteriology into the departmental curriculum and established a laboratory exclusively for bacteriological experimentation. The outstanding pedagogical reputation within the biological sciences would be later continued by Frs. Adelard Thuente (1910–62) and Bertram Niggemann (1914–89).

The physical sciences flourished as well in the early years of Saint John's under the aegis and visionary leadership of Abbot Peter Engel (1856–1921). Father Peter, an outstanding scientist of merit, designed and had built the first science building at Saint John's, later to be named in his honor as Engel Hall. He taught chemistry, astronomy, photography, established a meteorological station associated with the United States Signal Service and built the first observatory. Aside from these rather awesome feats, he served the monastic community as abbot for twenty-seven years. As one commentator aptly described Abbot Peter: ". . . he is not only deeply interested in that which is beyond the stars, but also in the stars themselves and what is below them."

The list is incredible and tasks impressive: Fr. Francis Merschman (1852–1916) taught physics and installed the first wireless telegraph station; Fr. Fridolin Tembreull (1876–1939) pioneered experiments in color photography and dutifully recorded meteorological data for seventeen years; Fr. Anselm Ortman (1872–1952) as a physicist emphasized and explored the experimental approach to teaching physics and also taught astronomy and applied his knowledge of astronomy to meteorology; Fr. Bernard Kevenhoerster distinguished himself not only in botany and chemistry but introduced geology into the curriculum as well. The distinguished tradition of the physical sciences would be later maintained by Fr. Severin Gertken (1881–1960) in chemistry, Fr. Polycarp Hansen (1884–1962) in physics, Frs. Bede Michel (1909–84) and Matthew

Kiess (1900–79) in chemistry. Father Matthew was instrumental in the planning and construction of the present science center.

These monks were pioneers who forged not only a strong presence of science at Saint John's in their creative ideas, inventive talents, and amazing resourcefulness, but brought about a fusion of scientific dialectics with Benedictine *labora*. While many of our graduates and associates, by their own testimony, have felt a ''sense of place'' at Saint John's, part of that tribute undoubtedly arises from the endeavor of those monks who created, from moving about in the world of the unknown to the known, a place of sense.

S AINT JOHN'S WAS THE SCHOOL I WANTED TO attend when I finished grade school. Coming from a Benedictine parish, it seemed natural to become interested in Saint John's. Living twenty-two miles from Saint John's on a farm between Saint Martin-Freeport-Albany-Farming (all of these Benedictine parishes), it became easy to become interested in Saint John's. The pastors of our parish—Frs. Clement Dimpfl, George Scheffold, Pius Meinz, Edwin Sieben, Cyril Ortmann, and others—were priests I heard my parents speak of with great respect and love. The parish was blessed with many vocations to the priesthood, brotherhood, and sisterhood. A cousin of mine, Fr. Arnold Mondloch, influenced me early in life. As a missionary in the Bahamas, he frequently came home to visit the relatives. When he returned, it seems all the boys who were baptized during the summer while he was at home were named Arnold. I was one of them. He died before I entered the novitiate, so I kept the name for religious life. At home we frequently heard our parents speak of *Die Benedicktiners*—and it was with great love.

In 1940 I entered Saint John's Preparatory. While I'm not a great one for remembering dates and names, I do remember the day I came to Saint John's as if it were yesterday—even though it is forty-nine years ago. I loved the prep school. Fr. Vincent Tegeder was the principal, and he gave me an excellent start as a shy farm boy. A note he sent to my parents after one month left a lasting impression of what a kind note means. My mother still has it; he wrote: "Arnold is doing just wonderful." It meant even more to my parents. What a lesson for all to remember—just what a short, kind note can do. Fr. Philibert Harrer of happy memory succeeded Father Vincent. It was he who was determined to help me with my German/English pronunciations—the *v*s and *w*s, the *t*s and *th*s needed to be corrected. It never totally disappears. I grew up hearing "Marriage is a holy 'wow' " (vow). After thirty-six years of marriage counseling, I have often wondered whether at times this pronunciation was at least somewhat correct.

Father Philibert asked me to come into his office three times a week and say a short poem—three times in succession without error. When I failed, I would hear: "Once more." This is the poem: "Theophilus of Thistles, that thruster of thistles, thrust three thousand thistles to the thick of his thumb." It may be easy for a reader, but it was murder for this writer. I still say it—faster than ever. I appreciate the personal interest he showed in me. I have always decided when I taught at the prep school and Benilde that I would try and help at least one student in a special way as Father Philibert did for me.

The prep school will always be my most memorable educational experience. Fr. Burton Bloms, as prefect, was just what I looked for. I had a competitive spirit in athletics. He encouraged me to excel but also directed me to become more interested in school work. Later on at ordination, my first assignment was at the prep school with Fr. Alfred Deutsch as dean. So that I wouldn't get sidetracked on sports, he told me: "Now I don't want you to be interested just in the athletes. I asked for you to be on the faculty because I feel you love young people and understand them." I appreciated his direction and compliment.

Later on when Father Otto, my brother, was ordained, I handed on that advice to him. It's no surprise how much influence monks really do have on one another. Father Otto, God rest his soul, and I were not only blood brothers; we were truly brothers in the Lord at work, prayer, and play. During my high school teaching days, I was able to share with many dedicated monks, laymen, and laywomen. This sharing in the monastery has been most helpful in sharing in the parish.

It is amazing how we can share our lives together in the monastery and then later find ourselves doing similar parish work. I have found this to be wonderful. It gives one many occasions to reminisce about shared monastic work and shared parochial work.

I would like to share some areas of monasticism that I find helpful in parish work:

1. The role of the abbot in a monastery is similar to a pastor in a parish.
2. The role of community in a parish is similar to a monastic community.
3. The role of collegiality in a parish is similar to a monastery.

Saint Benedict in chapter 2 of the *Rule* describes "what kind of man the abbot ought to be." What a challenging chapter for Benedictines who are engaged in pastoral work. The qualities enumerated by Benedict are as relevant for a pastor in a parish as they are for the abbot in a monastery. Benedict quotes the Apostle Paul: "You have received the Spirit of adoption as sons by virtue of which we cry, 'Abba—Father.'" A pastor of a parish must truly love all and be concerned about all regardless of age, background success, or response. Benedict speaks of equal love the abbot must have for all. A pastor needs to develop a good pastoral sense, a good pastoral practice. This demands a personal approach to needs of people. Benedict speaks of the abbot adapting himself to a variety of characters: "One he must coax, another scold, another persuade, according to each one's character and understanding." A pastor must "adjust and adapt himself to all in such a way that he may not only suffer no loss in the flock committed to his care, but may even rejoice in the increase of a good flock."

I can't imagine better direction for pastors than that. A true shepherd cares for people individually. Often we wish to be consistent, black or white, no grey areas, correct at all costs—and we lose compassion and sensitivity. In society today, more than ever, people come from various backgrounds, different religious practices, different ideologies. They seek guidance for greater meaning in life. A pastor truly must be a kind shepherd.

I was ordained in 1952. My first assignment was teaching and prefecting in the prep school. Fr. Florian Muggli, who was ordained the previous year, prefected in the college. Once a week he and I would visit in the evening with Fr. Walter Reger, who had many years of experience as a prefect. We shared our experience about students. We often discussed discipline and care for our students. At that time I found it difficult to understand that Father Walter didn't seem to be consistent at all times. In fact, at times, I left thinking his approach was weak and shallow. Why doesn't he take a consistent stand? In fact, at times, he just plain seemed to contradict himself. I often now in my prayers am thankful for my contact with him. Actually what he was doing was good "pastoral practice." He took into account different backgrounds, different circumstances. He truly exemplified compassion. This monastic experience has helped me as a pastor to be more sympathetic, understanding, and less judgmental. Benedict reminded the abbot

> what a difficult and arduous a task he has undertaken: ruling souls and adapting himself to a variety of characters. One he must coax, another scold, another persuade, according to each one's character and understanding. Thus he must adjust and adapt himself to all in such a way that he may not only suffer no loss in the flock committed to his care, but may even rejoice in the increase of a good flock (the *Rule*, chapter 2).

Good pastoral practice as described in the *Rule* will increase the flock not only in numbers but also in commitment and dedication. People are seeking for greater meaning to life. People are not satisfied just to "fulfill a law." No wonder we have two types of Catholics—Roman and "Roaming." A great number are looking for meaningful worship, meaningful relationships, and to be treated well. If they are not given this, they go elsewhere. Good pastoral practice consists of being thoroughly committed to the needs of people.

A monastic community living closely together shows how necessary it is to take care of all according to their needs. Sometimes monks spend the greater part of their lives in the monastery in education or in another capacity. Then they are assigned to parochial work. Some monks have felt the transition too difficult. They feel unprepared. Personally I have seen monks who in a very short time make the transition beautifully. Many of the same qualities are required regardless of assignment. In some other assignments additional education may be necessary. However, the attitude of being "pastoral" seems to transcend and help people overcome obstacles.

Certainly an example of a monk and educator who quickly became a marvelous pastor is Fr. Arno Gustin. In a short time in various assignments in the Crookston Diocese, he became an outstanding pastor and even in his retirement has not given up his pastoral zeal. I was pastor at that time at Holy Rosary Church, Detroit Lakes, also in the Crookston Diocese. It was a joy to visit with Father Arno and share pastoral experiences. Both of us had taught at Saint John's. Both of us could see the value of a monastic background in pastoral work. Every parish is a community. Every parish must be an education center. Every parish is a place of ministry. Where else could one really find a better place than a monastery to combine education, community, and ministry? I am grateful for this background as I try to do my part in developing Holy Name Parish into a community, a community that will continuously grow educationally and spiritually as well as a place of ministry—both in the parish and outreach programs.

A parish is a community of faith, worshiping and working together. Our motto *Ora et labora* teaches us a balance in life that I believe is helpful for parishioners in their lives. Celebration of the Eucharist on Sundays in the parish is the most important parochial event of the week. Liturgy is the action of the people who come together as an assembly. At Saint John's the abbey church exemplifies an assembly, architecturally and in prayer. It certainly wasn't difficult to build a new church at Holy Name after experiencing the power of assembly in the abbey church.

Another area of similarity between good parochial life and monasticism can be found in the concept of community. A parish ought to be a strong community where people come together to worship God and to support each other. Living in a monastery, being of help to one another, and praying and working together are very similar to parish life. I treasure and appreciate the type of living I experienced in the monastery because it is a great help in fostering similar life in a parish. Parishes that have developed a sense of community tend to become very active in outreach programs and social action. No one expressed this better than Fr. Virgil Michel. Although I had read some of his writings, his vision was a revelation to me at the fiftieth anniversary symposium in his honor in 1988 at Saint John's. I couldn't believe that almost all the significant new emphasis of Vatican II regarding norms of a good parish were expressed by him fifty years ago. Our seminary instructors at the time, Frs. Paschal Botz, Godfrey Diekmann, Gregory Roettger, Michael Marx, Colman Barry, etc. were giving us similar emphasis. All this has made me now as a pastor appreciative for having this theological background. All of this teaching became more of a reality with the documents of Vatican II.

Occasionally pastors feel that seminary teachers are "out of it," don't understand "pastoral life." I personally have found it different for myself. Theory and principles are very important. To translate this in the practical order is the job of a pastor more than a teacher. I am grateful for being a member of a religious community that emphasizes instruction and formation on a continuous basis. It may come as a surprise, but as a pastor I personally seek advice from someone trained in liturgy and theology more frequently than from another pastor. Some of my best feelings about what to do pastorally have come from Fr. Kilian McDonnell. A background of good theology is important in pastoral life. One can also learn much from monks who have special gifts of service to people and relate well to people. I always admired Father Otto, God rest his soul. How beautifully he related to people, especially the young.

Since Vatican II there has been more emphasis on collegiality. Parishioners have become part of decision-making. Parishioners are sharing more fully in all aspects of parish life: liturgy, business, education, etc. This tends to bind the people into a stronger community. Interestingly enough, seeking counsel and advice is part of good monastic life. Monks are called together for counsel, called together to hear issues, and called together to vote. There are many concepts pertaining to good parochial life that are similar to monastic life: collegiality, community, pastoral care, hospitality.

Certainly there are a great number of monastic insights that are helpful in parish life. Although one does not have the same type of community life as in a monastery, a monk can as a pastor be part of a Christian community in worship and work with his parishioners.

MAGNUS J. WENNINGER

THE SUMMER OF 1989 MARKED THE FIFTIETH anniversary of my entry into the novitiate of Saint John's Abbey. What a memorable day. Almost every detail of it remains etched in my memory.

To describe that day, however, would be to jump ahead in the story of my association with Saint John's. This actually began when I came in September 1933 at age thirteen as a student in Saint John's Preparatory. After an initial bout with homesickness, Saint John's quickly became my home. I came as a predivinity student, a resident of Saint Bede's Hall, where Fr. Pirmin Wendt was the head prefect and where I was quickly caught up in all the activities associated with boarding school life. By modern standards the discipline was strict. We never left campus, but the Benedictine family atmosphere made it tolerable, even enjoyable, at least so I found it to be.

Besides a host of good teachers like Frs. Marcian Peters in algebra, Joachim Watrin in geometry, Dominic Keller in dramatics, Vincent Tegeder in history, to name only a few, there was the intimate friendship I developed with other students in my class, one of the major influences that kept me coming back year after year to enjoy such close association in sports as well as in studies and in cultural activities. After high school I moved to Saint Anselm's predivinity college study hall for the next two years.

My decision to join the monastery was prompted primarily by this strong feeling I had by now developed that Saint John's was indeed home for me. I still had the priesthood in mind as my principal vocation, and with that ideal I entered the novitiate in a class of ten clerical novices. Each of us would have a different story to tell. Of the ten, three others besides myself are presently capitulars of Saint John's, one now belongs to Saint Augustine's Priory in the Bahamas, one to Abadia del Tepeyac in Mexico, and one to San Antonio Abad in Puerto Rico. One left after triennial vows, one was a novice from Saint Benedict's Abbey in Kansas, and one died in 1982. This class eventually received from some the epithet "Blue Ribbon Class."

The day we entered the novitiate seems as if it were only yesterday. My mother brought me from our home which was also The City Bakery in Park Falls, Wisconsin. We left early in the morning while my father and older brother were bringing the freshly baked bread out of the oven, arriving after a five-hour drive at Collegeville. My mother returned home after lunch. At the stroke of 3:00 p.m., the bell sounding the hour from the twin towers, we entered the monastery portal, now the entrance to the Abbot Alcuin conference room, to be greeted by Prior Rembert Bularzik. Abbot Alcuin was absent at the time. After a brief exhortation and a blessing, we were ushered into the novitiate quarters, still in the same location today, to don a Benedictine habit for the first time, without the hood, however, which was to be conferred ten days later at the ceremony of investiture by Abbot Alcuin.

Thus began a year-long time of absolute seclusion from the world, from the student body of Saint John's University, and even from association with any of the professed monks of the abbey. Frs. Basil Stegmann and Alto Butkowski were respectively our novice master and *socius*. How well I remember the day Father Alto told us that the Nazi armies had invaded Poland marking the outbreak of World War II. How well I remember our first Christmas in the monastery, the beauty of the chant at midnight Matins, sung just after the evening of Br. Stanislaus Zaworski's tragic death.

The novitiate was a year of formation, a term used more frequently now, in which we imbibed the teachings of Saint Benedict's *Rule* and learned how the wisdom of this teaching was applied in the centuries following his death (A.D. 547). This spiritual formation in monastic ideals continued through my next five years in the clericate, as it was then called, now Saint Luke Hall. Along with the study of scholastic philosophy as my major for the B.A. degree, I took a minor in education. Then after college graduation ceremonies, which my mother came to witness, I began the courses in theology leading to ordination. It seems Abbot Alcuin had already chosen me for a teaching career rather than for pastoral ministry. I was not asked or consulted—it was the custom at that time. The abbot's decision was for me a manifestation of the will of God. I taught one Latin class in the prep school during my last two years in the clericate.

During the summer of 1945, as the war was winding down, we were quickly prepared for ordination. This was conferred by Bishop Peter Bartholome of Saint Cloud in the first abbey church, now the Great Hall, on September 2, 1945. My parents, all my younger brothers, some uncles, aunts, and cousins came from Park Falls for the occasion. A week later I celebrated my first solemn Mass in our home parish. Three weeks later I was in Ottawa, Canada, studying in an M.A. program in philosophy, all arranged by Abbot Alcuin in preparation for my teaching career in the newly established Saint Augustine's Monastery and College in Nassau, the Bahamas. Here as a teacher of high school mathematics, in priestly ministry as occasion required, and as a regular member of that small monastic community, I spent the next twenty-five years from 1946–71. My account of these years can be found in Fr. Colman Barry's *Upon These Rocks,* the story of the Catholic Church in the Bahamas. From 1971–81 I was accountant and comptroller at Saint Augustine's.

After Vatican Council II came years of change and turmoil in every area of Catholic life. I personally look back upon the strong, basic formation I received as a young monk at Saint John's as the mainstay of my stability in the Benedictines, together with the primary source of spiritual strength, the grace of God. This is meant in no way to be judgmental of the motives of others who left the order during those years, neither of those in the Bahamas nor of those at Saint John's Abbey. I can speak only of my own experience. I know that it was to a large extent from my spiritual reading, our Benedictine *lectio divina,* that I came to a deep and firm acceptance of my vocation as a monk first, then as a priest, and finally as a teacher. None of these roles has been easy, but all have been richly rewarding.

As a monk I have been and still am strongly inclined toward a contemplative life-style. This was not the ideal that brought me to the monastery, but it certainly became an ideal during my clericate days. After ordination to the priesthood, I had no strong desire for pastoral ministry, although I was given the opportunity for it on weekend assignments at parishes in Nassau and on the Family Islands. Reading the spiritual classics became for me the way to bring harmony into what seemed to me to be conflicting ideals. Today I look upon the entire life-style and spirit of Saint John's as a portrayal of that harmony, sometimes shown in art works by the Benedictine motto *Ora et labora* (pray and work). Gregory the Great and Bernard of Clairvaux gave eloquent and moving witness to this in their writings.

My interests, however, are not exclusively in the realm of spiritual theology. When I began teaching mathematics in Nassau, I studied the subject matter pretty much on my own. My undergraduate courses were not in that field. It was Abbot Baldwin Dworschak who encouraged me to enroll for summer courses at Columbia Teachers College in New York. There I received an M.A. in mathematics education in 1961. It was also there that I became acquainted with polyhedron models. This interest led to the publication of works of mine in 1966, 1971, 1979, and 1983, for which I am best known, in fact internationally known. My 1971 book on *Polyhedron Models* was published in a Russian edition in 1974 and in a Japanese edition in 1979. My interest in polyhedron research and production continues to this day.

Saint John's has meant and still means a great deal to me. No matter what the future may hold, I am firmly convinced of the value of Benedictine ideals in any area of the world and in all walks of life. This is what our program for Oblates of Saint Benedict is designed to promote. I have only recently become director of Oblates at Saint John's, so I have little direct involvement in its origin or development here. It is my hope and prayer, however, that the spirit of the *Rule* of Benedict may become ever more widely known and followed. I never cease to find in the *Rule* deeper sources of inspiration for myself. This is especially true of the Prologue to the *Rule,* filled with so many references to the Word of God in

Scripture. And Saint Benedict's call is universal: "To you, there-fore, my words are now addressed, whoever you may be. . . ." (Prologue to the *Rule,* verse 3).

It is this spirituality of the *Rule* that I now seek to share with others, as it continues to filter through for me in my own experience. That it has some appeal is made evident by comments I receive, either about homilies I give or about the "Spirituality for Oblates" column that I write for the Saint John's Abbey *Quarterly.* I also ex-pressed what this is in an article entitled "The Spirit of the *Rule*" in the spring 1989 *Saint John's* magazine. When people ask what is an Oblate, I recommend two leaflets written specifically for Ob-lates or prospective Oblates: *Oblates of St. Benedict: An Introduction* and *Guidelines for Oblates of St. Benedict,* which are published by The Liturgical Press. How the *Rule* applies to Oblates is also admira-bly expressed in Esther de Waal's *Seeking God, the Way of St. Bene-dict* and Brian C. Taylor's *Spirituality for Everyday Living, An Adaptation of the Rule of St. Benedict,* also published by The Press. These authors are both in the Anglican or Episcopal Church tradition. I have come into contact with others, Lutherans too, who are drawn by the spiri-tuality of the *Rule.*

This spirituality, however, is not acquired by study or intellec-tual pursuit alone. It comes by dedication to a life of prayer. Prayer is not merely the saying of prayers or the reading of prayer formu-las but rather what may best be called living in a prayerful atti-tude, being attuned to the presence of God in every circumstance of life. This was the theme of the conferences I gave at the Oblate retreat at Saint John's in 1989. Personal prayer can be enriched by paying attention to the way in which great people of faith in the Bible and in Christian history prayed. Saint Benedict drew his inspiration from these sources, as they were known to him in his day. He transmitted it to us through the *Rule.* It lives today in any spirituality that draws its inspiration from these same sources, true to our Lord's words in Matthew's Gospel: "Every scribe who has been trained for the kingdom of heaven is like a householder who brings out of his treasure what is new and what is old" (13:52).

A practice I have found very helpful is that of keeping a jour-nal, a written record of personal reflections mixed with readings. While reading Karl Jaspers, an existentialist philosopher, I came upon this passage: "To apprehend thought with indifference prevents its appropriation." This passage came to mind later when I found a saying of Bernard of Clairvaux: "Instruction renders us learned but feeling—*affectio*—makes us wise." Or this one from Gregory the Great: "A person should speak not from mere knowledge (*scientia*) but from real sentiment, *sententia.*" I then recorded this reflection:

> In spiritual matters there must be a difference between forming a concept of a thing and a perception of that same thing. A concept is something purely intellectual. But a perception must go deeper into the soul, causing a change in one's inmost being. Every spiritual doctrine must be of these two modes. The first can be acquired by study, the second only in prayer.

Beginning in 1958 I was deeply moved by the works of John of the Cross, the sixteenth-century Carmelite poet and mystic. I have often heard it said that John of the Cross is difficult to read, too exalted in his mystical flights, too austere in his dark nights, beyond the realm of ordinary spirituality. I must say I have not found this to be so. Thus I was very pleased to find in the writings of Thomas Merton a study published in 1980 entitled "The Transforming Union in Saint Bernard and Saint John of the Cross." There is a remarkable unity of teaching in the classical literature of mysticism that has come down to us from the early Christian Masters as well as from Ignatius of Loyola, the sixteenth-century founder of the Society of Jesus. It is often taken for granted that Jesuit spirituality is quite different from Benedictine or Cistercian or Carmelite spirituality. But all of these have the same goal which comes at the end of the spiritual journey—the union of the soul with God—the very same desire Jesus expressed in his high-priestly prayer: "that they may all be one, even as thou, Father, art in me and I in thee" (John 17:21).

Saint Benedict sums up these thoughts in a beautiful passage at the end of the *Rule* in the form of two rhetorical questions which give the sources of any spirituality: "For what page or what utterance of the divinely inspired books of the Old and New Testaments is not a most unerring rule for human life? Or what book of the holy Catholic Fathers does not loudly proclaim how we may come by a straight course to our Creator?" As in the Prologue, Benedict made his call universal in the words: "To you, therefore, my words are now addressed, whoever you may be," so his last words in the *Rule* are: "Whoever you are, therefore, who are hastening to the heavenly homeland, fulfil with the help of Christ this minimum Rule." Benedict, the man of God, was filled with the spirit of all the just.

ANGELO G. ZANKL

As THE TRAGIC HAMLET STANDS ABOVE A newly opened grave to receive the body of his drowned Ophelia, Shakespeare has Hamlet utter this profound reality: "There's a Divinity that shapes our ends, rough-hew them how we will." The longer we live to "rough-hew" our life-span, the more we may be able to see God's finer shaping of it by using people and events.

Years ago when I entered the novitiate, the master admonished me: "You have a penchant for a prompt and profuse use of the perpendicular pronoun 'I.'" After looking up his words in the dictionary, I felt the first pang of his spiritual hammer and chisel beginning to shape my character.

Pope Leo XIII died in 1903. At that time I had an eleven-year-old sister, Veronica, who loved the pope and grieved over his death. At that time I was two years old and still carried about by Veronica. The year 1903 was also the height of the diphtheria epidemic in rural Almena, Wisconsin, where I was born. Diphtheria was generally fatal to children because a tough membrane formed over the throat which obstructed breathing. I caught the infection, Veronica at first did not. When I was old enough to understand, my mother told me that Veronica had said: "Please dear Jesus, rather let me die than Connel (my baptismal name) if he could become a pope like Leo XIII." My mother replied: "Oh that's impossible, but maybe he could become just a priest." After some hesitation Veronica agreed to that. Soon after, she caught the infection from me and died. Whether or not this episode influenced me in the more conscious early years of my life, I cannot tell. I had finished the sixth grade in public school when I saw a picture of a missionary on a small sailboat. I got the idea of being a missionary on a boat. Having grown to twelve years in dry non-maritime surroundings, I now recall that my primary motive was not so much to be a missionary as to be on the water and in a boat.

After looking through several boarding-school catalogues, I wanted to attend the school described as "A finishing School for Boys, Conducted by an Anglican Lady at Lakeville on the Mississippi." My fervent Catholic mother countermanded that place and decided to send me to Saint John's instead. "Besides," she added, "their catalogue shows there is a lake there and boats, too."

In September 1913 my mother took me as a boy of twelve to Minneapolis where we boarded the Great Northern to Saint Joseph. No passenger trains stopped at Collegeville then. At Saint Joe we hired a rig at the livery stable, a one-horse-and-surrey buggy with flat top and fringe, and drove the remaining four and one-half miles through the woods and on the now abandoned East Road. What a view it was to me as we came abreast of the old castellated water tower and our first observatory where the prep school is now. There were no other intervening buildings then, so when the wide frontage of the quadrangle with its twin towers rose into view, I was greatly impressed.

All arrangements for my schooling were made through Abbot Peter Engel, a kindly looking man with a full white beard. The total yearly cost of education in 1913 was $250 which included board, lodging, books, laundry, and tuition. Since my family could afford only half of that sum, Abbot Peter decided that I personally could make up the rest by waiting on tables and other chores.

I was enrolled in "pre-prep," a year's introduction to high school. The only distinct memory I have of the various subjects we studied is of Latin. Often I had my ears twisted by that first Latin teacher for failing to memorize the numerous and highly inflected declensions, case-endings, subjunctives, etc. Having grown up on a small farm, my whole ambit was about concrete entities, not semi-abstract ones like subjunctives.

For a flagrant flouting of important rules of the school, the custom of public corporal punishment was still in force. Of these rules, the smoking of a "coffin-nail" by a minor was deemed worthy of the biblical flogging of forty stripes, minus one. The prefect used a thumb-diameter leather tube into which Brother Shoemaker had sewn lead shot to give it more authority. The culprit got down on all fours, his coat tails were flipped up, and the leather lash was applied to that portion of the anatomy which nature has suitably cushioned. Needless to say I was not seduced by Lady Nicotine for quite some years.

An additional way of paying my half of the tuition opened in 1915. Damian Baker, Arthur Danzl, and I were chosen to assist Fr. Fridolin Tembreull in the darkroom of the Saint John's Photo Studio. The studio had been started by Fr. Peter Engel, later abbot of Saint John's (1894–1921). In my time the darkroom work became more intense because of students' growing needs. They came with their new box-cameras, and the only place to have their films developed and printed was the drugstore in Saint Cloud. Hitch-hiking fifteen miles one way in horse-and-buggy days? And in the winter? No way. So the three of us were instructed in all the elements of photography: mixing chemicals, developing films, and printing the snapshots.

We were then enrolling more and more students from the flat prairies of North Dakota and had to process their box-camera efforts. The prints had to pass Father Fridolin's inspection and muster before they could be sold. One time he flipped a large batch of prints through his fingers, then broke out in a hearty laugh. We all said: "What's wrong with them?" "Nothing," he said, "you can always tell when a kid comes from North Dakota; the only things he photographs are trees."

From this early introduction to the technology of photography, I have made it a life-long hobby and have gone all the way to optics, chemistry, composition, and finally to the never-ending debate whether or not photography is a legitimate art form. It is also a form of therapy in my debilitated and declining years.

Another early mentor of mine was Fr. Hilary Doerfler. When wire-telegraphy gave way to "spark telegraphy" or wireless, Father Hilary was like a boy with a new toy. Little commercial equipment was available at that time, so most of it had to be made in his Engel Hall basement shop. I can still picture him bent over his lathe winding coils of wire, his head enhallowed by thick white clouds of vile-smelling smoke from repeated black Manila stogies.

Saint John's was granted an experimental license in 1917, and Father Hilary wanted to test our newly developed facility of communication. On one April afternoon he asked another student, Herbert Richter, and me to pull a toboggan across the ice-covered Lake Sagatagan to Chapel Island and set up a portable transmitter and receiver. There Richter climbed a nearby tree to string an antenna wire and set up our "buzzer" transmitter and crystal and cat-whisker receiver. We sent our first and only message over the lake to Father Hilary in Engel Hall, when his surprising message came back to us: "Coming in loud and clear. Bad news: President Woodrow Wilson this noon declared U.S. at war with Germany. All amateur stations must dismantle. Come home at once. '30' " So began World War I at Saint John's in 1917 and also my life-long interest in electronics.

To be able to live in daily contact with men of learning is a privilege. We learn more from their philosophies than from their text books. One of these was Fr. Alexius Hoffmann, who wrote the first tentative history of Saint John's. A brilliant conversationalist on almost any topic, he was called a walking encyclopedia in his day. I had him as professor for only a limited time, but one admonition of his remained with me for the rest of my life. "Gentlemen, I want you to get into the habit of putting a date to everything you do— whether it is a paper you write, or a thing you make, or a shaving-cream can you buy, date it. You will never regret that." The main reason I have for anyone complimenting me on a good memory is that I got into Father Alexius' habit of dating everything I do.

So much has already been written about Abbot Alcuin Deutsch that I hesitate to add more. But I remember an early and typical indication of his vision. Before World War I he introduced a Jesuit expert in seismology to the students. These lectures were given in the old "exhibition hall" on the third floor of the quadrangle. As youngsters we were fascinated by the subject. This expert's parting advice to us was for each one to delve so deeply into one specific field and so completely immerse ourselves in it that the whole world would beat a path to our door, as it does to the door of the man who makes the better mousetrap. After the lecture Father Alcuin thanked the expert, but then came his astounding "Yes, but." In the presence of the seismologist, he said to us: "Young men, at this stage in your lives I want you to do just exactly the opposite. Do not limit yourselves to one specific interest. I want you to become interested in and examine everything. That's what the human mind is for, and for all truth and reality." After this confrontation I decided to follow Father Alcuin's counsel.

Before my entrance into the novitiate, Father Alcuin had noticed some evidences of artistic talent in me. When he was elected abbot upon the death of Abbot Peter in December 1921, he asked me to design the customary prelatial coat of arms for him. The motto Abbot Alcuin chose was *Non recuso laborem* (I shall not refuse the labor), a quotation from his patron Saint Martin of Tours. Monastic wags are always at hand, and this motto was soon translated into "I shall not refuse the honor." Other Benedictine and diocesan prelates afterwards requested coats of arms from me. In 1934 Fr. Walter Reger requested a new escutcheon for our university. It resulted in the present one: "Let us put on the armor of light," which appears to the present on university publications.

In 1921 there was a desire in the community for a building separate from the students' bathhouse at Lake Sagatagan. The decision was made to build it west of the students' facility, and I was asked to plan and design this new community bathhouse. The project was entrusted to the clerics. I had some controversy with a few of them about the chosen site on a sand hill. This objection was: "It's all quicksand and won't last." Some even quoted Scripture to that end. Others asked: "Have you ever tried to stand in a barrel full of ball-bearings?" My argument was there is a vast difference between "rolled" and "crushed" sand. Rolled sand has been swirled round and round in running water for ages till it approaches ball-bearing status. A structure on it will crack and sink. On the other hand, crushed sand has many facets and will pack hard, as marine pile-drivers know. The sand on our hill is the glacial crushed type. And the bathhouse has had no structural cracks after sixty-seven years. When it was finished, I chiselled the date 1922 with a cold-chisel on the stone in the tower.

In my middle years I was invited to give lectures and conduct summer liturgical workshops in various Catholic colleges. Eventually I was elected president of the National Catholic Art Association. In 1944 I was told to look into the book *Who's Who in America* and was surprised to find my name there. I suspected an enterprising Dominican nun who wanted the association to thrive. When I accosted her, she denied it and knew of no one else who might have been implicated. At any rate, after a second year's publication, I requested the publisher to withdraw my name.

When Christian art at Saint John's is considered, it would be a major omission not to record the contributions of our former Br. Clement Frischauf. A quiet, gentle, and humble man, Brother Clement had spent twelve years in the mural decoration of Monte Cassino Archabbey in Italy; then more years in South America, and in the Bronx, New York City. He transferred his vows to Saint John's in the early '30s. His imposing figure of Christos Pantocrator in the Great Hall is his masterpiece here. And he did it all alone. At age seventy-three he climbed the high scaffolding every weekday to finish it. I had the privilege of helping him decide about the reverently hovering angels in the mural. He thought their faces should be shown, but we finally agreed that their faces should be veiled in the presence of their eucharistic King.

Brother Clement exercised a profound influence on me. Once it was necessary for him to correct me after my failing deliberately to keep an appointment for consultation. He did the correcting so kindly and gently—no anger, resentment, vindictiveness—almost like God's own corrections. He grieved not because I had hurt him but because I had hurt myself by my infidelity.

In February 1944 Monte Cassino was bombed into rubble by our United States Air Force, and the twelve years of loving labor of his was forever lost. Perhaps as a solace he attended our orchestra's rendition of his favorite composer, Papa Haydn, that evening. On his return to his cell, he slipped on a patch of ice between Benet Hall and the quadrangle, suffered a skull fracture, and died. Little had he dreamed that from 1963 onward, when the site of his masterpiece became the present Great Hall, many more thousands of people, believers and non-believers, would confront that great and awesome face of the Redeemer than would have if that old edifice had remained a church.

Another major instrument in God's hands for my shaping was our novice master Fr. Athanase Meyer. The year of spiritual training in the novitiate is intensive. At its end one is intended to be ready for a lifelong commitment to the religious vows that are to be taken.

In the '20s novitiate it was my assignment to serve Fr. Cornelius Wittmann. He was the last survivor of the original five monks who came to Minnesota from Pennsylvania in 1856 to begin monastic life in this "Indianbush." It was my "obedience" to wheel him daily from his cell to the chapel for Mass and back. Little conversation between us was possible since he was very deaf and almost totally blind. I did not realize then, as I do now, that I was to be a living link between the origin of this place and the present. That is the wonder of a monastic community: a living continuity for ages, as long as it "truly seeks God!" Father Cornelius died in 1921.

Father Athanase's method of shaping us novices was firm, but at the same time so gentle that the desired correction was effective. It was, for example, the custom for our group of fifteen novices to be led after supper on a brisk walk to the cemetery and back. One evening two of us, Herbert Richter and I, spotted what looked like small melons growing next to the gravel path to the cemetery. We managed to fall back to the rear of the line, and each of us snatched a small melon and hid it behind his scapular. This made us look somewhat pregnant, but all went well until we returned from the walk. In the dormitory we tried to stab our knives into the melons and found them so hard and white that there was no question of eating them. What to do? We couldn't dispose of them in a wastebasket. That would give us away. Richter, being more imaginative than I, suggested taking the evidence into the water-closet, the name for toilets in those days, chopping up the melons into small pieces and flushing them away. These toilets had the water reservoir overhead that I thought would furnish a vigorous enough flushing when the chain was pulled. Richter being the smarter one, pulled the chain after each few slices and so easily disposed of his melon. I was stupid enough to cut up the whole melon, then pull once. Result: a hopelessly clogged toilet. In due course the novice master summoned the Brother Plumber to remove the obstacle. Let me add I found out later that our long-time gardener, Br. Leo Bettendorf, was wise to the temptations of novices, planting these inedible citrons near the well-traveled gravel path and planting the ordinary melons much farther down in the garden near Lake Watab.

I waited nervously for the "shoe to drop," but the master said not a word about it for several weeks. Then one day his spiritual conference was about the Holy Spirit and the channels of grace. Father Athanase particularly warned us never to place any obstacle to the channels of grace, for that would grieve the Holy Spirit and stop all his action in us. Then the master stared straight at me and said: "It's just like putting watermelons into the toilet and plugging it up, isn't that so, Frater Angelo?" There was not another word from him, just a stunned silence among us all.

The year of the novitiate was followed by the usual studies in philosophy and theology. My theological studies for five years were at Saint Vincent Pontifical Seminary at Latrobe, Pennsylvania. On returning home I began to teach systematics or dogmatic theology in the seminary here, replacing Fr. Alexius Hoffmann who had become an invalid. My span of teaching years was interspersed with short periods of parochial assistance, convent and hospital chaplaincies.

In 1951 Abbot Baldwin appointed me pastor of Saint Clement's Parish in Duluth. When that city became an ocean port with the opening of the Saint Lawrence Seaway in 1959, Bishop Thomas Welch of Duluth added the additional function of port chaplain to my duties.

As professors in the classrooms we deal primarily with adolescents and young people and their developing sense of responsibility. As pastors we deal with the entire life-spans of people from birth through the maturing years with their heavy burdens up to their passage from time-existence to eternal-existence. For this reason I believe the last twenty-nine years as pastor and hospital and convent chaplain in Duluth have been most formative for me. Experiences in these fields have ranged from tragic to banal, from crushing frustration to pure delight. For example, a dying suicide had consumed a whole can of lye to end her domestic troubles. Neither coaxing nor prayers on my part changed her mind, she said: "No, Father, Satan has claimed me for his own, and I'm going back to him." Or a deathbed marriage to settle inheritance questions, or patient listening with drooping eyelids to the tedious litany of aches and pains of the elderly. Nurses dub these lengthy jeremiads "organ recitals."

Before Vatican Council II parish priests spent many long hours in the dark confines of confessionals. These hours were truly illuminating about human nature. These ranged from the reluctant withholding of absolution to obstinate sodomists, now called "gays," to the joyful light dusting of God's terrestrial angels, our children. I can recall one child's confession prepared by the sisters for her First Communion:

> Bless me Father for my sins. This is my last—I mean my first—confession. Then I tell my sins: I fighted with my brother Tommy, sassed my Mommy back, I tripped on my cat's tail, it scratched me and I got mad. Then I say my contrition—"O my God I'm hardly sorry for all my sins and I promise to end my life. Amen." Father, I'm gonna be much more better now.

When I had reached age eighty-six, Abbot Jerome Theisen told me it was time to enter our health care center at the abbey, and as he hopefully stated, "to give a good example to the younger monks." After thirty-eight years outside the monastery, I also felt it was time to come home to benefit from the good example of the younger monks. The community by-laws state that the novitiate is a place where they are to eat, sleep, and meditate. That is basically what I am again doing now in our health center. Remembering my boyhood whimsy of wishing to be near a lake and boats, I see after a span of eighty-nine years what a magnanimous sense of humor God has. For twenty-nine years he gave me the pleasure of seeing the varied sunrises over Lake Superior, the "unsalted sea of the North." And boats? Not just a little sailboat, but ships of all sizes, from Leif Erickson's replica that sailed to Norway in 1986 to the behemoths, some longer than three football fields, that carry Minnesota iron ore to the Eastern states and abroad.

Shakespeare referred to the Divinity that shapes our ends but fails to mention, as I have tried to indicate, that the same Divinity uses others to perfect and polish us. As the end of my own shaping nears, I gratefully give thanks for all whom God has used in this task: bishops, five abbots, priests and monks, my former seminarians and all students, doctors and nurses, penitents, parishioners, parents, and children. May the Lord fittingly reward them all.

CONTRIBUTORS[1]

COLMAN J. BARRY '43, regents professor of religious history, president of Saint John's University, visiting professor at several American universities, founding dean of the School of Religious Studies at The Catholic University of America, editor, author and lecturer, is the president of the Hill Monastic Manuscript Library.

DENNIS BEACH '82, instructor in English and prefect in Saint John's Preparatory School, has served as academic dean in the prep school, is managing editor of Saint John's Abbey *Quarterly*.

SILVAN BROMENSHENKEL '42, missionary in the Bahama Islands for over forty years, has served on a number of the Family Islands, as prior of Saint Augustine's Monastery and teacher in Saint Augustine's College, is pastor of Our Saviour's Church on the landfall of Christopher Columbus, San Salvador Island.

ALBERIC R. CULHANE '53, associate professor of theology in the college of arts and sciences of Saint John's University, writer, archaeologist, editor of the Saint John's Abbey *Quarterly*, acting president of Saint John's University, is assistant to the president of Saint John's University for university relations.

1. The numbers following the names of contributors indicate the year in this century that these members of the Saint John's community made their vows as monks.

ALFRED H. DEUTSCH '34, regents professor of English of the college of arts and sciences of Saint John's University, served as dean of the Saint John's Preparatory School and dean of the school of divinity of Saint John's University, novice master, monastic chronicler, is the author of Collegeville stories such as *Bruised Reeds* and *Still Full of Sap, Still Green*. He died September 30, 1989.

DANIEL D. DURKEN '50, writer, novice master, abbey personnel director, associate pastor, director of The Liturgical Press, dean of men of the college of arts and sciences of Saint John's University, where he is an associate professor of theology.

BALDWIN W. DWORSCHAK '27, sixth abbot of Saint John's, president of the American Cassinese Congregation of Benedictines, participant in Vatican Council II, cooperated with Bauhaus architect Marcel Breuer in the planning and construction of nine Collegeville buildings, including the second Saint John's Abbey and University Church.

ARNO A. GUSTIN '27, professor emeritus of education, registrar, dean and president of Saint John's University, first president of Mary College, Bismarck, North Dakota, was pastor of Sacred Heart Church, Roseau, Minnesota.

OLIVER L. KAPSNER '23, emeritus professor of logic in the college of arts and sciences of Saint John's University, catalog librarian at Saint John's University, The Catholic University of America, Library of Congress, Saint Vincent College, was the first field director of microfilming manuscripts in libraries and archives of Austrian monasteries to establish the initial collection of the Hill Monastic Manuscript Library.

JOHN KULAS '51, associate professor of German language and literature in the college of arts and sciences of Saint John's University, writes on the relation of Saint John's monastery and schools to its neighborhood as a graduate of Saint John's Preparatory School, college of arts and sciences of Saint John's University, school of divinity of Saint John's University, and as a native of Stearns County from Albany, Minnesota.

EMERIC A. LAWRENCE '29, professor of French and theology in the college of arts and sciences of Saint John's University, exchange professor of theology at Luther College, Decorah, Iowa, and Concordia College, Moorhead, Minnesota, chaplain at Saint Scholastica Convent, Duluth, is an author of several volumes of homilies and spiritual meditations widely used in Christian ministry.

NEAL HENRY LAWRENCE '55, served in the United States diplomatic service in the Far East, joined the Saint John's community and is a pioneer member of Saint Anselm's Priory, Tokyo, dependent foundation of Saint John's Abbey, whose story he tells from his personal perspective.

OMER W. MAUS '39, has served in urban pastoral and orphanage ministries, with the Chippewa Indians at Saint Mary's Mission on the Red Lake Indian Reservation, is chaplain at the Minnesota Correctional Facility, Saint Cloud.

AIDAN McCALL '48, associate professor of classics and African literature in the college of arts and sciences of Saint John's University, veteran faculty resident in the dormitories, former dean of men and vice-president of student affairs of the college of arts and sciences of Saint John's University, is doing research in Afro-American Studies at the Schaumberg Institute, New York City.

KILIAN W. McDONNELL '46, professor in the school of theology of Saint John's University, author, ecumenist, founder of the Institute for Ecumenical and Cultural Research, is active both in the charismatic movement and national and international inter-faith dialogues.

RAY PEDRIZETTI '54, associate professor of classics and philosophy in the college of arts and sciences of Saint John's University, served as a prefect and faculty resident in the college dormitories as well as abbey junior master.

RYAN T. PERKINS '78, has a master's degree in theology from the school of divinity of Saint John's University, studied religious history at the University of Notre Dame, served in the abbey archives and is a Catholic chaplain at the Newman Center of the University of Minnesota.

JAMES PHILLIPS '70, has worked at Saint Augustine's Monastery, Nassau, Bahamas, has served as an abbey sacristan, is a prefect in Saint John's Preparatory School and a nursing aide in the monastery's health care center.

MARTIN RATH '50, served for thirty-three years at Saint John's in the bookstore and as postmaster before studying for the priesthood at Sacred Heart Seminary, Hales Corner, Wisconsin. Following ordination he has worked in pastoral ministry at Saint Bernard's Parish, Saint Paul, Minnesota, and as chaplain at Saint Therese Residence, Minneapolis. He is pastor of Most Holy Redeemer Church in Ogema and the mission of Saint Ann's in Waubun, Minnesota.

DIETRICH T. REINHART '72, assistant professor of history in the college of arts and sciences of Saint John's University, has been director of liturgy in Saint John's Abbey, and is academic dean of the college of arts and sciences of Saint John's University.

MARTIN E. SCHIRBER '29, professor emeritus of economics, dean of the college of arts and sciences of Saint John's University, worked in the National Catholic Rural Life Conference, organized Rural Life Conferences at Saint John's and has been active in the development office at Saint John's and with the J-Club.

HUBERT SCHNEIDER '31, came to the Saint John's Community from the Benedictine parish of Meire Grove in Stearns County. After his profession of vows, Brother Hubert was assigned to the carpenter shop. He has served there for fifty-nine years and remains today our master craftsman and instructor in the woodworking arts.

DON TALAFOUS '47, associate professor of theology in the college of arts and sciences of Saint John's University, writer, faculty resident on the first and second floors of Benet Hall, has worked in pastoral ministry as university chaplain with several generations of Johnnies.

VINCENT G. TEGEDER '31, dean of Saint John's Preparatory School, professor emeritus of American history, chairman of the department of history of the college of arts and sciences of Saint John's University, writer, is the archivist of Saint John's Abbey and University.

JEROME THEISEN '52, eighth abbot of Saint John's and chancellor of Saint John's University, associate professor of theology in the school of theology of Saint John's University, author, has served as novice master, chaplain at Saint Benedict's Convent, associate director at the Institute for Ecumenical and Cultural Research, and exchange professor at Luther College, Decorah, Iowa.

HILARY D. THIMMESH '48, associate professor of English, dean of the college of arts and sciences of Saint John's University, administrator of Saint Martin's Abbey, Lacey, Washington, is currently president of Saint John's University.

SIMEON J. THOLE '56, instructor of English and prefect at Saint John's Preparatory School, subprior of Saint John's Abbey, is chaplain with the Benedictine sisters of Mount Saint Benedict, Crookston, Minnesota.

CYPRIAN V. WEAVER '66, assistant professor of biology in the college of arts and sciences of Saint John's University, has been conducting a diabetes-related research program for the last thirteen years.

ARNOLD WEBER '46, instructor in social sciences at Saint John's Preparatory School, lecturer, retreat facilitator, principal of Benilde-Saint Margaret High School, Saint Louis Park, Minnesota, is pastor of the parish community of Holy Name, Medina, Minnesota.

MAGNUS J. WENNINGER '40, instructor in languages and mathematics in Saint John's Preparatory School and instructor in philosophy at the college of arts and sciences of Saint John's University and in Saint Augustine's College, Bahamas, director of Oblates, is internationally known through his creative work and publication on the topic of polyhedrons.

Angelo G. Zankl '21, enjoys the longest and most diverse ministry of contributors to this volume. Professor of dogma at Saint John's Seminary, professor of art and architecture and dean of men of the college of arts and sciences of Saint John's University, pastoral assistant and pastor in Dakota and Minnesota parishes, chaplain at Saint Scholastica Convent, Duluth, he continues in retirement to practice his many skills in such fields as photography, clock work, and heraldry.

ACKNOWLEDGEMENTS

The editor is grateful to his confreres who contributed essays for this book; to Marianne Hansen, who helped prepare the manuscript; to Fr. Alberic Culhane, Julian G. Plante, and Sr. Dolores Schuh, who read the proofs; to Mark Twomey and John Schneider of The Liturgical Press, who provided editorial assistance; to Colleen Stiller, Sue Pitschka, Monica Weide, Deb Lampert-Pflueger, and Monica Bokinskie of The Liturgical Press, who typeset and keylined the copy; and to Br. Robin Pierzina, who, with the assistance of Glenn Beltt, Don Bruno, Lee Hanley, Br. Alan Reed, Michael Scully, Kathryn Stommes, Br. Placid Stuckenschneider, and Fr. Vincent Tegeder, selected the photographs. This book was set in Baskerville type by The Liturgical Press and printed on Satin-Kote Opaque paper by Sentinel Printing Company, Inc., Saint Cloud, Minnesota.